GEORGIAN ARCHITECTURE

GEORGIAN ARCHITECTURE

James Stevens Curl

David & Charles

BY THE SAME AUTHOR

The Life and Work of Henry Roberts (1803–76), Architect. The Evangelical Conscience and the Campaign for Model Housing and Healthy Nations (Chichester: Phillimore & Co Ltd, 1983)

The Londonderry Plantation 1609–1914. The History, Architecture, and Planning of the Estates of the City of London and its Livery Companies in Ulster (Chichester: Phillimore & Co Ltd, 1986)

The Art and Architecture of Freemasonry. An Introductory Study (London: B.T. Batsford Ltd, 1991, and New York: Overlook Press, 1993 – winner of the Sir Banister Fletcher Award for Best Book of the Year, 1992). *See also* the new edition, published by B.T. Batsford, 2002

Egyptomania. The Egyptian Revival as a Recurring Theme in the History of Taste (Manchester: Manchester University Press, 1994)

The Oxford Dictionary of Architecture (Oxford: Oxford University Press, 2000)

The Honourable The Irish Society and the Plantation of Ulster, 1608–2000. The City of London and the Colonisation of County Londonderry in the Province of Ulster in Ireland. A History and Critique (Chichester: Phillimore & Co Ltd, 2000)

The Victorian Celebration of Death (Thrupp, Stroud: Sutton Publishing Ltd, 2000)

Kensal Green Cemetery. The Origins & Development of the General Cemetery of Souls, Kensal Green, London, 1824–2001 (Edited) (Chichester: Phillimore & Co Ltd, 2001)

Classical Architecture. An Introduction to its Vocabulary and Essentials, with a Select Glossary of Terms (London: B.T. Batsford Ltd, 2001)

Death and Architecture. An Introduction to Funerary and Commemorative Buildings in the Western European Tradition, with Some Consideration of their Settings (Thrupp, Stroud: Sutton Publishing Ltd, 2002)

Piety Proclaimed. An Introduction to Places of Worship in Victorian England (London: Historical Publications Ltd, 2002)

Contributor to: *The Encyclopedia of Urban Planning* (New York: McGraw-Hill Inc, 1974); *The Survey of London* (London: The Athlone Press for the GLC, 1973, 1975, and 1983); *Transactions* of the Ancient Monuments Society (London: Ancient Monuments Society, 1977); *National Trust Studies* (London: Sotheby Parke Bernet, 1980); *Contemporary Architects* (London: Macmillan Press, and Chicago and London: St James Press, 1987); a new edition of J. C. Loudon's *On the Laying Out, Planting, and Managing Cemeteries, and on the Improvement of Churchyards* (Redhill: Ivelet Books Ltd, 1981); *Macmillan Encyclopedia of Architects* (London: Macmillan, 1982); the *Buildings of England* Series (Harmondsworth: Penguin Books Ltd, 1983, 1984, and 1991); 'The Work of Michael Sandle' in *The Geometry of Rage* (Bristol: Arnolfini Gallery, and Glasgow: Third Eye Centre, 1984); the Catalogue *Charles Sergeant Jagger: War and Peace Sculpture* (London: Imperial War Museum, 1985); *Influences in Victorian Art and Architecture* (London: Society of Antiquaries of London, 1985); *O Ewick is so Lanck. Die Historischen Friedhöfe in Berlin-Kreuzberg* (Berlin: Beuermann, 1987); *The Book of London* (London: Weidenfeld & Nicolson, 1989); *The Victorian Façade: The Work of William Watkins and his Son* (Lincoln: Lincolnshire College of Art & Design, 1990); *Simon Stringer, Sculptor* (Uppingham: Goldmark Gallery, 1990); *Contemporary Masterworks* (Chicago and London: St James Press, 1991); *L'Egitto fuori dell'Egitto. Dalla riscoperta all'Egittologia* (Bolonga: Cooperativa Libraria Universitaria Editrice Bologna, 1991); *Louis Visconti (1791–1853)* (Paris: Délégation à l'Action Artistique de la Ville de Paris, 1991); *The Rattle of the North: an Anthology of Ulster Prose* (Belfast: Blackstaff Press, 1992); *International Dictionary of Architects and Architecture* (Detroit, Mi: St James Press, Gale Research Inc, 1993); *L'Égyptomanie à l'épreuve de l'archéologie* (Brussels: Éditions du Gram, and Paris: Musée du Louvre, 1996); *Culture and Identity in Late Twentieth-Century Scotland* (Phantassie: Tuckwell Press, 1998); *A Republic for the Ages. The United States Capitol and the Political Structure of the Early Republic* (Charlottesville, Va: University of Virginia Press, 1999); *Giovanni Battista Piranesi* (Uppingham: Goldmark Gallery, 2000); and many journals, including, *Country Life, The Architects' Journal, Journal of the Royal Society of Arts, Interdisciplinary Science Reviews, Annals of Science, Architectural History, The Journals of Garden History, The Guardian, The Scotsman, Progressive Architecture, Bauwelt, Connaissance des Arts, RIBA Journal, The Antiquaries' Journal, RTPI Journal, The Architect, Official Architecture and Planning, The Oxford Mail, The Music Review, The Oxford Magazine, Journal of the Oxford Society, Isis, Town and Country Planning, The Architect and Building News, The Times, The Oxford Times, Project Scotland, The Leopard, Garden History, The Scottish Civic Trust Yearbook, the Ecologist, the Scottish Review, Hertfordshire Countryside, Leicestershire and Rutland Society of Architects Yearbook, Pharos International, Bradford Telegraph and Argus, Hampshire: The Country Magazine, RIBA East Midlands Yearbook, The World of Interiors, Chowkidar, Osaka Port Promotion Authority Journal, Leicestershire and Rutland Heritage, The Spectator, Planning Perspectives, Journal of Design History, SPAB News, The Literary Review, The Architectural Heritage Society of Scotland Newsletter and Annual Report*, and many others.

A DAVID & CHARLES BOOK

Copyright © James Stevens Curl 1993, 2002

First published in the UK in 1993
First published in paperback in 1993
This new edition paperback published in 2002

James Stevens Curl has asserted his right to be identified as author of this work in accordance with the Copyright, Designs and Patents Act, 1988.

A catalogue record for this book is available from the British Library.

ISBN 0 7153 0227 2 (paperback)

Typeset in 10/12 pt Caslon 540
by ICON GRAPHIC SERVICES, EXETER.
Printed in Singapore by CS Graphics Pte Ltd
for David & Charles
Brunel House   Newton Abbot   Devon

FRONTISPIECE *Mussenden Temple, Downhill, Co Londonderry, by Michael Shanahan* (JSC).

In Memoriam
John Edwards Gloag
(1896–1981)

'How was it that architects, designers, craftsmen, and their patrons never seemed to put a foot wrong in the Georgian period? What was the secret of their capacity for good design, their sense of style, and their impeccable judgement?'

JOHN GLOAG: *GEORGIAN GRACE*
(LONDON: ADAM & CHARLES BLACK, 1956) p xvii

Preface and Acknowledgements

This book is intended to provide the general reader with an overview of Georgian architecture within the limitations of length and number of illustrations imposed. I do not pretend that the book is a work of original scholarship, for the very simple reason that the architecture of the reigns of the first four Georges has been very thoroughly examined by numerous writers, and there are scholarly monographs on many of the outstanding architects of the period, but I have attempted to cover all the main stylistic aspects. There are still some mysteries, however, and I have given reasoned hypotheses where appropriate.

Throughout I have used the old Counties to describe the locations of the buildings mentioned. This I have done for two reasons: first of all, I detest meaningless names like 'Cumbria' and 'Avon'; and secondly the *Buildings of England* series is still arranged County by County. In my view the tinkering with historic boundaries in the 1970s was an act of vandalism and foolishness. The old County boundaries are related to the Diocesan boundaries, and they have profound *historical* meaning and relevance.

Georgian Architecture is dedicated to the memory of my friend John Gloag, who wrote with warmth and perception about the Georgian period, and who made a considerable contribution to the understanding of taste and architecture in this country.

I acknowledge my debt to the sources quoted in the references, Select Bibliography, and captions of the illustrations. Like many architectural historians, I owe much to Sir Howard Colvin, whose *A Biographical Dictionary of British Architects 1660–1840* (New Haven and London: Yale University Press, 1995) is an indispensable source of biographical, documentary, and factual information: I have drawn on his work for many details concerning the careers of several of the protagonists who contributed in no small measure to the excellence of Georgian architecture, and I am personally grateful to him for his generosity over the years. I thank Mr Timothy Auger, Editorial Director of B.T. Batsford Ltd, and Mr Simon Houfe

for permission to quote from and reproduce illustrations from the late Sir Albert Edward Richardson's *Monumental Classic Architecture in Great Britain and Ireland*, and Mr Houfe again for permission to quote from the same author's *An Introduction to Georgian Architecture*. I remember Sir Albert (1880–1964) with special affection because he gave me encouragement very early in my student days, and his life and work were inspirations in the 1950s and the dark days of the 1960s.

Mr Dan Cruickshank granted permission to quote from his work, including the splendidly useful *A Guide to the Georgian Buildings of Britain and Ireland* (London: George Weidenfeld & Nicolson Ltd, in association with the National Trust and The Irish Georgian Society, 1985) and *Life in the Georgian City*, written with Mr Neil Burton (London: Penguin Group, 1990): the former book contains a comprehensive gazeteer which, with Pevsner's *Buildings of England and Buildings of Scotland* series, should accompany any enthusiast (if that is the right word in the context of eighteenth-century creations) in search of the pleasures of Georgian buildings and landscapes.

Help with illustrations and other matters was given my Mr C. Bell, General Manager of the Belfast Charitable Society, Clifton House; by Mr Robert H. Bonar and the Rev W.D. Patton of the Presbyterian Historical Society or Ireland; by Mr Geremy Butler; by Miss Kitty Cruft of the Royal Commission on the Ancient and Historical Monuments of Scotland; by Miss Iona Cruickshank; by John Hughes Photography; by Mr Ralph Hyde and the staff of the Guildhall Library, City of London; by Mr Anthony F. Kersting; by Mr John Killen of the Linen Hall Library, Belfast; by Mr Ian Leith of the Architectural Section of the Royal Commission on the Historical Monuments of England, by the Ulster Museum, Belfast; by Mr Rodney C. Roach; by *Country Life*; and by Mr Peter Thornton, Mrs Margaret Richardson, and Miss Christine Scull of Sir John Soane's Museum. John Murray (Publishers) Ltd kindly allowed me to quote from Professor J. Mordaunt Crook's *The Dilemma of Style* (1987), for which I am grateful.

JAMES STEVENS CURL
Burley-on-the-Hill, Rutland; Peterhouse, Cambridge;
and Holywood, Co Down, 1989–2002

About the author

JAMES STEVENS CURL is Professor of Architectural History at The Queen's University of Belfast. Among his recent books are *The Victorian Celebration of Death* (2000), *Oxford Dictionary of Architecture* (2000), *The Honourable The Irish Society and the Plantation of Ulster 1608–2000* (2000), *Classical Architecture* (2002), and *The Art and Architecture of Freemasonry* (2002). He has contributed to and edited the scholarly monograph, *Kensal Green Cemetery: The Origins & Development of the General Cemetery of the Souls, Kensal Green, 1824–2001* (2001). A prolific author, he has been described as 'one of the few architectural historians who manages to absorb prodigious research which he imparts effortlessly in sustained and lively narrative'.

CONTENTS

List of Illustrations

Sources are given in abbreviated form in parentheses after each caption, with negative numbers when applicable. These abbreviations are as follows:

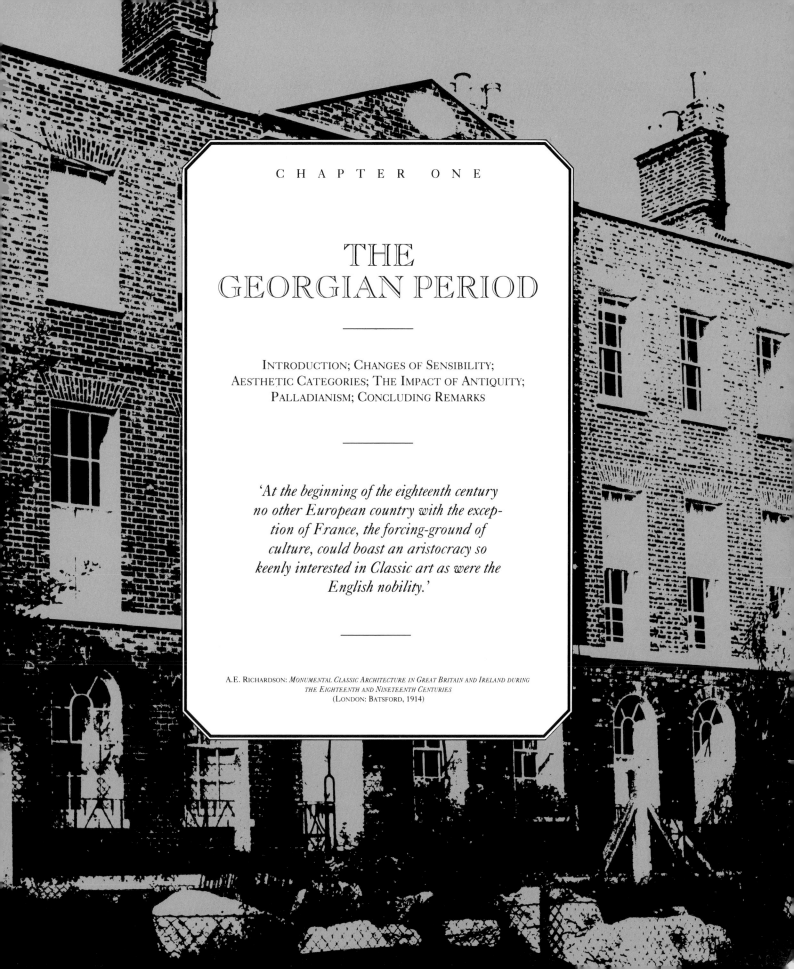

CHAPTER ONE

THE GEORGIAN PERIOD

INTRODUCTION; CHANGES OF SENSIBILITY;
AESTHETIC CATEGORIES; THE IMPACT OF ANTIQUITY;
PALLADIANISM; CONCLUDING REMARKS

*'At the beginning of the eighteenth century
no other European country with the exception of France, the forcing-ground of
culture, could boast an aristocracy so
keenly interested in Classic art as were the
English nobility.'*

A.E. RICHARDSON: *MONUMENTAL CLASSIC ARCHITECTURE IN GREAT BRITAIN AND IRELAND DURING
THE EIGHTEENTH AND NINETEENTH CENTURIES*
(LONDON: BATSFORD, 1914)

PLATE 1 *Duncan Terrace. Islington, London, dating from 1791, probably designed by James Taylor (c 1765–1846): a typical Georgian brick-fronted terrace of houses with sash-windows and fanlights* (JSC).

Introduction

The term 'Georgian Architecture' seems to conjure up in the minds of many people an impression of a modest brick-fronted house (PLATE 1) with white-painted sash-windows, a doorcase probably with a fanlight, and perhaps the travesty of Georgian architecture favoured by estate agents and speculative builders today. Yet there was far, far more to Georgian architecture, for it encompassed a great range of styles, including Gothick, *Chinoiserie*, the 'Indian' or 'Mughal' style, Palladianism, the Revival of Classical Antiquity, the Greek Revival, and much else. The sheer variety of styles was amazing, and it must not be forgotten that the Georgian period also saw the Industrial and Agrarian Revolutions, and so the landscape was transformed and (in the case of the landscape) *designed* during that time. Indeed, it was during the reign of George III that the foundations of an industrialised economy were laid with the development of steam power: the Stockton and Darlington railway was operative in the reign of George IV. Improvements in agriculture were also very considerable.

What do we mean by the 'Georgian period'? It is as well to remind ourselves of this at the outset. The Georgian Age began with the accession of George Lewis, Elector of Hanover (1660–1727) as King of Great Britain and Ireland on the death of Queen Anne on 1 August 1714. In the next year (1715) the Jacobite Rebellion began in Scotland, but ended in 1716, and the Hanoverian Succession was for a time assured. King George I was succeeded by his only son, George Augustus (1683–1760) in 1727, who reigned as King George II: the Jacobite Rebellion of 1745-46 was a serious threat to the Hanoverians in his reign as well, but the destruction of the remnants of the Jacobite army at Culloden ushered in an era of relative stability. The King was succeeded by his grandson, George William Frederick (1738–1820), eldest son of Frederick Lewis, Prince of Wales (1707–51): the new King reigned as George III, but later became incapacitated, partly through increasing blindness, and partly through a growing tendency to derangement, which became acute in 1810. From 1811, George Augustus Frederick, Prince of Wales (1762–1830), became the Regent. During this time the Prince Regent was much occupied with the plans for the laying out of Regent's Park and the surrounding terraces. The Prince succeeded his father as King in 1820, reigning until his death in 1830 as King George IV. Thus, the Georgian period lasted from 1714 to 1830, and the last twenty years or so of the time, dominated as they were by the exotic and showy tastes of the Prince (which included a strong preference for French *Empire* furniture and motifs), produced styles of architecture and design which we call 'Regency'. Of course 'Regency' did not stop in 1830, for aspects of design continued into the reigns of King William IV (1830–37) and Queen Victoria (1837–1901), but we now designate the slightly heavier and more robust design from 1830 as 'William IV' or 'early Victorian'.

With the accession of Victoria, of course, the very close connection of the Throne with the Electorate of Hanover ended. The first two Georges had been born in Osnabrück and Hanover respectively, but George III was born in Norfolk House, St James's Square, and George IV was born in St James's Palace. The 'foreignness' of the first two Georges, and the strength of Jacobite sympathies, meant that the right of both to reign was disputed. This weakness of the Crown increased the influence of the supporters of the Hanoverian Succession, and indeed political power was vested exclusively in the few noble families which claimed to represent the principles of the 'Glorious Revolution' of 1688. The affairs of the nation were therefore controlled by the Whig Oligarchy, which by 1760 had ceased to represent principle, but was cemented by connections, and operated by means of bribery and other corrupt practices. George III, however, did not have the same need as his predecessors for Whig support, and his title to the Throne was not in dispute: he therefore attempted to break the power of the Whig Oligarchy, whose country houses are still one of the great glories of Britain. As will be described below, Whiggery and Palladianism were associated very closely, and it was no coincidence that the decline of Palladian authority coincided with the reign of the new King. If Palladianism had been the dominant style of the reigns of the first two Georges, a far wider choice of styles was available during the reign of George III: Picturesque eclecticism had arrived.

Changes of Sensibility

During the course of the eighteenth century, the problem of transporting heavy goods was made very much easier by the construction of the canal system, with which James Brindley (1716–72) was so intimately concerned from the 1750s, especially in connection with the plans of Francis Egerton, Duke of Bridgewater (1736–1803). Even before then, the first vessel passed through the Newry Canal, Co Down, in 1742, and in 1753 an Act of Parliament[1] was passed to render the River Lagan navigable and to create a passage by water from Lough Neagh to Belfast. The canals had a very profound effect on the economy, and were closely associated with the first phase of the Industrial, Commercial, and Agrarian Revolutions that were to transform and enrich Britain.

Importantly, too, sensibilities changed, and an appreciation of the possibilities of the Picturesque and of Nature as having aesthetic qualities grew. During the long reign of George III (1760–1820) the first steps were taken by which a growing part of the populace – educated, curious, and affluent – would demand political clout. The reforms enacted under William IV were being argued about in the reigns of George III and IV, and it was under William IV that the Throne was stabilised for young Princess Victoria.

There are those who still refer to the Victorian Age as the period when the Industrial Revolution, the railways, slums, the urban poor, and dark, disagreeable urban fabric somehow came into being, spoiling beyond redemption a mythical dream of a pre-industrial Britain. Such a view is overly simple. The Industrial Revolution had begun some eighty years before Victoria ascended the throne.

Daniel Defoe (c 1660-1731) published his *A Tour Through the Whole Island of Great Britain* in three volumes in 1724–27. This is a very interesting view of the state of things in the early-Georgian period, for the Scottish Highlands were not Sublime, but a 'frightful country', not just because they were bleak, mountainous, and terrifying, but because there was no industry there. The Lake District had not then had a Wordsworth to sing its praises, so it was 'barren and wild, of no use or advantage to man or beast', because it was completely undeveloped. Yet somewhere like Halifax could be admired, for its surrounding hillsides were white, not with sheep or flowers, but with newly woven cloth laid out to bleach in the sun. To Defoe child labour was not an affront, but a glorious sight, because it was clear evidence that there was plenty of work for all, and that the district was prosperous. Indeed, the fact that children had a value in that they could work may have made it more attractive to have them and keep them alive, and this, in turn, probably contributed to the great rise in population that was a feature of the nineteenth century.

Britain in the early-Georgian period was very different from what it is now. The vast majority of the population lived in the country, and the countryside had no mystique, nor was it viewed through the rosy spectacles of a town-dweller of the 1990s. Most people lived in it, and it was cold, boring, dark, and ugly: there was also a great deal of it, and the wilder and less populated parts were regarded with horror. It must be remembered that the parliamentary Union with Scotland was very new (1707), although the Crowns had been united since the accession of King James I and VI in 1603. The wild Highlands, so soon after the Jacobite Rising of 1715–16, would therefore have seemed very alien to English eyes, and Defoe had nothing good to say about them. He noted with approval, however, the crumbling decayed walls of British towns and cities, while ruined castles pleased him because

they proved Britons no longer needed to defend themselves from each other (a prematurely optimistic view considering that the 1745–46 Rising was still to come).

Yet by the middle of the century perception of the countryside was changing as aesthetic sensibilities became attuned to a new way of looking at things. This was one of the most remarkable transformations of the Georgian Age.

Aesthetic Categories

It was during the Georgian period that aesthetic categories were established as standards of taste. The three categories were the Beautiful, the Picturesque, and the Sublime. Ever since the Florentine Renaissance, Architecture had aspired to an expression of the ideal, with systems of proportion based on anthropometric perfection. In the eighteenth century, however, the Scottish writers Archibald Alison (1757–1839), Alexander Gerard (1728–95), David Hume (1711–76), Francis Hutcheson, the Ulster-born Scot (1694–1746), Henry Home, Lord Kames (1696–1782), and Dugald Stewart (1753-1828)[2] developed theories of Beauty and Association: Beauty, they claimed, was relative to the sense of the mind that perceived it, and was not an absolute, for each mind saw a different Beauty. Edmund Burke (1729-97) was to produce *A Philosophical Enquiry into the Origin of our Ideas of the Sublime and Beautiful* in 1756, one of the most important aesthetic documents of the period.

According to Burke, Beauty and Sublimity were evoked because of invariable and certain laws, and he ascribed differences of aesthetic judgement to differences in sensibility or powers of observation. Burke[3] did not accept that architectural Beauty was connected with the proportions of the ideal human body; he denied that there was an 'inner sense' of Beauty; and he rejected the notion of mathematics as a measure of Beauty. Beauty, to Burke, was a property which causes love, and it consists in relative smallness, smoothness, absence of angularity, and brightness of colour. Hutcheson argued that Beauty in objects was derived from a compound ratio of uniformity and variety: when the uniformity was equal, Beauty lay in the variety, and where variety was equal, Beauty lay in uniformity. This really is the basis of Palladian composition, especially in large façades where the overall uniformity and regularity of the entire composition is enhanced and made interesting by the invention and scope of the architectural detail.

Alison held that proportion was merely fitness for the ends of stability and support, so it was not a constant or series of constants. Therefore architectural Beauty and proportion were not created by mathematical means, but by an association of fitness of form, shape, size and scale for the function: proportions, openings (such as windows and doors), and masses of wall looked right because they *looked* as though they would work. Alison believed that when any object was presented to the mind, a train of thought was awakened 'analogous to the character or expression of the original object'.[4] He also referred to the connection between the sign and the thing that is signified, and argued that the apprehension of Beauty is accompanied by pleasure, which he termed the 'emotion of Taste'. Qualities of matter were not Beautiful or Sublime in themselves, but they were the 'Signs or Expressions of Qualities capable of producing Emotion'. Alison believed that previous writers had been in error in supposing that aesthetic enjoyment was simple: he argued that it is induced only when the emotion was followed by the 'Excitement of a peculiar exercise of the Imagination' involving an associative train of thought and imagery activated by the object studied in the first place. Such a view, of course, pre-supposes a level of education and sensibility in the person experiencing the emotion which would have been normal among professional, aristocratic, and upper-middle classes then, but which would be elusive (to be charitable) today.

The Picturesque was a standard of taste, largely concerned with landscape, which relied not on the precision of proportion and measurement, but on more emotional responses to associations evocative of persons or events. The Picturesque (from *Pittoresco*, meaning 'in the manner of the painters') was also associated with carefully contrived compositions, particularly those of Claude Lorraine (1600–82), Salvator Rosa (1615–73), Gaspard Dughat, also called Poussin (1615–75), and Nicolas Poussin (1593–1665), and was essentially an anti-urban aesthetic concerned with individuality: it was linked with notions of pleasing the eye, with singularity, and with impinging upon the sensibilities with all the power of a fine landscape painting. To Sir Uvedale Price (1714–1829) the Picturesque comprised all the qualities of nature and art that could be appreciated in studies of paintings executed since the time of Titian, and he argued in his *Essay on the Picturesque* of 1794 in favour of 'natural' beauty, deploring contemporary fashions, such as those established by Lancelot 'Capability' Brown (1716–83) for laying out grounds, because they were at variance with all the principles of landscape painting. Price's arguments were set out by his friend and neighbour, Richard Payne Knight (1750–1824) in his didactic poem, *The Landscape*, of 1794. Price and Knight had a considerable influence over the design of gardens and landscapes in later years, and helped to create a climate in which the asymmetrical, serene, reposeful, and informal aspects of much architectural and landscape design developed in the nineteenth century. The asymmetrical villas of John Nash (1752–1835), for exam-

PLATE 2 *Cronkhill, Shropshire, by John Nash, of* c *1802. An asymmetrically composed Italianate villa* (JSC).

ple (PLATE 2), were a by-product of the Picturesque, and the freeing of architectural composition from the tyranny of symmetry was undoubtedly due to ideas of the Picturesque. The term suggested variety, irregularity, roughness of texture, and it was associated with the power to stimulate imagination.

Thus the eighteenth century saw an increased emphasis on the appreciation of the visual qualities of nature and on the creation of a Beautiful and Picturesque landscape to improve the dull, monotonous, boring countryside that was a feature of the early part of the century. The agreeable countryside with its hedges and carefully planted woods was *designed* in the Georgian period, and was associated with agrarian reform as well as with the desire to create harmonious landscapes and views from the great new houses of the Whig Oligarchy. James Thomson's (1700–48) *The Seasons* of 1726–30 celebrated rustic scenes in a way that was unfamiliar, and helped to create a new fondness for the countryside that spread to Continental Europe as well.

Burke, in his *Philosophical Enquiry*, associated the third category, the Sublime, with Terror. Wild, grand, stupendous, and terrifying aspects of nature were celebrated by many artists during the eighteenth century as indicative of the Sublime. Splendour, darkness, vastness, blackness, flaming chimneys, and gigantic buildings could suggest the Sublime. Ideas of exciting pain, danger, terror, powerful emotion, feelings, or astonishment could be associated with the Sublime. Power, strength, violence, noise, smoke, energy, light, all suggest Sublime terror. Vacuity, darkness, solitude, and silence were just as important in considerations of the Sublime, as Burke reminds us, while hugeness, height, ruggedness, enormous chimneys, and infinity all suggest the Sublime, which was, in essence, the extraordinary, the surprising, and the marvellous. Uniformity, uninterrupted progression (like a vast scheme for a factory façade), and repetitive architectural motifs (such as arcades, colonnades, and windows) also indicate the Sublime. Any structure or landscape that is vast, and which suggests that it came about through the action of immense forces, great numbers of labourers, and gigantic endeavour, suggests the *awefulness* of the Sublime. Noble severity, a new toughness, and a suggestion of bustle, energy, and force were all Sublime. Joseph Wright of Derby (1734–97) suggested the power of the Sublime in many of his paintings, notably those of industrial or scientific subjects, where realism and emotion are strongly represented. Joseph Mallord William Turner (1775–1851) suggested the Sublime in his extraordinary visions of ship-wrecks, storms, and steam-powered trains and ships, while the great Prussian architect, Karl Friedrich Schinkel (1781–1841), who visited England in 1826 (that is, in the reign of George IV), noted the industrial buildings of the north – the immense factories, chimneys, and viaducts – and he likened the great number of chimneys to obelisks. To Schinkel the thousands of smoking obelisks and pottery kilns were grand and 'Egyptian': he understood the excitement of the Sublime in the hugeness of new buildings in Manchester, the potteries at Etruria in Staffordshire, the tremendous vaults of the London docks and warehouses, and the expression of power in iron cranes and mighty industrial architecture.[5]

Burke recognised the power of suggestiveness to stimulate the imagination, and that in nature, as in art, 'a judicious obscurity in some things contributes to the effect of the picture' because dark, confused, uncertain images have a 'greater power on the fancy to form the grander passions than those which are more clear and determinate'. Burke's work made a great impression on Immanuel Kant (1724–1804), whose *Observations on the Feeling of the Beautiful and Sublime* (1764) and *The Critique of Judgement* (1790) are important systematic studies of the theory of art and beauty, and are key works on aesthetics. To Kant, Beauty was not reducible to rules, but results from a direct response to feeling, and is not derived from empirical conformity. Kant saw the Sublime as attached to relatively formless phenomena, and giving a suggestion of infiniteness, such as a storm, a vast mountain-range, the angry sea, or huge thundering waterfalls. Kant observed that the most important distinction between the Sublime and the Beautiful was that a beautiful natural object, such as a flower, conveys a finality in its form, giving us an object in which to delight because the object is preadapted to our judgement, but another object might outrage our imaginations because it creates apprehension, excitement, or terror, and cannot be contained within any precise boundaries by its uncontrollable, formless, violent nature.

Thus it was that eighteenth-century sensibilities began to appreciate the untamed grandeur of nature in all its terrible splendour. The climate was created in which rugged and mountainous scenery, such as that of the Lake District and the Scottish Highlands, could be admired for its Sublime qualities rather than dismissed as 'frightful' or 'dismal'. Fashionable Sublimity was intimately connected with the cult of the Picturesque, and led directly to the Romantic Movement, to an appreciation of Gothic, and to an exploration of the irrational, as in horror novels, that was far removed from the Apollonian clarity of Reason, Optimism, and the European Enlightenment. The way began to be cleared for the remains of a Medieval Catholic past to be viewed as novelties, with delicious shivers of apprehension, and finally with an altogether kindlier eye.

The Impact of Antiquity

One of the most important and significant aspects of Georgian taste was the enormous influence of Classical Antiquity. Classical Roman literature about villa and rural life was read to foster the ideal of contentment through the harmonious balance of 'natural' landscapes and a judiciously planned dwelling, the whole presided over by a benevolent Deity. Roman literature contained descriptions of villas and of life in the country: the most important source was found in the letters of Gaius Plinius Caecilius Secundus (Pliny the Younger [c AD 62–114]), while Quintus Horatius Flaccus (Horace [65–8 BC]), Marcus Valerius Martialis (Martial [c AD 40–104]), and Publius Virgilius Maro (Virgil [70–19 BC]) were also read for their celebrations of the beauty of gardens and landscapes. The problem was how a Georgian landowner could re-create the country villa of Classical Antiquity, for it was fairly obvious that the ideal of the 'happy man' and the benevolent Creator could not be achieved by means of regular walks, topiary, and the formal geometry of the seventeenth-century garden.

It was thought that the great Renaissance gardens in Italy

PLATE 3 *Downhill, Co Londonderry. The vista from the courtyard of the house to the Mussenden Temple, high above the sea. Note the rugged rustication and crenellations. This is an example of the Sublime* (JSC).

Picturesque: they were Sublime. Some stunning juxtapositions involving landscapes of the Sublime variety were created at Powerscourt, Co Wicklow; Inveraray, Argyll; and Downhill, Co Londonderry (the latter the most spectacular of all, sited high above the north coast of Ulster) (PLATE 3). Thus Classical ideals of landscape acquired a peculiarly British air, and the Antique themes were transported into new realms of the creative imagination.

Mention has been made of landscape painting as a source of Georgian landscape-design, especially the views with distant temples and Arcadian scenes. Certainly many of these paintings provided ideal images of the Classical landscape, with a finely balanced juxtaposition of hills, ruins, temples, water, and planting, and gardens such as Stourhead in Wiltshire look very like such compositions, so they may have been influenced by the paintings. Alexander Pope (1688–1744) was adamant in declaring that gardening was landscape painting, while Horace Walpole, (1717–97) Fourth Earl of Orford from 1791, observed that William Kent's (*c* 1685–1748) training as a painter influenced his designs for gardens. Yet, if one looks carefully at paintings of the period showing country gentry with their horses and dogs, set in Italianate landscapes reminiscent of Poussin or Claude, the point comes across strongly that the landowner, with his new Classical house and Picturesque garden, was identifying with Antiquity and creating a new Augustan Age in Georgian Britain. In a sense, the country and its setting not only realised a painting in real life, but enabled the collections of sculpture, paintings, engravings (notably those of Giovanni Battista Piranesi [1720–78] – the Venetian etcher, archaeologist, artist, and architect – with their Sublime and over-scaled visions of Roman ruins), architectural drawings, books of architectural designs, and views of gardens to be housed in a suitable setting. Therefore, the country house and setting were not only created to suggest the translation of the country house of a Pliny or a Virgil to Britain, and the aspirations of the educated British to be seen as modern Romans (with all the virtues of the Ancients), but were a sort of memento or souvenir of the Grand Tour. Furthermore, the Classical house and garden set in a wild and rugged landscape (such as that of the Scottish Highlands or mountainous Ireland) could suggest the bringing of civilisation to parts of the British Isles where the benefits of Roman rule had never been brought before, so the idea of a modern Augustan age was fostered. Works of Antiquity, such as sculpture, cinerary urns, and sarcophagi, would be shown off in a setting intended to re-create both Antiquity and Renaissance Italy, and so the entire ensemble was a variety of mnemonic, a Temple of Memory. The effect was even more startling in a wild, Sublime landscape.

This point is made clear in William Mason's (1724–97) *The English Garden*, published in York in 1783, (although the four

were based on the Antique, and so wealthy Britons on the Grand Tour (an essential part of the Georgian gentleman's education) studied Italian gardens, read their Pliny, Horace, Martial, Virgil, and others, and transplanted a mixture of Classical allusions and Italian garden-design to the British Isles. One of the features of many British gardens was the incorporation of extensive views over the countryside, often framed by artfully planted clumps of trees, so that the working, productive farmland was included in the Picturesque view. Pliny the Younger was enthusiastic about such a scheme of things, which he enjoyed at his country houses, while views of distant countryside were features of many Italian gardens, notably at the Villa d'Este at Tivoli and from the gardens on the Palatine Hill in Rome. The so-called 'English' landscape was therefore based on Antique and Italian precedents, adapted to British climate, topography, and use. Where mountainous landscapes surrounded the house and garden, of course, the distant views over the countryside were more than parts came out in 1772, 1777, 1779, and 1782 respectively): in this work the garden is seen as a memory system, deliberately contrived like a theatrical set. Now this point needs emphasis, for William Kent had worked on theatrical sets in Italy as well as in England, [6] and gardens were often shown as backdrops in the theatre. In Italian gardens theatres were often found, and entertainments of a theatrical type were given in the open air. As Inigo Jones's (1573–1652) designs for Masques found their way into the collections of Richard Boyle, Third Earl of Burlington and Fourth Earl of Cork (1694–1753), it is highly unlikely that early seventeenth-century styles of theatrical design did not have some influence on Burlington or on his protégé, William Kent, and therefore on the Palladian Revival generally. The episodic *scenic* nature of early-Georgian gardens such as those of Chiswick, the Leasowes, Rousham, or Stowe suggests places designed as theatrical set-pieces or as backdrops to civilised life.[7] Of course a series of episodes on a route or routes also suggested a journey, a miniature Grand Tour, or even condensed Classical mythology or the essence of Antiquity and Arcady, experienced in an English garden. With Chinese pagodas and Gothic ruins, as well, an even wider set of allusions could be created.

The Georgian period also saw a tremendous growth of interest in the planting of trees, shrubs, and other plants from outside the shores of the British Isles. This interest was not only scientific (the century was noted for its curiosity about virtually everything), but because of the shortage of timber that had caused concern ever since late Medieval times. The native woodlands had been largely destroyed for purposes of building, for ships, and to make pike-staves and charcoal.[8] The Georgian enclosures, the revolution in agriculture, and the requirements of private hunting enabled a huge programme of planting to take place, and new woodlands and copses, as well as extensive planting of hedgerows (often of shrubs interspersed with trees), were created. Many trees were imported from Mediterranean countries and from North America, and a far greater variety of planting than had been historically the case became possible, so the background colouring of the landscape was changed. Importing trees, moving grown specimens, and changing the very shape of the countryside were no cheap undertakings and it is clear from contemporary accounts that armies of gardeners planted new trees, changed contours, and realised the designs of the landscape gardeners.

Thus, in the eighteenth century, prospects were opened or created; the newly made rationally hedged and fenced countryside was called in to play a role in the long vistas as well as its part in more efficient agriculture; new woodlands were planted; and the old formal regularity of gardens was obliterated. Classical temples were set against a backdrop of foliage;

new and surprising episodes were created; grottoes, rockworks and ruins were built; and waters were dammed, creating new lakes and waterfalls to delight, enhance the picture, and transport the senses and the imagination.

At first, Classical architecture was dominant for garden-buildings, such as temples and belvederes, then a more native note was struck by incorporating genuine ruins of old abbeys and the like into the landscape design (as at Studley Royal in Yorkshire), then by building sham ruins and follies in the 'Gothick' taste. So the native northern architecture began to assume an important role in the design of gardens, with the Italianate and Classical elements. During the second half of the eighteenth century three further movements rose to preeminence. The first was the style of landscape devised by 'Capability' Brown which tended to emphasise the natural features of a site while eliminating all formal elements such as statues, urns, temples, inscriptions, and any geometrical gardens. In other words he revealed the forms of the landscape, but his work was often perceived as dull, and looking too much like ordinary countryside. Unfortunately, the removal of the objects which served as mnemonics, and which stimulated the imaginations of those enjoying the gardens, made the iconographical part of garden-design obscure. Although Brown had been head gardener at Stowe from 1741 to 1751, he rejected the programme suggested by the Elysian Fields, the Temple of Ancient Virtue, the Temple of Modern Virtue (ruined, and with a headless bust of Sir Robert Walpole, First Earl of Orford [1676–1745], to make a strong and moral point), the Parish church, and the Temple of British Worthies (PLATE 4). Brown's style may reflect a change of sensibility, a decline of interest in the Grand Tour and in Classical learning, and a growing belief in the private, individual thought of the human brain, as opposed to the public reaction. The plainer style of Brown gave the individual's mind and eye a wider scope for imagination, unprompted by Classical allusion or inscription, which diluted the connections with Arcady and with Augustan Rome. Thus greater numbers of associational ideas could be induced, but in the process the connection with Antiquity and with Italy was weakened, and indeed confusion could result. The second was the growing taste for the exotic, especially for *Chinoiserie* and Orientalism generally, as exemplified in Sir William Chambers's (1723–96) work at Kew Gardens. The last was the application of Picturesque principles to garden design, dominated by Knight, Price, and Humphry Repton (1752–1818). The latter designer was most successful at relating his landscapes to the buildings, and reintroducing terraces, flower-beds, trellis-work, and conservatories.

Ultimately, these changes widened choice to a bewildering degree, and opened up a range of stylistic possibilities that virtually submerged the connection with Classical Antiquity.

Palladianism

PLATE 4 *Temple of British Worthies, Stowe, Buckinghamshire, by William Kent, of 1733. Note the stepped pyramid at the centre of the composition* (AFK G27847).

In architecture, too, the impact of Antiquity was extremely important. When the Georgian period began, the Baroque style had been firmly established ever since the Restoration of the Monarchy in 1660. Sir Christopher Wren (1632–1723), William Talman (1650–1719), Nicholas Hawksmoor (*c* 1661–1736), Sir John Vanbrugh (1664–1726), James Gibbs (1682–1754), and Thomas Archer (*c* 1668–1743) were the giants who dominated British architecture during its Baroque period.

Wren's architecture was strongly influenced by the work of Claude Perrault (1613–88) and by other French architects, but Gibbs had trained under Carlo Fontana (1638–1714) in Rome, and it shows, especially in his church of St Mary-le-Strand in London of 1714–17 (PLATES 5 AND 6). Archer had travelled widely in Europe too, and that shows as well, the dominant influences being Gianlorenzo Bernini (1598–1680) and Francesco Borromini (1599–1667). Both Vanbrugh and Hawksmoor employed large masses of masonry, extremely emphatic elements such as oversized keystones, and frequent references not only to Antiquity (the Mausoleum at Halicarnassus on the tower of the church of St George, Bloomsbury (PLATE 7), or the belvederes at Blenheim Palace (Oxfordshire) which were based on a Roman temple at Bordeaux recorded by Perrault in his edition of Vitruvius of 1673) but to Roman Baroque, to English Jacobean Architecture (especially Wollaton), to the Grand Manner of the reign of King Louis XIV at Versailles (the plan of Blenheim), and to Medieval architecture (the broach spire of Christ Church, Spitalfields, and Vanbrugh's own house at Greenwich).

Yet in 1715 Lord Burlington, Colen Campbell (1676–1729), and their associates sought to return to principles established by Vitruvius (Marcus Vitruvius Pollio), who flourished in the time of Julius Caesar and Augustus, and who wrote *De Architectura*, a work on architecture drawn from Greek sources, now lost, and from his own experience. This work is the only one of its kind to have come down to us from Antiquity, and appears to date from 16–14 BC. Those Antique principles were perceived as perfectly enshrined in the works of Andrea Palladio (1508–80), the most influential of Italian Renaissance architects, who revived the symmetrical planning of Classical Roman architecture, and who himself made detailed studies of Antique buildings which survived in whole or in part. His buildings in and around Vicenza include several villas with temple-front porticos which he erroneously thought were used on Roman villas, and his work was admired for its

The West end

The South side

PLATE 5 *St Mary-le-Strand, London of 1714–17, by James Gibbs, from Plate 17 of Gibbs's* A Book of Architecture (SM).

PLATE 6 *Side elevation of the church of St Mary-le-Strand, London, from Plate 19 of Gibbs's* A Book of Architecture (SM).

relative clarity of expression and harmony of proportions. In 1554 he published *Le Antichità di Roma* and *Descrizione delle Chiese... di Roma*, provided illustrations for the 1556 edition of Vitruvius, and, in 1570, brought out his enormously important *Quattro Libri dell'Architettura*, which contained theory as well as celebrations of his own buildings.

Inigo Jones had travelled in Italy, and had acquired sufficient expertise to bring the latest Italian designs to England, and between 1605 and 1640 he staged many Masques, plays, and other entertainments for the Courts of James I and VI (1603–25) and Charles I (1625–49). Following a second jour-

ney to Italy in 1613–14 during which he acquired a detailed knowledge of the theory and grammar of Classical architecture not only by visiting buildings, but through the various architectural volumes he bought, including Palladio's *Quattro Libri...*, he changed the face of English architecture. His buildings, including the Queen's House, Greenwich (1616–19), the Queen's chapel, St James's Palace (1623–25), the Banqueting House, Whitehall (1619–22), and St Paul's church and Piazza, Covent Garden (1631–2 and 1631–7 respectively), must have looked shockingly new in a country used to overloaded Elizabethan and Jacobean architecture.

They represent the first Palladian Revival buildings in Northern Europe, but they remained, in the words of Howard Colvin, [9] 'isolated monuments of an art which few even of Jones's own staff at the Office of Works could emulate. On contemporary English taste their influence was limited, because Jones himself designed very little outside the immediate circle of the court, and his style was too esoteric to be easily absorbed by provincial master builders', until Burlington revived Palladianism nearly a century later.

So why did the protagonists of Palladianism have such success from 1715, and turn the clock back nearly a century to re-establish a style which Jones had introduced? The answer seems to lie in the fact that the 'Glorious Revolution' transformed the Whigs from an opposition to leadership of the nation. By the time of the Hanoverian Succession in 1714 Whigs were determined to support that Succession, to give allegiance to a species of liberal Anglicanism as the ideological support for Court and Government, and to use Freemasonry as the vehicle for the transmission of their ideology.[10] Freemasonry had been brought south with the Stuart Court, and it had long been associated with the Scottish Royal House. Sir Robert Walpole was a Freemason, and his Houghton Hall in Norfolk was one of the great Palladian mansions of the period. The 1715 Jacobite Rebellion threatened the Whig Oligarchy as much as the Hanoverians, and it was no accident that Grand Lodge was established in 1717, the year after the Rebellion was suppressed. This was to enable the Craft to be purged of all Jacobite elements and to line it up firmly on the Protestant-Hanoverian-Whig side, a point that comes out in *The Constitutions of the Freemasons* of 1723, by which date the Craft was aggressively Hanoverian, supporting the Establishment, and with its leadership drawn from the great Whig Oligarchy and from the Newtonian scientists.[11]

Just as Georgian Freemasonry was Royalist and supportive of the Hanoverians, the Palladian style had strong Royalist associations, for it had, after all, been the Court style of James I and VI and Charles I. It seems that the second Palladian Revival, led by Lord Burlington (himself a Whig) and his circle, was at least partly promoted to demonstrate the historical and dynastic links of the Hanoverians with the Stuarts through the line of Princess Elizabeth (1596–1662) – eldest daughter of King James I and VI, and later Electress Palatine – and therefore to declare the legitimacy of the Succession after the catastrophes of the reign of Charles I, the Civil War, the Commonwealth, and the uncertainties of the reigns of the last Stuarts, especially relating to religion and groups to be favoured. Palladianism was therefore almost an official style, favoured by the Whig Oligarchy, which was also firmly behind a purified Freemasonry.[12] It was no wonder that, in the years following 1715, it found favour as *the* country-house

PLATE 7 *The church of St George, Bloomsbury, London, by Nicholas Hawksmoor, of 1716–31, with a prostyle hexastyle Corinthian portico based on a Roman temple front, and a spire derived from descriptions of the Mausoleum at Halicarnassus. An example of a Baroque church, though with Antique influences* (AFK H1768).

style: Baroque, after all, had associations with the Tories, with Absolutism, with France, and, above all, with Popery. The new climate established from 1714 *needed* a style that would convey continuity, yet would be somehow purer, connected with Antiquity, and suited to the aspirations of the Georgian Age. Palladianism answered all those requirements: if ever there was an 'early-Georgian' style, it was the second Palladian Revival.

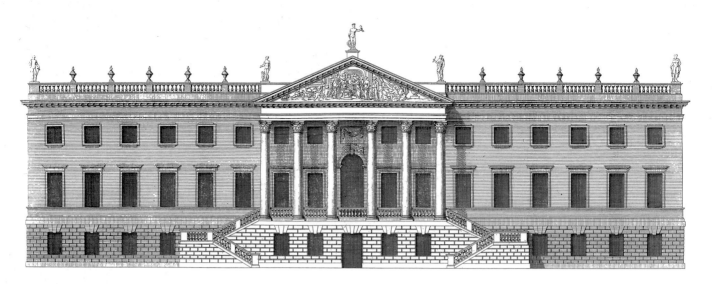

Concluding Remarks

PLATE 8 *The first design for Wanstead, Essex, by Colen Campbell (*c *1714), showing the* perron *and hexastyle portico at* piano nobile *level, from* VB, *Vol I, Plate 22* (SM).

The Tories, who had gained power in 1710, intended that the new London churches should be truly monumental (PLATE 7), to suggest the power of the Tory High-Church Establishment, so architecture as political propaganda was already on the eighteenth-century agenda. Lord Shaftesbury (1671–1713) wrote in 1712 the treatise *Concerning Art, or the Science of Design*, published in 1714, in which he castigated Baroque because it was not rational, and was indicative of subversive Continental influences, notably those emanating from France. He attacked Wren (whose architecture was strongly influenced by France), and argued for the establishment of a 'National Taste'. The Whig Shaftesbury aroused a response. In 1715 the first volume of Colen Campbell's *Vitruvius Britannicus, or The British Architect*, appeared: Campbell was patronised by the great Whig aristocrat John Campbell, Second Duke of Argyll and Duke of Greenwich (1678–1743), and the book illustrated the most important works of architecture built in England from the early seventeenth century, including Campbell's own Wanstead House, Essex (*c* 1713–20). Wanstead was austere, with a horizontal emphasis and a huge hexastyle portico (the first country-house portico was at The Vyne, Hampshire, of *c* 1655) at *piano-nobile* level (PLATE 8). In his preface, Campbell attacked the prevailing love of foreign architecture, especially the 'affected and licentious' work of Bernini, Fontana, and Borromini, and extolled 'Antique Simplicity'. Palladio he presented as a great contrast to Baroque corruptions, more correctly connected with Antiquity, and he especially praised Palladio's influence on Inigo Jones. Then Giacomo Leoni (*c* 1686–1746) published the English transla-

tion of Palladio's *Quattro Libri*... from 1715 to 1720, and the Italian Alessandro Galilei (1691–1737) was invited to England in 1714 as part of the attempt to encourage a more correctly Classical architecture.

Galilei was invited by John Molesworth (*ob* 1726), who, with his father (*ob* 1725) – created First Viscount Molesworth in 1716 – Sir Thomas Hewett (1656–1726), and Sir George Markham, formed the 'new Junta for Architecture', the aim of which was to introduce a true Classical style to supplant the tainted Absolutist and Papist Baroque. Hewett was appointed Surveyor-General of the King's Works in 1719, succeeding William Benson (1682–1754) and his deputy, Colen Campbell. Benson had managed to get Wren removed from the office in 1718: under Hewett's influence architects sympathetic to the Palladian style were favoured, and obtained the plum public posts. Campbell's presentation of the works of Palladio, Jones, and John Webb (1611–72) together with the swift acquisition of all the influential positions by Whigs, led to the adoption of Palladianism as *the* style of the early-Georgian period, notably for country houses and public buildings. Apart from Burlington, Shaftesbury, Campbell, and Kent, Henry Herbert, Ninth Earl of Pembroke (1693–1751) and the cousins Roger (1695–1749) and Robert (*c* 1702–54) Morris were among the leaders of the revolution which supplanted the inventive English Baroque style in favour of rule-book Palladianism involving a synthesis of the works of Palladio and those of Inigo Jones. The objects included the creation of a National Style and the cutting of the ties of dependence in matters of taste on Roman Catholic France. As we shall see, the movement was remarkably successful.

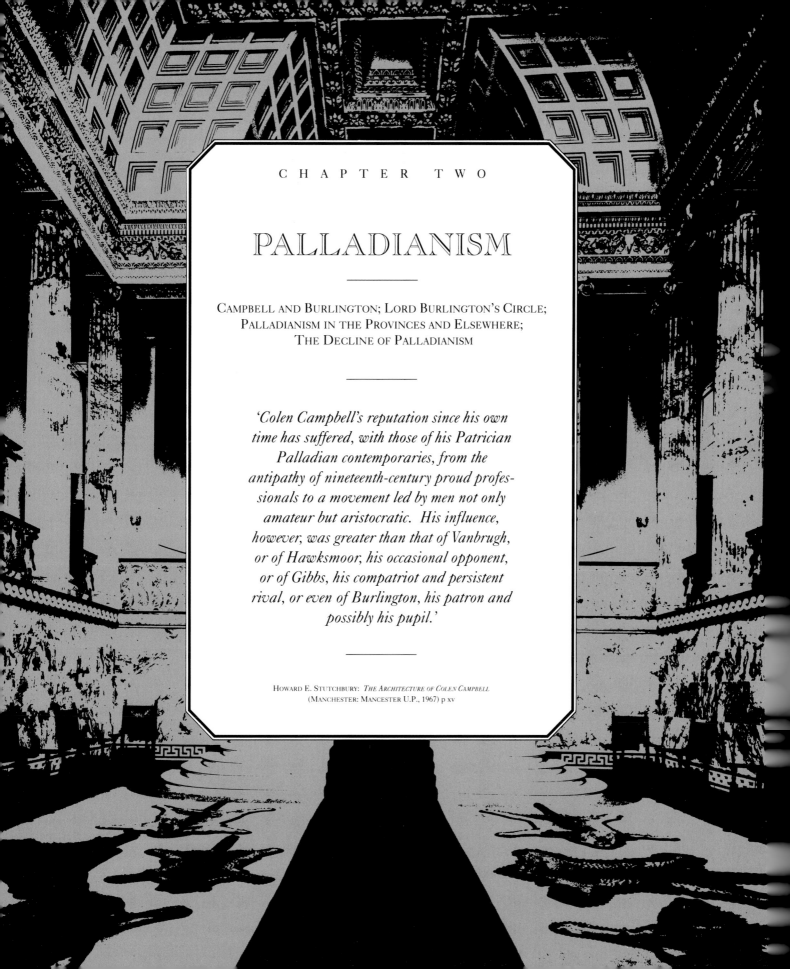

PALLADIANISM

---

*'Colen Campbell's reputation since his own
time has suffered, with those of his Patrician
Palladian contemporaries, from the
antipathy of nineteenth-century proud profes-
sionals to a movement led by men not only
amateur but aristocratic. His influence,
however, was greater than that of Vanbrugh,
or of Hawksmoor, his occasional opponent,
or of Gibbs, his compatriot and persistent
rival, or even of Burlington, his patron and
possibly his pupil.'*

HOWARD E. STUTCHBURY: *THE ARCHITECTURE OF COLEN CAMPBELL*
(MANCHESTER: MANCESTER U.P., 1967) p xv

Campbell and Burlington

T he origins of Palladianism have been outlined in the previous chapter, and the main protagonists identified. The Earl of Shaftesbury argued that the visual arts should have a basis in truth rather than in fancy, and that they should therefore be based on sound precedents, and those models of perfection were found in Classical Antiquity and in Vitruvius. Inigo Jones had not cared for heavily ornamented buildings which 'wear brought in by Mihill Angell and his followers', and an 'aboundance of dessignes' did 'not well in sollid Architecture'. He went on to compare how

*'euery wyse ma(n) carrieth a grauiti in Publicke Places, whear
ther is nothing els looked for, & yt inwardly hath his
Immaginacy set free, and sumetimes licenciously flying out... So
in architecture yᵉ outward ornamentes oft to be Sollid, propor-
sionable according to the rulles, masculine and unaffected'.[1]*

The search for what Shaftesbury termed a 'National Taste'[2] led men against the Court Architecture of William and Mary (1688–1702), and Anne (1702–14), and there was clearly a change of feeling opposed to the Baroque of Wren, Vanbrugh,

Hawksmoor, Archer, and Gibbs. Shaftesbury specifically denounced Wren's additions to Hampton Court, and declared the 'Publick' would hardly be able to bear a 'new Cathedral' like St Paul's. John James (*c* 1672–1746), in a letter[3] to the Duke of Buckingham in 1711, expressed the hope that for once in his life he might have the 'Opportunity of shewing that the Beautys of Architecture may consist with ye Greatest plainness of the Structure', something he held had 'scarce ever been hit by the Tramontani unless by our famous Mr. Inigo Jones'. In spite of this, James's buildings, such as St George's, Hanover Square, of 1720–25, looked anything but Palladian, and only his Wricklemarsh at Blackheath of *c* 1725 had any claim to be Palladian.

Peckwater Quadrangle at Christ Church, Oxford, built by William Townesend from 1707, was completed in 1714, and is the first Palladian palace-fronted composition in England even earlier than Campbell's and Wood's more famous contributions. Peckwater is constructed around three sides of a quadrangle, with three matching elevations, rusticated ground floor, Giant Order of Ionic pilasters rising through the upper storeys, and with pediments carried on hexastyle engaged

Ionic temple-fronts. The designer was Henry Aldrich (1648-1710), Dean of Christ Church, a man steeped in Classical learning, and the author of *Elementa Architecturae Civilis*, published in 1789. Colvin has noted that the façades of Peckwater, designed in 1706, 'anticipate those of Queen Square, Bath, by some twenty years, and entitle Aldrich to be regarded as one of the forerunners of the Palladian movement which he did not live to see' (PLATE 9).

However, early and important though Aldrich's work was, it was eclipsed by the contribution of Colen Campbell, who was not only well connected, but arrived on the scene at exactly the right moment. Campbell came of the Campbells of Cawdor Castle, and seems to have been a lawyer at first. He may have been associated with James Smith (*c* 1645–1731), Architect, of Edinburgh, described by Campbell in *Vitruvius Britannicus* as the 'most experienced Architect' in Scotland. Smith knew Italy, and he may have been the formative influence on Campbell. The latter arrived in London late in 1711 or early in 1712, in which year he submitted several designs to the Commission for Building Fifty New Churches in or near the Cities of London and Westminster or their suburbs. As has been mentioned earlier, the Tories (who were also High Churchmen) came to power in 1710, the Act[4] for building the churches was passed in 1711, and a Commission was established which included Sir Christopher Wren, Sir John Vanbrugh, and Thomas Archer. This Commission appointed Nicholas Hawksmoor and William Dickinson (*c* 1671–1725) Surveyors. Dickinson took up another position in 1713, and was succeeded by James Gibbs, (another Scot), who designed St Mary-le-Strand (PLATES 5-6) but who was deprived of office in 1716 as a Papist and suspected Jacobite. Campbell probably was the fellow-countryman Gibbs claimed intrigued to have him removed. Gibbs was replaced by John James. The change of Government and the accession of George I had severe repercussions, but Hawksmoor and James remained in office until the Commission was wound up in 1733.

Campbell commenced the collection of drawings for the plates in his volume, and the first book of *Vitruvius Britannicus* appeared in 1715. Other volumes appeared in 1717 and 1725, and all were published by subscription. *Vitruvius Britannicus* was supposed to be a comprehensive collection of modern British architecture, but was essentially propaganda for the superiority of 'Antique Simplicity' over the Baroque, and presented the 'renowned Palladio' and the 'famous' Inigo Jones as exemplary figures. Campbell celebrated Palladian architecture at exactly the right moment, for taste was veering away from the style of Wren, and the change of political climate gave him the opportunity to advertise his own architectural work. Designs were published, addressed to prominent Whigs, and the first volume was dedicated to King George I, who responded to the flattery with gifts of money.

When William Benson managed to persuade the Whig ministry to dismiss Wren from the surveyorship of the Works in 1718, and get himself appointed instead, Campbell was made Chief Clerk and Deputy Surveyor, but both Benson and Campbell were sacked in 1719, because, in the words of Hawksmoor, Benson had 'got more in one year' for 'confusing' the King's Works than Wren did in '40 years for his honest endeavours', and because Benson tried to insist that the House of Lords was about to fall down: Benson and Campbell had ambitious plans to provide a vast new Palladian Palace of Westminster, and tiresome old buildings stood in the way of their scheme, which, in the event, was not realised.

In 1719 Benson was involved in the building of Stourhead House, Wiltshire, by his brother-in-law, the banker Henry Hoare, to designs by Campbell (PLATES 10–11). The latter had built Shawfield Mansion, Glasgow, in 1711–12, and Wanstead House, that great and early Palladian pile, was begun c 1713 to designs by Campbell for Sir Richard Child, and illustrated in its various forms in *Vitruvius Britannicus*, Vol I, plates 21–26 (PLATES 8 AND 12) and Vol III, plates 39–41 (PLATE 13). Campbell also produced a design for a house for John Hedworth at Chester-le-Street, Co Durham, in 1716, illustrated in Vol II, plate 88, and a house in Eastgate, Beverley, Yorkshire, in 1716–17, illustrated in Vol II, plate 87. In 1717–24 the Rolls House, Chancery Lane, was built to Campbell's designs, illustrated in Vol III, plates 44–45, and in 1718 he designed Ebberston Lodge, near Scarborough illustrated in Vol III, plate 47. It would be difficult to overestimate the effect *Vitruvius Britannicus* had on taste, for the volumes were instrumental in publicising the style and Campbell's own work. A revolution had begun.

Palladianism also received a valuable boost when Giacomo Leoni published *The Architecture of A. Palladio, Revis'd, Design'd, and Publish'd by Giacomo Leoni, a Venetian: Architect to his most Serene Highness, the Elector Palatine*, with a text in English, French, and Italian, the first volume of which appeared in 1715, and the fifth in 1720. This was not only the first adequate edition of Palladio's *Quattro Libri* to appear since 1642, but had new illustrations by Leoni which replaced Palladio's woodcuts. Although Leoni was rather free in his interpretation of the illustrations, which had taken him several years to prepare, there was no doubt that his pictures were more attractive and informative than the originals, and the book was an instant and influential success. A second edition, with text only in English, came out in 1721, and a third, with notes and remarks of Inigo Jones taken from papers in Worcester College, Oxford, appeared in 1742.

The publication of the first volumes of *Vitruvius Britannicus* and of Leoni's *Palladio* provided two standard books of the English Palladian Revival. The *Palladio* was eventually superseded by Isaac Ware's (*ob* 1766) edition of Palladio's

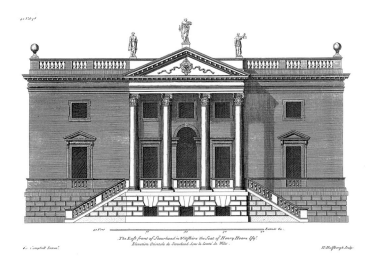

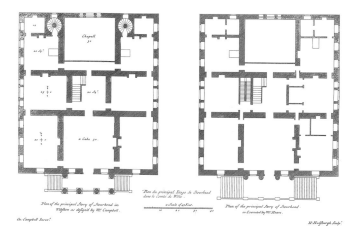

PLATE 10 *East elevation of Stourhead, Wiltshire, by Colen Campbell, from* VB, *Vol III, Plate 42. Note the prostyle tetrastyle Composite portico, rusticated base, and clearly defined* piano nobile *level* (SM).

Plate 11 *Plans of the principal floor of Stourhead, Wiltshire. On the left is Campbell's design, and on the right is Hoare's executed design. From* VB, *Vol III, Plate 41. Note the clear geometry of the dispositions of rooms and openings* (SM).

Four Books of Architecture of 1738, with new plates engraved by Ware: this later publication was a scholarly book, which can still be admired as a reliable work. However, Campbell's *Vitruvius Britannicus* and Leoni's *Palladio* were probably the catalysts that stimulated the interest of the Third Earl of Burlington and Fourth Earl of Cork. Burlington was to become the chief Arbiter of Taste during the early-Georgian period, and was the High Priest of Palladianism. He had made the Grand Tour in 1714–15, and designed the Bagnio or Casina at Chiswick House, Middlesex, his first essay in architecture, in 1717, but it was only after the publication of Leoni and Campbell that he returned to Italy in 1719 to see the buildings by Palladio in and around Vicenza for himself. He returned to England with William Kent, who was to carry out various commissions for painting ceilings, but who was later to turn to architecture. Burlington was now badly bitten by the Palladian bug, and, with Campbell, sought to make Palladian architecture the National Style, carrying it on from the auspicious beginnings established in the seventeenth century by Inigo Jones. He sacked Gibbs, who was working on the Earl's house in Piccadilly, and appointed Campbell as his architect.

In 1720–21 Burlington purchased drawings by Inigo Jones and John Webb from John Talman (1677–1726), eldest son of the architect William Talman, the leading Whig architect of the 1680s and 1690s. These drawings were published by William Kent as *Designs of Inigo Jones* in 1727, with several plates of designs by Burlington included, as well as the drawings by Palladio which Jones had bought in 1614. Burlington had found Palladio's drawings of Roman *Thermae* and other Antique buildings in the Villa Maser in 1718, and had purchased some of them from the Bishop of Verona: a selection of these drawings was published by Burlington as *Fabbriche Antiche disegnate da Andrea Palladio* in 1730. Various drawings in Burlington's collections were published by Hoppus in *Palladio* (1735), by Ware in *Designs by Inigo Jones and Others* (1743), and by Vardy in *Some Designs of Mr. Inigo Jones and Mr. William Kent* (1744). Ware dedicated his 1738 *Palladio* to Burlington.

Burlington fell out with Campbell in the 1720s, and began to practise as an architect, assisted by Henry Flitcroft (1697–1769), who became known as 'Burlington Harry', and who rose to become Comptroller of Works as a result of Burlington's patronage. Burlington also retained the services of Daniel Garrett (*ob* 1753) and of a draughtsman, Samuel Savill. Burlington designed the new dormitory at Westminster School (1724) (PLATE 14), designs for which had been made earlier by Wren and Dickinson, so this marked an important moment in his single-minded campaign to restore Vitruvian principles as practised by Jones, Palladio, and Vincenzo Scamozzi (1552–1616). Burlington's knowledge of Antique architecture came largely from his study of Palladio's

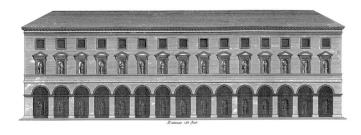

PLATE 12 *The second design for Wanstead, Essex, by Colen Campbell (c 1714–15) showing the cupola. The composition owes something to Vanbrugh's Castle Howard. From* VB, *Vol I, Plate 25 (BAL/RIBA).*

PLATE 13 *The third design for Wanstead, Essex, by Colen Campbell, of 1720, a variation on the second design, but omitting the cupola over the hall, and with towers at each end (which were not built). This was the model for English Palladian country houses for the next century, and the composition was the precedent for many buildings, including Georg Wenzeslaus von Knobelsdorff's Berlin Opera House on the Unter den Linden, of 1740. From* VB, *Vol III, Plate 39-40 (BAL/RIBA).*

PLATE 14 *Burlington's design for the dormitory block at Westminster School, of 1722–30, from William Kent's* Designs of Inigo Jones, *Vol II, Part 2, Plate 51 (SM).*

illustrations which provided many familiar English Palladian motifs such as the Diocletian or 'Thermal' window, coffered vaulted ceilings, and the closely spaced columns of the so-called 'Egyptian' Hall: other 'Palladian' motifs came from drawings by Jones and Webb. Characteristic Palladian features recur in Burlington's Architecture of the 1720s and 1730s: his Tottenham Park, Wiltshire, of 1721 has towers derived from Wilton House, Wiltshire, embellished with the Serliana or Palladian/Venetian window; at Chiswick Venetian windows are incorporated, and the Thermal window occurs in the clerestory of the central Octagon (PLATE 15); and at York, the Assembly Rooms of 1731–32 were an archaeological reconstruction of the Vitruvian 'Egyptian Hall' as interpreted by Palladio (PLATE 16). By then all the themes of the Second Palladian Revival had become familiar and were common currency: the style for Whig country houses and public buildings was established.

Burlington, the 'Palladio and Jones of our times', as Scipione Maffei described him, had become *the* authority on matters of architectural style and taste, and his advice was sought by anyone who mattered in Georgian England. His protégé, William Kent, had by this time become an architect, and in 1726 Kent became Master-Carpenter to the Board of Works, rising in 1735 to be Master-Mason and Deputy Surveyor. As a member of the Board of Works, Kent designed his celebrated Horse Guards, Whitehall (designed in 1748 but built 1750–59) (PLATE 17), Royal Mews (1731–33), and Treasury Buildings, Whitehall (1733–37).

Although Burlington had abandoned Campbell for Flitcroft and Kent, Campbell had a series of rich, influential Whig patrons who kept him busy: they included John Aislabie (1670–1742), Henry Hoare (*ob* 1725), the Earl of Pembroke, and Sir Robert Walpole. His Wanstead House was a model for a whole series of great houses, including Wentworth Woodhouse, Yorkshire, by Flitcroft, of *c* 1735 (PLATE 18), Nostell Priory, Yorkshire, by James Paine (1717–89), *c* 1737, and John Wood the Elder's (1704–54) Prior Park, near Bath, of 1735. However, Campbell's smaller Palladian villas at Newby (Baldersby) Park, Yorkshire (1720) (PLATE 19), and Stourhead, Wiltshire (1720) (PLATES 10–11) were even more influential. His mighty Houghton Hall, Norfolk, begun in 1722 (with modification to corner towers in 1735 by Gibbs, and to the interior by Kent), was one the grandest houses of the Palladian Revival and of the Whig Oligarchy (PLATES 20–21). In 1722–25 Campbell produced the very remarkable Mereworth Castle in Kent, and with its formal symmetrical plan, central domed rotunda, and Ionic hexastyle porticoes, based on Palladio's Villa Capra near Vicenza (PLATES 22–24).

Burlington also designed Chiswick Villa in *c* 1723, inspired by the Villa Capra, but it has an octagonal central space lit

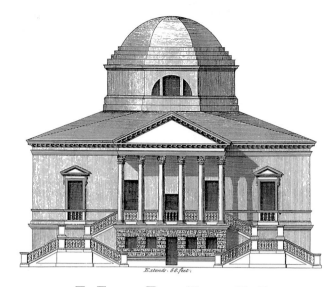

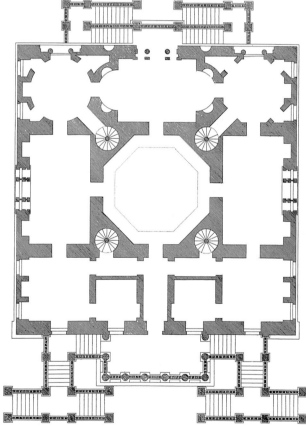

PLATE 15 *Lord Burlington's villa at Chiswick: main elevation and plan. Note the Thermal window in the octagon, the* perron, *and the prostyle hexastyle portico at* piano-nobile *level. Note the sequence of rooms on the garden-front based on Palladio's plan for the Palazzo Thiene, Vicenza. From* Designs of Inigo Jones, *Plate 71* (SM).

PLATE 16 *The interior of the Assembly Rooms, York, by Lord Burlington, based on the 'Egyptian Hall' of Vitruvius, as interpreted by Palladio* (RCHME YC 1373).

PLATE 17 *Horse Guards building, Whitehall, London, by William Kent, of 1748–59, from* VB, *Vol V, Plates 7–8* (BAL/RIBA).

PLATE 18 *Wentworth Woodhouse, Yorkshire, by Henry Flitcroft ('Burlington Harry'), of* c *1735, one of the grandest Palladian compositions derived from Wanstead* (JSC).

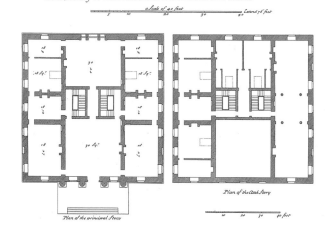

PLATE 19 *Newby Park, Yorkshire, of 1720, by Colen Campbell, from VB, Vol III, Plate 46* (SM).

PLATE 20 *Houghton Hall, Norfolk: the south front as designed by Colen Campbell, and begun in 1722. Note the tetrastyle portico at* piano-nobile *level, the* perron, *the towers at the corners derived from Wilton House, Wiltshire, and the Serlianas set in the* piano-nobile *front of the towers. From* VB, *Vol III, Plate 33* (SM).

PLATE 21 *Houghton as built. Note that the portico is now engaged rather than prostyle, and the Jonesian towers have been replaced by Baroque cupolas by Gibbs, 1725–28, 'obstinately raised...in defiance of all the virtuosi'* (JSC).

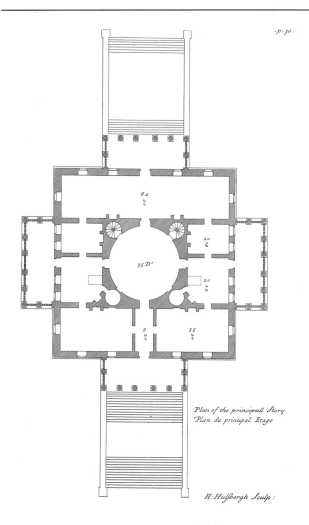

p:30.

Plan of the principall Story
Plan du principal Etage

H. Hulsbergh Sculp:

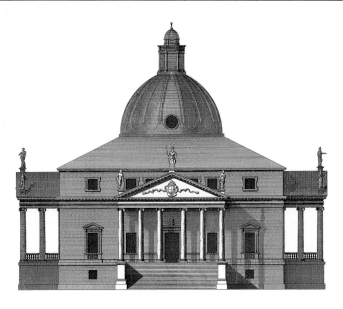

PLATE 24 *Elevation of Mereworth
Castle, near Maidstone, in Kent,
from* VB, *Vol III, Plate 37* (SM).

PLATE 22 *Plan of the* piano-
nobile *level at Mereworth Castle,
Kent, by Colen Campbell, from* VB,
*Vol III, Plate 36. Note the four
prostyle hexastyle porticoes, central
rotunda, and resemblance to
Palladio's Villa Capra near
Vicenza* (SM).

p:38.Vol:3.d

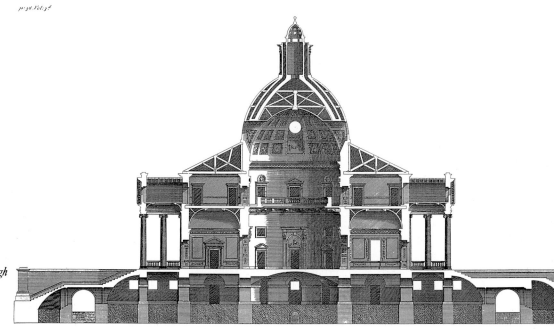

PLATE 23 *Section through
Mereworth Castle, Kent,
from* VB, *Vol III, Plate
38* (SM).

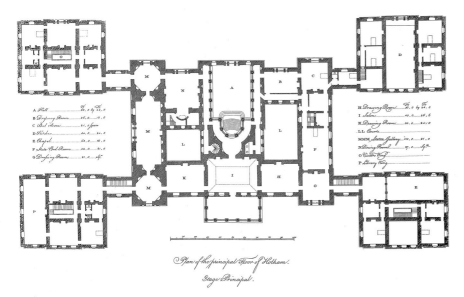

from above, only one hexastyle Corinthian portico at *piano-nobile* level reached by a *perron*, and a sequence of three rooms on the garden-front, the centre rectangular with apses at each end, flanked by circular and octagonal chambers (PLATE 15). These three rooms are derived from Palladio's Palazzo Thiene in Vicenza, which had been created to suggest an Antique sequence of rooms. Burlington's use of geometry influenced later architects, notably Robert Adam.

William Kent may have designed the remarkable stables at Houghton, with their severe, plain brickwork, and Antique air, and we know he designed ceilings and chimney-pieces for the great house. But his most stunning exercise in Palladianism is undoubtedly Holkham Hall, Norfolk, of 1734, with contributions from Lords Burlington and Leicester (the client): the final work was realised under the direction of Matthew Brettingham (1699–1769). Holkham is a remarkable composition, with a central block to which are attached four pavilions or wings, each symmetrically arranged and capable of standing alone as a Palladian exemplar (PLATES 25–26). The *piano nobile* is set above a rusticated base, and there are four towers at each corner of the central block. The attic-storey is clearly

expressed, and there are several Serlianas or Venetian windows. Lord Leicester had made the Grand Tour, and wished to have a house to set off his newly acquired collections of paintings and Classical sculpture. Kent designed an entrance-hall of immense grandeur and gravity, with a coffered ceiling, an Order of Ionic columns sitting on a mighty base faced with slabs of pink Derbyshire alabaster, and a stair leading up to the *piano-nobile* level on which the Ionic columns stand (PLATE 27). The curved apsidal end holding the stair has a screen of columns derived from Palladio's San Giorgio Maggiore in Venice; the frieze of garlands, bucrania, and *putti* is derived from the Temple of Fortuna Virilis in Rome; and the columnar arrangement suggests, in part, the majesty of a Roman basilica. This basilican plan was described by Vitruvius and reconstructed by Palladio in his *Quattro Libri...* The voids behind the apse were described as 'places for filth', so Kent placed water-closets in his voids at Holkham. Everything in this Stone Hall is dramatic and grand, yet the ensemble is under great control, derived firmly from Classicism, and stripped of all Baroque rhetoric.

Kent was a designer with a greater range of expression than

either Burlington or Campbell. At Esher Place in Surrey he added in *c* 1733 Gothick elements to 'Wolsey's Tower', thereby demonstrating a sensitivity to historical precedent worthy of a Vanbrugh. At Stowe, Buckinghamshire, he designed garden-buildings, including the Temple of Venus (*c* 1730), the Temple of Ancient Virtue (*c* 1734), the Temple of British Worthies (*c* 1735) (Plate 4), Congreve's Monument (1736), and the Oxford Gate, Hermitage, and Shepherd's Cove. Gibbs also designed several buildings for the gardens at Stowe, including the remarkable Gothick Temple of 1741–44 (PLATE 28). At Claremont in Surrey and Rousham in Oxfordshire, Kent also designed garden-buildings, and showed that his training as a painter enabled him to compose scenes in the manner of a Claude or a Poussin. His Elysian Fields at Stowe, for example, mingle architecture and landscape in a manner to suggest Arcady and Antiquity. At Stowe, the Temple of Ancient Virtue is derived from Roman circular temples such as that of Vesta at Tivoli.[5]

It was apparent that the Palladian Revival had evolved into something rather like Holy Writ, with rules and laws governing its proportions and details: any deviation was seen as evidence of ignorance or worse. The argument included the theory that in Antiquity laws of architecture had been evolved which were basically demonstrated in the three *Roman* Orders: Doric, Ionic, and Corinthian. Each of these Orders had a significance. Doric was masculine, strong, and unaffected; Ionic represented wisdom; and Corinthian suggested beauty and femininity. These notions are enshrined in the lore of Freemasonry, of course,[6] which fitted in very 'neatly' (to use a favourite Georgian all-purpose word) with Whig aspirations and influence. The laws of architecture had been revived by Palladio, who demonstrated that the architecture of Antiquity, as described by Vitruvius, and which could be studied in Rome itself, up to a point, could be recovered, and could be used for modern buildings. The principles, the eternal verities of architecture, as perfected in Antiquity, had been rediscovered and refined by Palladio, and had been brought to England by Inigo Jones in the reign of James I and VI. The re-establishment of an ordered Government, the securing of the Protestant and Hanoverian Succession, and the elimination of threats of Absolutism and Popery, with the Whig Oligarchy firmly in charge, demanded a 'National Style' of architecture, and that style was Palladianism, making clear the legitimate descent from the Stuart line without all the difficulties experienced in the reigns of Charles I (1625–49), Charles II (1660–85), and James II and VII (1685–88).

The Palladians introduced several new notions, including the uniform terrace of houses with no columns or pilasters (that is, astylar), which first appeared in a design by Colen Campbell in 1717 at 31–34 Old Burlington Street, London. Even Inigo Jones's houses set on the arcades which became known as 'piazzas' had pilasters at the upper levels, but Campbell's plain brick façades only had string-courses, a crowning cornice, moulded architraves, and doorcases with consoles and cornices. Giacomo Leoni designed the first town mansion in a terrace with an Antique temple-front at Queensberry House, 7 Burlington Gardens of 1721, and Burlington himself designed the first astylar Palladian town mansion at Mountrath House, 30 Old Burlington Street, of 1721.

One of the most influential of Palladian exemplars was the house Burlington designed for General George Wade (1673–1748) in 1723 that stood at 29 Great (now Old) Burlington Street, and was closely based on a design by Palladio in His Lordship's collection (PLATE 29). The lowest storey was heavily rusticated with five arches behind which was the central entrance with two windows on either side, all rectangular, with the tympana above decorated with cartouches and swags. The five bays above were rusticated, with arches, and an Order of unfluted Roman Doric pilasters was attached to the rusticated walls, carrying a Doric entablature with bucrania. In the centre arch of the first floor was a favourite Palladian motif, the Serliana or Venetian window,

PLATE 27 LEFT *Interior of the Hall at Holkham* (RCHME BB66/3638).

PLATE 28 *The Gothick Temple, or Temple of Liberty, at Stowe, by Gibbs, with lantern pinnacle-towers by Sanderson Miller* (AFK G27852).

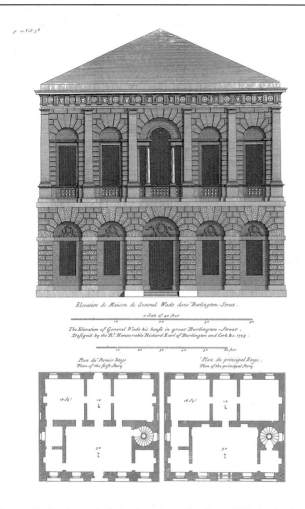

p. to Vol.3.

Elevation de Maison de General Wade dans Burlington Street.

a Scale of 40 feet

The Elevation of General Wade his house in great Burlington-Street.
Designd by the Rt Honourable Richard Earl of Burlington and Cork &c. 1723.

Plan du Premier Etage.
Plan of the first Story.

Plan du principal Etage.
Plan of the principal Story.

PLATE 29 *Burlington's design for a house for General Wade, showing the elevation to Burlington Street and the two floor plans. Note the rusticated ground floor and the Order of Roman Doric pilasters above, with the central Serliana set in an arch. From* VB, *Vol III, Plate 10* (SM).

many town-houses, including Campbell's Burlington House, Piccadilly (1718–19) and Leoni's Queensberry House, and remained an exemplar throughout the century, influencing Sir Robert Taylor (1714–88) at Heveningham Hall, Suffolk (1778–80) (PLATE 30), and Sir William Chambers at Somerset House, The Strand (1776–96). But the importance of the Wade house was the layering or modelling of the façade, the use of the Venetian window in the arch, and the scholarly archaeological approach to the design involving not only imitation of the best exemplars, but refinement of tried motifs from Palladio, Jones, and Webb, who were the admired architects of previous generations. Having created refined buildings based on approved precedents, the new works of the Palladians then became models themselves, and were copied again and again.

Lord Burlington's Circle

As has been made clear, however, the success of Palladianism was not solely because exemplars were admired and published (although the fact of their publication undoubtedly helped the dissemination of Palladian motifs): it was to a very large extent due to the creation of a 'Circle' which embraced the architects Campbell, Kent, Flitcroft, and Roger Morris. The latter was not merely an orthodox Palladian (as at his charming Marble Hill, Twickenham, of 1724–29), but the inventor of a villa style of his own (notably Combe Bank, Sundridge, Kent, of *c* 1725, and Whitton Place, Middlesex, of *c* 1732). Morris also used a Tuscan portico for the stable-block at Althorp, Northamptonshire, of *c* 1732 (PLATE 31), which looked back to Jones's St Paul's, Covent Garden, and which, as Mr. Colvin notes, 'has no obvious parallel in contemporary Georgian Architecture'.[7] Another important architect-member of Burlington's Circle was Isaac Ware, who, as it has been observed, brought out a new edition of Palladio's *Four Books...* in 1738 with illustrations by himself, but in 1733 he also published *Designs of Inigo Jones and Others*, which contained patterns for chimney-pieces and other details by Jones, Burlington, and Kent. In 1735 he published *The Plans, Elevations and Sections of Houghton in Norfolk*, Kent and Campbell's great house, and in 1756 he brought out *A Complete Body of Architecture*, a huge work in which is enshrined virtually all Georgian architectural theory.

Now these architect-members of the Circle all rose in their careers through the patronage and political clout of Burlington, and all helped to promote the architecture and ideas which his Lordship had espoused. It was not merely

set in an arched recess. This Serliana set in an arch was used again and again in the course of the century.

Wade's house was illustrated in *Vitruvius Britannicus* Vol III (1725) PLATE 10. Now it is also clear that Burlington was influenced by John Webb's Queen's Gallery at Somerset House of 1662, which also had an arched rusticated ground floor and Giant Order (this time Corinthian) of pilasters rising through the first and second floors. Webb's building was also published in *Vitruvius Britannicus*, and it, in turn, seems to have been based on Palladio's Palazzo Iseppo Porto, Vicenza, of around 1549, judiciously spiced with a hint of Donato Bramante's (1444–1514) Palazzo Caprini in Rome of 1513: it was unusual to have such a clear descendant of the Inigo Jones style appearing in Restoration times, when the dominant themes were French Baroque. Webb's Queen's Gallery was a precedent (as Mr. Cruickshank has pointed out) for

practice and buildings which helped the cause, however: in Georgian times, as before and after (it is just as true today), publications and good illustrations were essential to promote style, motifs, and theories. *Vitruvius Britannicus* in its various editions was, of course, extremely important, and the other publications mentioned above all played their parts. Robert Morris, related to Roger, was a theorist of great significance; his *An Essay in Defence of Ancient Architecture or, a Parallel of the Ancient Buildings with the Modern: showing the Beauty and Harmony of the Former, and the Irregularity of the Latter* (1728), *Lectures on Architecture, consisting of Rules founded upon Harmonick and Arithmetical Proportions in Building* (1734), *An Essay upon Harmony, as it relates to Situation and Building* (1739), *The Art of Architecture, a Poem in imitation of Horace's Art of Poetry* (1742), *Rural Architecture* (1750), *The Architectural Remembrancer: being a Collection of New and Useful Designs, of Ornamental Buildings and Decorations for Parks, Gardens, Woods, etc., to which are added, A variety of Chimney-Pieces, after the Manner of Inigo Jones and Mr. Kent* (1751, reissued as *Architecture Improved* in 1755 and 1757), and many other essays, letters, and sundry writings contributed to Palladian literature.

The *Essay in Defence...* was a polemic, a savage assault on Baroque buildings recently built, which were verbally demolished and compared unfavourably with Palladian compositions. The *Lectures...* included expositions of proportional systems taken from Palladio's seven 'ideal room' proportions in *Quattro Libri....* Morris advocated the division of the internal and external parts of the building by 'harmonick'

PLATE 30 *Heveningham Hall, Suffolk, by Sir Robert Taylor, of 1778–80, one of the grandest of Georgian houses with interiors by Wyatt and Rebecca. The central part is based on Webb's Queen's Gallery at Somerset House of 1662, and the end pavilions are clearly based on Palladian exemplars* (AFK H19552).

PLATE 31 *The stable-block at Althorp, Northamptonshire, by Roger Morris. Note the Tuscan portico based on Inigo Jones's church of St Paul, Covent Garden, which is in turn taken from Palladio's version of a Tuscan portico* (RCHME AA67/1864).

proportions rather than *measurements* in feet and inches. Just as in 'musick' there were seven notes in a scale, so in architecture there were seven proportions which could be used to produce every building ever designed. He therefore chose the cube, one and a half cubes, and double cubes as basic room proportions, and also suggested ratios of three cubes long, two cubes wide, and one cube high (3–2–1), with variants of 4–3–2, 5–4–3, and 6–4–3 as those necessary to produce harmoniously proportioned volumes or rooms. Now the square, as the basis for the chosen cube, could also contain within it a circle, and this, in turn could be the base of a drum on which a dome could be constructed. Morris gave his proportional system authority by basing it on Palladio's ideas, which, in turn, he claimed were based on Antique, and, eventually, God-given principles. He argued that in Classical Antiquity the Ancient Greeks had evolved the language of architecture, deriving the finely proportioned stone elements from trees and from naturally occurring objects which they refined, and that Greek ornament and architectural elements were further refined, codified, and transformed into even greater perfection through the 'sublime genius' and 'indefatigable care and industry' of Andrea Palladio. Morris's works are important publications because they encapsulate the theories of Palladianism: other texts produced under Burlington's aegis tended to be engravings of architectural subjects *sans* text (or with minimal text), but Morris wrote copiously on Palladian laws and aesthetic theory, emphasising the canonical nature of the Orders and the superiority of Classical simplicity over Baroque and other extravagances.

Isaac Ware, in his version of Palladio's *Quattro Libri...* (which by 1738 had attained canonical status), also illustrated seven 'ideal room' proportions. The first room was circular, rising to a height equal to its diameter before the hemispherical dome began to spring, so a rotunda consisting of a drum roofed with a hemisphere would be one-and-a-half diameters high from the floor to the highest point of the dome. The circle could fit within a square, so the next room would be square on plan with a vaulted ceiling of a hemi-dome springing from a point the same height as the side of the square – an alternative roof was a segmental vault springing from a line coincident with the highest point of the semicircular roof. The third room had a plan consisting of a square plus a third of a square, so was rectangular: the roof vault sprang from a point the height of the original square. The next plan was rectangular, based on a square plus a rectangle, the proportions being based on a cube extended by the square root of two. The last three rooms had plans of a square plus half a square, a square plus two-thirds of a square, and two squares. Ceiling- or vault-heights were related to the proportional system, which was an architectural interpretation of Venetian musical theories involving major and minor thirds. Plans of

rooms, plans of entire houses, sections, and elevations could be designed using proportional relationships, and so a relatively simple formula provided the basis for whole houses and other buildings. These numerical systems, of course, also relate to Freemasonic notions of numbers and their inner, hidden meanings. It was a tenet of early Renaissance theorists that if rooms or buildings had dimensions 1–2, 2–3, or 3–4, they would be harmoniously proportioned, and this system was regarded as the key to the proportions of Roman architecture and to the balance of the entire universe. Once music became more complex, so did architectural proportion, and Palladio's use of 5-6, 4-5, and so on opened up new and endless possibilities for new refinements, subdivisions, fractions, and multiples involving every part of the building.

Another important writer of the Circle was Robert Castell (*ob* 1729) whose *The Villas of the Ancients Illustrated* of 1728 was a major study in which he proposed reconstructions of Roman villas based on the descriptions in texts from Roman Antiquity. Castell printed the source-material in the original Latin (with English translations), but perhaps even more influential were the beautiful plates by Pierre Fourdrinier (or Fourdrinière) which illustrated the villas of Antiquity in their settings, and these views and landscapes resembled some of the man-made gardens and parks of the early-Georgian period. This superb and luxuriant volume contained a remarkable attempt at a reconstruction of Pliny the Younger's celebrated villa at Laurentium, one of the most important Classical exemplars in the imaginations of designers at the time. Indeed, Pliny's villa was held in the highest regard, as an almost unattainable ideal, superior to anything possible in the eighteenth century, yet striven for and sought, like some lost perfection, infinitely beautiful and set in a landscape of Arcadian loveliness. In spite of its dedication to Burlington however, the book was undersubscribed, and failed to bring financial rewards to its author, who died of smallpox in the Fleet Prison, where he had been incarcerated for debt: at the time of his death he was working on a translation of Vitruvius.

Burlington and his Circle believed that in buildings there were proportions that pleased the eye, just as in music there were harmonies and relationships of tones and semi-tones that enchanted the ear, but that any deviation or experiment from these perfect proportions, derived from Antiquity and perfected by later artists, was not to be tolerated. However, Lord Kames, in his *Elements of Criticism* of 1762 (one of the most thorough treatises on aesthetics and criticism, which, with Alison's *Essays on Taste*, was the major philosophical text of the eighteenth century on those subjects until it was eclipsed by the works of German writers), argued that proportions in buildings and their relationships were not immutable, because as the beholder walks about, the proportions of the rooms and façades change, and that, in reality, if the eye were capable of judging ideal proportion, the observer would only be satisfied if he stood in one spot from which the proportions could be ascertained as 'agreeable'.

William Hogarth (1697–1764) was to lampoon Palladianism, its pushiness, its tyranny, and its pretensions to moral superiority in his picture *Taste in High Life*, and, in his publication *The Analysis of Beauty* (1753), he examined aesthetic theory, and argued that the views of a practising artist should, in a just world, carry greater weight than the theories of the connoisseur and dilettante. He satirised academicism and those who worshipped at the altar of Taste, and he argued for a 'precise serpentine line', fluid and even Rococo, as a key to beauty, which should be individual, subjective, and dependent on the eye of the beholder. Formidable forces were being marshalled against the pre-eminence of the Palladians.

Palladianism in the Provinces and Elsewhere

Writers such as Alexander Pope helped to create a climate in which Classical allusions could flourish; and Pope, it should be remembered, created a remarkable garden at Twickenham in which an elegiac note was struck. Allan Ramsay (1686–1758) was the poet of elegiac landskips and of Palladianism in Scotland. Under the aegis of Sir John Clerk of Penicuik (1676–1755), Scotland's Arbiter of Architectural Taste from the 1720s, Anglophile, and Whig, a Circle was formed which included Ramsay, the antiquarian Alexander Gordon, and the architect William Adam (1689–1748) who became in 1728 Clerk and Storekeeper of the Works in Scotland, and in 1730 Mason to the Board of Ordnance in North Britain in which capacity he was able to carry out large schemes for military fortifications. Adam did not slavishly follow the severe English Palladian style, but freely adapted elements from many sources, especially those of Gibbs and Vanbrugh.

In the English Provinces there were many Tory landowners and merchants who resisted the blandishments of Palladianism, tainted as it was with Whiggery. Baroque motifs were still occurring in provincial towns as late as the 1750s, and great Baroque buildings such as Blenheim Palace clearly influenced local builders.[8] While conservatism and local tastes undoubtedly accounted for much, the importance of architectural pattern-books cannot be overstated in the spreading of accurate motifs. While *Vitruvius Britannicus* and *Designs of Inigo Jones* promoted Palladianism, a great architect who had been elbowed aside by the Palladians, James Gibbs, produced

what was probably the single most important pattern-book of the Georgian period, his *A Book of Architecture* of 1728, a folio volume of 150 plates of his own designs, which came out in a second edition in 1739. In 1732 he produced his *Rules for Drawing the Several Parts of Architecture*, which appeared in further editions in 1738 and 1753. Gibbs's name had been left out of Campbell's *Vitruvius Britannicus*, so Gibbs's response was to devote the whole of *A Book of Architecture* to publicising his own very considerable skills as a designer: he included monuments, chimney-pieces, garden-buildings, urns, cartouches, and so on, and therefore combined a portfolio of his own designs with a high-quality pattern-book. It has long been recognised as the most widely used architectural book of the century, and was the source of countless features of Georgian architecture on both sides of the Atlantic. Stylistically his work was strongly influenced by Baroque and Palladian devices from Italy, while his church steeples owe a great debt to Wren.

As has been mentioned above, the 'Junta' was responsible for introducing Alessandro Galilei to the British Isles, and in 1718 Galilei visited Ireland at the invitation of the Molesworths who had their seat near Dublin. For Speaker Conolly (*ob* 1729) Galilei designed Castletown, Co Kildare, the first great Palladian Palace in Ireland, with its massive central block and low wings connected by curved colonnades. Galilei returned to Italy, and the executive architect was (Sir) Edward Lovett Pearce (*ob* 1733), who had studied in Italy, and who had been taught by Vanbrugh, his father's first cousin. Pearce became the leading Palladian architect in Ireland, and was in touch with Lord Burlington's Circle. These influences are clear in his architecture, for his best work merges Palladianism with certain Baroque flourishes that recall Vanbrugh. His finest work is the Parliament House in Dublin (1729) (PLATE 32), and he was responsible for Bellamont Forest, Co Cavan, of *c* 1730, Ireland's first Palladian villa.

The other great Palladian architect in Ireland was Richard Castle, Cassel, or Cassels (*ob* 1751), a German who settled in Ireland, and who introduced the Baroque ellipse in the plan of Ballyhaise House, Co Cavan, of *c* 1733, which was on axis behind the entrance-hall, and which produced a bow in the centre of the garden-front (PLATE 33): this motif was often used in Irish houses thereafter, and bows often occur at the ends of country-houses in Ireland. Of course Vanbrugh had used bows at both Blenheim and Castle Howard, but English Palladians did not care for such 'impure' devices. Ellipses, however, were used by Borromini and Bernini, and appeared north of the Alps in works by Johann Bernhard Fischer von Erlach (1656–1723) and Johann Lukas von Hildebrandt (1668–1745), among others. It would seem that Cassels imported the ellipse from Germany to Ireland and married it

PLATE 32 *Sir Edward Lovett Pearce's Parliament House in Dublin of 1728. It is a monumental composition with projecting wings. From Richardson* (BTB/SH).

to the Palladian language. The attractiveness of the bow was undeniable, and second-generation Palladians such as Taylor and Ware started to incorporate bows in their designs from around 1750. Cassels's most celebrated designs include Powerscourt, Co Wicklow, of 1731–40, with a central three-storey block nine windows wide, with a five-bay pedimented centre-piece, and two-storey pavilions linked to the main block. Inside was a hall encrusted with shells, like German Grotto Halls in Baroque palaces, while the saloon was a version of a Vitruvian 'Egyptian Hall'. Cassels's Russborough, Co Wicklow, completed in 1748, has a central block joined by two Doric quadrant colonnades to wide wings, and the stair-case-hall has Rococo plasterwork.

Many distinguished provincial designs belong to the Palladian stable. John Carr (1723–1807) was responsible for Constable Burton, Yorkshire, of *c* 1762–8, illustrated in *Vitruvius Britannicus*, Vol V, plates 36-37, which has an Ionic portico at *piano-nobile* level with a recess behind, clearly based partly on Palladio's Villa Emo. However, Carr also incorporated Gibbsian motifs in this house.

In Bath, John Wood the Elder was to build several well mannered structures, but his chief claim to our attention is that he grouped together ordinary terrace-houses and gave

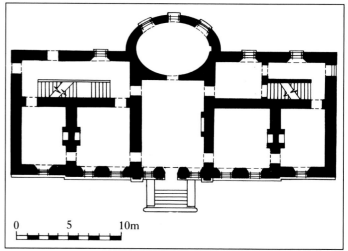

PLATE 33 *Plan of Ballyhaise House, Co Cavan, of* c *1733, built to designs by Richard Cassels. Note the elliptical saloon expressed outside with a bow* (JSC).

them an architectural treatment to suggest that they formed a palace. His first completed scheme was Queen Square (1729–36), each house being sub-leased to owner-builders or builder-tradesmen who had a free hand in the planning, but who had to follow Wood's elevations: in this respect London practice was copied. Wood's greatest urban scheme was the

Circus (PLATE 34), begun in 1754, but conceived earlier: it was completed by John Wood the Younger (1728–81), and it followed the general arrangement of a Roman amphitheatre, except that instead of having, as at the Colosseum, a convex façade facing outwards, the façades were concave, facing inwards. As with the Colosseum, however, superimposed Orders were used, with Doric at the bottom, then Ionic, then Corinthian, and between the paired columns were the window- and the door-openings. The Circus entered into the language of Town Planning, and was an important precedent.

Wood was a Freemason, and in his *The Origin of Building, or the Plagiarism of Heathens Detected*, of 1741, he endeavoured to show that Classicism owed its origins to the Divine Revelation of the Three Orders to the Jews for the Temple of Solomon. His son continued to work at Bath, culminating in Royal Crescent (PLATE 35), which was even grander than the Circus, and was built 1767–75. Royal Crescent has a Giant Order of engaged Ionic columns rising from the *piano-nobile* level to the crowning entablature, and sitting on a plain ground-storey. Camden Crescent of *c* 1788, by John Eveleigh, is a surprisingly late and very grand Palladian crescent with a pedimented centre-piece of four bays (leaving a column in the middle, which a true Palladian would have eschewed as a solecism), and with a three-bay pavilion at each end (PLATE 36, page 44). The Order is Corinthian.[9]

PLATE 35 *Royal Crescent, Bath, by John Wood the Younger, 1767–75* (RCHME A45/5921).

PLATE 34 *The Circus, Bath, from 1754, by John Wood. From Richardson* (BTB/SH)

PLATE 36 *Camden Crescent, Bath, by John Eveleigh. Note the centre-piece of four bays* (JSC).

The Decline of Palladianism

There were plenty of conventional Palladian fronts, like that of Castle Ward, Co Down, of 1760–73, a seven-window-wide house with a rusticated base and a central pedimented three-bay arrangement with arches on the ground floor, and a Giant Order of four engaged Ionic columns rising from a *piano-nobile* level to the entablature (PLATE 37). The surprising thing about Castle Ward is the garden-front, which faces Strangford Lough (PLATE 38): it has crenellations and Gothick windows not unlike those of the Orangery at Frampton Court, Gloucestershire of *c* 1750, perhaps designed by one of the Halfpennys, with John as the more likely candidate. The whole is of Bath stone imported in

one of Bernard Ward's ships. In the grounds is a garden-temple with façade based on Palladio's *Il Redentore* in Venice, probably *c* 1750. The architect of this lovely house is unknown, but the spectacular udder-like plaster fan-vaulting of the sitting-room does suggest some kind of unusual flair. Could Ward have got a Bath architect, such as one of the Woods, to design this house? Or could the most likely candidate be Richard Jones (*n* 1703), who built Prior Park to designs by John Wood the Elder, and also the Palladian Bridge in the grounds, which may have been designed by Wood (after Palladio), but is very similar to the bridge at Wilton designed by Roger Morris for the Ninth Earl of Pembroke in 1736-37 and illustrated in *Vitruvius Britannicus* Vol V (1771) plate 89? (PLATE 39).

Jones is known to have designed the sham castle on Claverton Down around 1762, so he could have turned his hand to that sort of Gothick at Castle Ward. Some of the udder-like forms of the interior are suggested by William Kent and the Hon Richard Bateman's Shobdon church, Herefordshire, of 1746–56[10] (PLATE 40), but there is no documentary evidence available as yet to tell us who designed Castle Ward. Yet there could be another candidate for Castle Ward: James Bridges, who practised in Bristol between 1757 and 1763, and who designed the Royal Fort (a house for a merchant in Bristol of before 1760) in the Anglo-Palladian

PLATE 37 *Castle Ward, Co Down: the Palladian front of 1760–73* (JSC).

PLATE 38 *The Gothick front, Castle Ward, Co Down* (JSC).

PLATE 39 *The Palladian Bridge, Wilton, by Roger Morris* (JSC).

PLATE 40 *Church of St John the Evangelist, Shobdon, Herefordshire, by the Hon Richard Bateman, possibly with William Kent, but certainly with elements copied from designs by Kent, notably John Vardy's* Pulpit for York Minster, *of 1744, after Kent* (JSC).

PLATE 41 *Royal Fort, Bristol, by James Bridges. This may have been the model for Castle Ward, as there are several similarities between the two buildings. It was built before 1760* (JSC).

style (PLATE 41). Now the Royal Fort looks rather like Castle Ward (the position of the central bay is significant), and the Bristol house has riotous Rococo interiors, probably by Thomas Paty (*c* 1713-1789). Both Bridges and Paty designed in the Gothic style (St Nicholas, Bristol, designed by Bridges in 1760, was finished by Paty, who designed St Michael's church, Bristol, of 1775-77, and Bridges was also responsible for St Werburgh, Bristol, of 1758-61), and both were capable of competent Classical work. The dates fit, and there was a Co Down-Bath-Bristol connection, even the Halfpennys having connections with Ulster. Shobdon, too, has Ulster links through the Chichesters and other families.

The Palladian dominance, even tyranny, seemed to be firmly established in the reigns of George I and II, although Chinese and Gothic tastes continued to be manifest at the same time. There were plenty of pattern-books and the realised copies from those books were visible throughout the land. Yet Palladianism was to falter, and it fell from the elevated uplands of canonical correctness and aesthetic superiority it had enjoyed since around 1720. Taste changed in the late 1740s, and around 1750 (Burlington died three years later) it was clear that the Whig 'National Style' had become only one of several architectural options open to designers. The idea of some sort of canonical system in architecture, a kind of standard of Taste or aesthetic absolutism, fell from grace. In the second half of the eighteenth century notions of Classical proportions as absolutes were partly abandoned, and 'architecture' ceased to mean solely Classical architecture. Personal opinion began to defeat the imposed authority of Palladianism, and personal preferences demanded a multiplicity of stylistic possibilities. It was the beginning of Romanticism.[11]

C H A P T E R   T H R E E

THE ROMANTIC REVOLUTION

INTRODUCTION; THE EXOTIC AND THE GOTHICK TASTE;
THE CASTLE STYLE; *CHINOISERIE* AND ORIENTALISM.

*'During the eighteenth century romantic
attitudes transformed architectural
composition. Picturesque values (that is,
architecture as scenery) and associationist
aesthetics (that is, architecture as
embodied memory) broke up the canonical
harmonies of classicism. Diversified
patronage encouraged the pursuit of
novelty. And the progress of architectural
archaeology multiplied the range of
available options.'*

J. MORDAUNT CROOK: *THE DILEMMA OF STYLE. ARCHITECTURAL IDEAS FROM THE PICTURESQUE TO THE
POST-MODERN* (LONDON: JOHN MURRAY, 1987) PP 13-14.

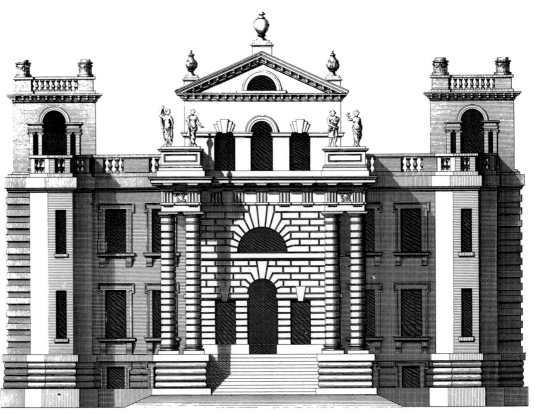

The North front of Seaton Delaval in the County of Northumberland the Seat of Francis Delaval Esq.ᵣ   design'd by S.ᵣ John Vanbrugh K.ᵗ 1721.

Elevation Septentrionale de Seaton Delaval dans le
Comte de Northumberland Maison de Delaval Esq.ᵣ

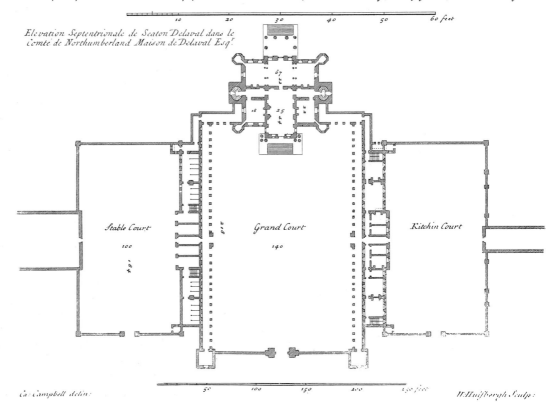

PLATE 42 *Plan, showing the Grand, Stable, and Kitchen Courts, with the house, at Seaton Delaval, Northumberland, by Sir John Vanbrugh, of 1720–28. Note the fortress-like corner elements, which turn out to be canted bays on the elevation. The attic storey recalls Elizabethan prodigy-houses such as Wollaton Hall, Nottinghamshire. From* VB, *Vol III, Plate 20* (SM)

Introduction

Romanticism suggests the level of feeling at a certain period, and it was regarded as being the opposite of Classicism. It seems that an idea of the past embraced a type of nostalgia which became more obvious as the limitations of the present were perceived. Just as Antiquity captured the imaginations of many Georgians, so the Medieval period began to be appreciated. Romanticism was an attitude of mind that saw a ruined temple as more significant than one in perfect condition because it suggested the passage of time, melancholy, longing, and human condition, yet by its ruined state and its associations it enhanced the spirit and the mind. But the partially destroyed cannot be Classical, because something that is Classical is whole, complete, and perfect, implying the best of its kind, and denoting clarity, logic, symmetry, harmonious proportions, and recognised canons of form and detail connected with the Orders. Classicism, in a nutshell, implies perfection, clarity, restraint, and beauty of form. Therefore the sensibility that found a ruined temple beautiful is essentially Romantic, even though the temple might once have embodied Classical perfection. It follows that an asymmetrical composition, in which Classical elements were deliberately composed in an un-Palladian manner, could be described as 'Romantic Classicism': examples can be found in the works of Nash and others. On the Continent, the greatest Romantic Classicist of all was Karl Friedrich Schinkel (1781–1841).

Longing for the past, and a taste for the distant or the exotic, could encapsulate a great range of styles, and while the Picturesque movement evoked Arcadian landscapes and a lost Antiquity, it was but a short step to Anglicise the vision by incorporating Medieval ruins of castles and monasteries in such a Picturesque ideal. Alexander Pope, John Dyer (1699–1758), and David Mallett (c 1705–65) were partly inspired by Melancholy, which once more became fashionable, though John Milton (1608–74) and Edmund Spenser (c 1552–99) had often drawn on Melancholy as a stimulus for their writings. Deserted graveyards, presided over by hooting owls (themselves harbingers of Death), ivy–draped Gothic ruins, the eerie light cast by the moon, ghosts of monks and nuns, and much else became staple fare in Gothick novels, and stimulated the creators of Picturesque gardens to produce strange and powerful images. Furthermore, if one had no real ruin on one's estate, it was always possible to build one. Robert Blair's (1699–1746) didactic poem, *The Grave*, of 1743, is a celebration of death, of the solitary tomb, and of the anguish of loss and mourning:

'Well do I know thee by thy trusty yew
Cheerless, unsocial plant, that loves to dwell,
Midst sculls and coffins, epitaphs and worms:
Where light-heel'd ghosts, and visionary shades,
Beneath the wan cold moon (as fame reports)
Embody'd, thick, perform their mystic rounds.
No other merriment, dull tree, is thine.'

Edward Young (1683–1765) published his *The Complaint, or Night Thoughts on Life, Death, and Immortality* in 1742–45, another didactic poem, which was extremely important in creating a new and tender sensibility towards the dead and burial-places: it was particularly significant in France and Germany during the Enlightenment. In *Night Thoughts* the eighteenth-century reader could indulge a taste for the imagery of graveyards, ruins, solitary watchers by the melancholy tomb, obscurity, and darkness: he could, like Werther, be

'Led softly, by the stillness of the Night,
Led... o'er the pleasing Past,...
And finds all Desart now, and meets the Ghosts
Of...departed Joys, a numerous Train!'

Even more important to English sensibilities was the *Elegy in a Country Churchyard* of 1750, by Thomas Gray (1716–71), in which the melancholy mood conjures up thoughts prompted by the sight of the graves of the humble dead, excluded in life from material rewards and glory, yet even glory is mortal.

In order to understand that remarkable phenomenon, the Romantic Revolution, we need to retrace our steps to examine the architectural legacy *before* Palladianism enjoyed its triumph. With Vanbrugh's mighty Castle Howard in Yorkshire, English Baroque matured, for in that great building many themes were merged: monumentalism, the French Baroque compositions of Vaux-le-Vicomte and Marly, and a reminiscence of the principle of grander Palladian compositions. But it is the overpowering hall, with its massive masonry with arched openings revealing the stairs, and its tall cupola (which clearly influenced Wanstead II [PLATE 12]) with high-level windows, which really had no precedent. Vanbrugh, assisted by Hawksmoor, began work building this great pile in 1700. These themes were developed at Blenheim Palace, Oxfordshire, in 1705–16, with its huge *Cour d'Honneur* flanked by the kitchen and stable courts, and the great house on the south-eastern side. The house has four corner-towers surmounted by belvederes with finials that could easily have been by Borromini, and a central hall with broken pediments that, in general massing, recalls something of Jacobean prodigy-houses. We know that Vanbrugh sought to connect his architecture with English castles, the massive-

PLATE 43 *Sir John Vanbrugh's own house at Greenwich of 1717, a remarkable evocation of the Medieval past* (JSC).

ness and brooding grandeur of which he suggested at Seaton Delaval, Northumberland, of 1720–28 (PLATE 42). We know he appreciated old buildings, and often wished to retain ruins and old structures in the landscapes of his great houses. He therefore was a pioneer of the English Picturesque-Romantic tradition. The silhouettes of his great houses, if one half-closes one's eyes, seem to be reminiscent of some great late-Medieval or late-Tudor pile. His own house of 1717 at Greenwich was a remarkable tribute to the Medieval past, with its crenellations, towers, and fake machicolations, and reflected its creator's passion for Architecture, Theatre, and War (PLATE 43). Vanbrugh wrote that the 'castle air' made a 'very noble and masculine shew', and was extremely tough and vigorous, although the 'air' was suggested by silhouette and composition rather than by quotation of detail.

It is clear that Hawksmoor, like Vanbrugh, was fascinated by the Medieval Gothic past, and he actually designed Gothic buildings, working on Beverley Minster, Yorkshire, in 1716–20; designing All Souls' College, Oxford, in 1716–35 in a Gothic style, the towers of which are loosely derived from Beverley Minster (PLATE 44); and finalising the western towers of Westminster Abbey (1734), completed by John

James. Now of course another great English Baroque architect had designed in Gothic: Sir Christopher Wren had built Tom Tower, Christ Church, Oxford (1681–82), the Gothic steeple of St Dunstan-in-the-East, and St Mary Aldermary, Bow Lane, which are not undistinguished examples of the style. At St Sepulchre, Holborn, Wren reconstructed the Medieval Gothic church in 1668–80, incorporating most of the surviving fabric of the old building.

James Gibbs designed two outstanding buildings for the Universities of Oxford and Cambridge. The first was the Senate House at Cambridge of 1722–30, with its Giant Corinthian Order, central engaged temple-front with pediment, alternating triangular and segmental pediments over the windows of the lower floor, and the semicircular-headed windows above, the whole capped by a noble entablature over which is a balustrade: it is the finest Georgian building in Cambridge. At Oxford, he designed the Radcliffe Camera, or library, of 1737–48, which is probably his best work (PLATE 45). It consists of a rusticated polygonal base, articulated with arched openings and pediments, over which is a Giant engaged Order around the drum which is pierced with two storeys of windows. There is a massive entablature with balustrades capped with urns, and from the perimeter rise curved buttresses with support the clerestory drum from which rises the great dome over which in turn is a lantern. Gibbs's Italian training is clear from this masterpiece, yet it is derived in part from unrealised designs for the library by Hawksmoor of 1712–15 and 1733–34 which in turn derive from Wren's design for a mausoleum for King Charles I (not built). The Camera owes more, perhaps, to St Peter's Basilica in Rome than to St Paul's in London.[1]

Now Gibbs had survived as an architect in spite of Whiggery, his own unsuitability as a Scot, a Papist, and a probable Jacobite, and all the intrigues of the Palladians. He showed his respect for his Italian training and for Wren. With his Gothick Temple at Stowe (PLATE 28) he showed he was not to be trapped in Classicism either: the date was significant, for in the 1740s the tide was starting to run against the Palladians. Appropriately, the Gothick Temple was called the 'Temple of Liberty': it is a triangular building with pentagonal turrets at two corners, and a taller tower over the third at the rear. Surprisingly, the detail is more Second-Pointed than Perpendicular, which is unusual for the Georgian period, but the details are ill observed. Now this Gothick Temple is one of the first-generation Georgian 'Gothick' buildings to be erected, for the Gothick craze was relatively young, so it is important. Was it in some way an allusion to that extraordinary Triangular Lodge at Rushton, Northamptonshire, of 1594, built by Sir Thomas Tresham (*c.*1543–1605), which, with its three-sided plan, triangular windows, trefoils, three triangular gables on each side, and much else, is a marvellous

PLATE 44 *All Souls' College, Oxford, of 1716–35, by Hawksmoor* (AFK G14780).

PLATE 45 *The Radcliffe Camera, Oxford, of 1737–48, by James Gibbs* (JSC).

example of an Elizabethan emblematic conceit, for the threes are a play on Tresham's own name and on his emblem, which was the trefoil? The building was also a deliberate advertisement of the Roman Catholic faith of the Treshams (the threes suggest the Trinity, and the building symbolises the Mass as well), and was a protest against persecution and against the destruction of the symbols of the Old Faith.

Yet Richard Temple, Lord Cobham (*c* 1669–1749), Gibbs's patron at Stowe, was a Whig, so he would not have shared Tresham's problems, but he was clearly a man who saw the value of variety in allusion, and it would not be unseemly to be as eclectic as possible in such a garden. Cobham, after all, was a friend of Pope and Congreve, as well as of other literary men, and fought valiantly against the protection by the Government of the Directors of the South Sea Company. His independent stance could well have caused him to make such a statement of defiance, for he had fallen from the favour of both Walpole and the King. The Temple bore the legend THANK GOD I AM NOT A ROMAN, which is amusing considering

Gibbs's religion by birth and the location of his training. It is more likely a deliberate statement against the square and circle, against Classicism, against conformity, and against Absolutism. Furthermore, seven statues of Saxon deities stood sentinel around the Temple, which probably connects it with John Wood's *An Essay towards a Description of Bath* of 1742 in which he sought connections (as in his 1741 *Origin of Building*) with British as opposed to Classical Antiquity, yet linking the two.

The Exotic and the Gothick Taste

It is clear that even the Palladians adopted a fairly free attitude towards garden-building, which could be seen as frivolous, lightweight, amusing, diversionary, and exotic contrasts in the settings of Palladian houses. At Stowe, for example, a variety of garden-buildings could be seen as Picturesque events in the carefully composed landscape-garden. Thus it was that architects could experiment with curiosities, with unusual references to Antiquity, with Baroque extravaganzas, with Gothic, with allusions to ruins and a medieval past, and with styles derived from eastern countries, such as China.

Alexander Pope was responsible for Alfred's Hall in Cirencester Park, Gloucestershire, a castellated Gothick folly of 1721, which was even earlier than Gibbs's Temple at Stowe, and before that, in *c* 1717, a Gothic garden-building was erected in the formal garden at Shotover in Oxfordshire, probably to designs by William Townesend (*ob* 1739). The Shotover temple has a vaulted arcade of three arches on the ground floor flanked by two polygonal towers, and the castellated gable above was pierced by a wheel-window. This building seems to have been a deliberate expression of Whiggery in a Tory stronghold, and therefore the style could vary in meaning, depending on circumstance. Kent designed a number of Gothick buildings, including a gateway at Hampton Court (1732), and several Gothick garden-buildings at Richmond Gardens, Surrey (1730–35).

As we have seen, professional pattern-books, antiquarian studies, and theoretical works proliferated in the eighteenth century, and were responsible for the dissemination of style, detail, and notions of 'correct' proportion and advanced 'Taste'. Batty Langley (1696–1751) was one of the most successful authors producing pattern-books. His works include important books such as *A Sure Guide to Builders, or the Principles and Practice of Architecture made easy for the Use of*

Workmen (1726 with subsequent edition, revised, in 1729), *Practical Geometry, applied to the Useful Arts of Building, Surveying, Gardening, and Mensuration* (1726 and 1729), *The Builder's Chest Book, or a Compleat Key to the Five Orders of Columns in Architecture* (1727 and 1739, but also published in Dublin as *The Builder's Vade Mecum* of 1729 and 1735), *New Principles of Gardening; or the laying out and planting of Parterres, Groves, Wildernesses, Labyrinths, Avenues, Parks, etc.* (1728), *The Young Builder's Rudiments, or the Principles of Geometry, Mechanicks, etc., Geometrically Demonstrated* (1730 and 1734), *The Builder's Compleat Chest Book* (1738), *The City and Country Builder's and Workman's Treasury of Designs* (1740, 1745, 1750, 1756, 1770), *The Builder's Compleat Assistant* (1741 and 1766), *The Builder's Jewel, or the Youth's Instructor, and Workman's Remembrancer* (1741 and many subsequent editions), and much more. All these books were widely used by craftsmen, builders, architects, and others.

There is no doubt that Langley was of great importance in showing, in simple, clear terms, how Classical architecture could be drawn and built. With his brother Thomas (1702–51), an engraver, he established a school offering lessons in architecture and draughtsmanship, and he was a convinced Freemason, signing himself 'Hiram' in *The Grub Street Journal* of 1734, and calling his (perhaps unfortunate) sons Euclid, Vitruvius, Archimedes, and Hiram. His two folio volumes, *Ancient Masonry* (1734–36), collected a huge amount of material from Hans Vredemann de Vries (1527–1606) to James Gibbs, and, consequently, it was 'one of the largest and most comprehensive treatises in the literature of English architecture'.[2] In spite of his strange name, Langley was anything but 'batty', and his books are, to this day, highly intelligent and useful, especially in respect of drawing the Orders and other Classical detail. Indeed, his methods are often easier and more practical than those advocated by more celebrated writers of the period, and his works deserve a more serious assessment than they have enjoyed at the hands of snooty commentators.

There was obviously a crying need in the eighteenth century for instruction in architecture and draughtsmanship, and, like so many in the Georgian period, Langley rose to the occasion. Eileen Harris has described[3] how, hurriedly, 'designs were copied, engraved and printed, some upside down and mis-numbered, several with as many different pieces as possible on a single sheet. Provided with an equally slapdash, piratical text by Batty, they were issued whole or in parts to carpenters, joiners, masons, cabinet-makers and other craftsmen'.[4] But such methods were usual at a time when the treatment of other men's works was, to be charitable, cavalier. Any successful book would be pirated at once, and if anyone of distinction died, the hacks employed by booksellers and publishers would be required to produce immediate copy,

Batty and Thomas Langley Invent and Sculp. 1741.

PLATE 46 *A Second Gothick Entablature and Capital for Batty Langley's 'First Order' of Gothick. It is clearly a type of Doric, with quatrefoils instead of metopes, and Gothick triglyphs. All mouldings are Classical. From* Ancient Architecture Restored..., *Plate 3* (SM).

PLATE 47 *The Gothick Tower at Edgehill, Warwickshire, of 1745–47, by Sanderson Miller* (JSC).

PLATE 48 *Arbury Hall, Warwickshire, c 1748–70, showing the south front by Sir Roger Newdigate, Bart, and Sanderson Miller* (JSC).

which was then rushed out as the 'true' memoir: it was said by Carruthers, in his *Life of Pope* (1857), that Edmund Curll's (1675–1747) biographies were 'one of the new terrors of death'.[5]

Many commentators, including Wittkower,[6] have seen Langley as a mere hack, vulgarising architectural theory, but such a view fails to take into account the very real need to have simple pattern-books available for artisans and students. Langley published simplified methods of mensuration using proportional methods (it should be remembered that draughtsmen worked with dividers and compasses rather than scales), and these were easy to use and understand, so the cry of 'vulgarity' is probably unduly sniffy. Most people are useless at design, and most architects (then as now) lack distinction in that field: the provision of pattern-books for whole buildings and every conceivable part of a building ensured that even bad designers and builders with no aesthetic eye would have a sporting chance of getting things reasonably right, and for that service Langley and his contemporaries deserve our respect and thanks.

It is clear that many of the superior tones adopted by critics of Langley were prompted because of Langley's foray into the morass of Gothic designs, for today he is remembered mostly for the book he published with his brother in 1741–42: this was *Ancient Architecture Restored and Improved by a Great Variety of Grand and Usefull Designs, entirely new in the Gothick Mode for the Ornamentation of Buildings and Gardens*, which was reissued in 1747 as *Gothic Architecture, Improved by Rules and Proportions in many Grand Designs of Columns, Doors, Windows, Chimney-Pieces..., Temples and Pavillions, etc*. It is unfortunate that this little book has been given so much publicity in the twentieth century when Langley's many achievements in the dissemination of Classical Architecture are looked down upon, or forgotten, or underestimated, and especially when it is remembered that the book was not particularly successful when it came out. 'Langley Gothick' has had a bad press, and for this Horace Walpole and Thomas Gray can be fairly blamed, although Walpole had considerable impudence in criticising Langley, for he was clearly indebted to him: this is probably due to the unpleasant faults of his snobbery and

Plate 49 *The Dining-Room at Arbury Hall, Warwickshire, of 1765–88, by Sir Roger Newdigate, Bart, and Henry Keene. It is one of the most delicate and perfect of all Georgian Gothick interiors* (Country Life).

jealousy.[7] In fact, although Langley's *Ancient Architecture Restored* enjoyed neither a good reputation nor great commercial success, it was an important source-book for Walpole, Sanderson Miller, Shenstone, and many other heroes of the early Gothic Revival.

Langley's work was an attempt to make Gothic architecture intelligible to an age steeped in Classical principles, and so he sought to describe Gothic in terms of formulae akin to the Classical Orders. The illustrations were amazing and unscholarly inventions in which most of the mouldings were still Classical, and Langley's 'First Order' of 'Gothick' had foiled channels in triglyphs and quatrefoils in metopes, making his 'First Order' a kind of Gothicised Doric (PLATE 46), and his 'Fifth Order' a very elongated slender thing connected in terms of proportion to Corinthian, but really unrecognisable as either Corinthian or Gothic (apart from the circular column with colonnettes attached by bands to the shaft). It would seem that Langley did not bother to measure, survey, and draw from real Gothic examples, but merely gave buildings a cursory glance and applied his impressions to Gothicising the Orders. Langley believed that Gothic was a corruption of Roman architecture, and was therefore capable of being 'improved' by the superimposition of Classical and Palladian principles. In the early-Georgian period, indeed, 'Gothic' was a term of abuse, and was seen as a deviation from the principles of Antiquity and Good Taste. Chambers's *Encyclopaedia* of 1742 defines a 'Gothic column' as a 'round pillar in a Gothic building, either too thick, or too small for its height'.[8] In other words, it was deformed, and could be dismissed, just as 'Gouty' Greek baseless Doric would be looked down upon for a time.

Like his other books, however, Langley's 'Gothick' was widely imitated, and examples of architecture based on the engravings in his book can be found in Calton Hill Cemetery, Edinburgh, the Gothick Octagon at Bramham Park, Yorkshire, and many other places.[9] The first important point to note about Langley's Gothick, therefore, is that its engaging and pretty style was an invention of his, and was copied all over the place, but only for garden-buildings, chimney-pieces, house, tombs, doorcases, and windows. Professor Alistair Rowan has demonstrated that Langley responded to the fashion established earlier by Pope, Kent, and others, and it would be far fairer to regard Langley's Gothick as an attempt to categorise and systematise the style invented by Kent and others.[10] It is absurd to take the strictures of Walpole and Eastlake seriously, for they were looking at Gothic from a different point of view: Langley was actually trying to make Gothic intelligible and respectable by showing a way in which it could be analysed and codified on principles derived from Classicism. Yet Kent and Gibbs, no less, produced, 'unscholarly' Gothick that owed very little to Medieval precedent, and

the Georgian Gothick must be seen as essentially amusing, applied to incidentals, and calculated for novelty, as in garden-buildings. It is a branch of Rococo, and is capricious, light, and fanciful.

In spite of his strictures, Walpole and his friend John Chute owned copies of Langley's book, which was clearly influential in the creation of both Strawberry Hill and for the unexecuted remodelling of Chute's seat, The Vyne, in Hampshire.[11] Sanderson Miller (1716–80) had a copy of Langley, and it obviously helped Miller when designing the Gothick front at Radway Grange, Warwickshire, of 1744–46, the octagonal castellated Gothick tower at Edgehill, Warwickshire, of 1745–47 (PLATE 47), and advising Sir Roger Newdigate, Bart (1719–1806), over the Gothick work at Arbury Hall, Warwickshire, of *c* 1750–52 (PLATES 48–49).

Miller had a vast acquaintance among aristocratic friends and neighbours, and soon the Squire of Radway was being consulted by all those who wished to embellish their properties with 'Gothick' architecture. Miller's buildings were far more truly Picturesque than the efforts of Kent, and his Edgehill tower (PLATE 47) was of great significance as an exemplar. Miller also was adept at designing 'ruins', consisting of towers and castles, of which the Gothic 'castle' at Hagley Park, Worcestershire, was the most important, for it was greatly admired, and was regarded as having the 'true rust of the Barons' Wars'. Such 'fictitious' ruins were designed not only to delight the eye or terminate a vista, but to act as mnemonics of past ages, customs, and manners, and give pleasure by means of an association of ideas.[12] Miller was also to design the Great Hall and Gothic Gateway at Lacock Abbey, Wiltshire, in 1754–55, and may also have added the two lanterns to Gibbs's Gothick Temple at Stowe in 1756 (PLATE 28). His works, which are many, are listed by Howard Colvin.[13]

Miller's huge network of friends, and the sensations aroused by his early experiments, made his influence widespread. His friend, Richard Jago (1715–81), the author of the long poem *Edge-Hill*, seems to have been the link between Miller and William Shenstone (1714–63), poet, who adorned his estate at The Leasowes near Halesowen with an elegiac funerary urn and much else, and who wrote to Jago asking him if he had mentioned

'a treatise that your Mr. Miller had, where the author endeavours to vindicate and establish Gothic architecture? And does not the same man explain it also by draughts on copper plates? That very book, or rather the title and the author's name, I want – by the assistance of some such treatise, I could sketch out some charming Gothic temples and Gothic benches for garden-seats'.[14]

It is obvious from this that Miller was publicising Langley's book, and that intelligence of the work was communicated to his friends, who in turn told others. By 1749 Shenstone had built his first Gothick structure at The Leasowes. Shenstone, in turn, corresponded with many landowners keen to improve their estates, and, like Miller, seems to have given advice on Gothick buildings to a great number of people. Horace Walpole, also, propagated the Gothick Taste, and so successful was he that he was able to boast that he 'preached so effectively that...every pagoda took the veil'.[15] This was a reference to the Chinese Taste, which had been in vogue, was to remain so, and of which more anon. Walpole, Miller, and Shenstone are only three of many we know who took up Gothick and promoted it, thereby undermining Palladianism. Thus, Langley was just as significant in promoting the Gothick among aristocratic and influential classes as he was in influencing architects, builders, and artisans.

In 1752 appeared *Rural Architecture in the Gothic Taste* by William Halfpenny (*alias* Michael Hoare) (*ob* 1755) and his son, John, which contained further variations on the Kent style of Gothick (PLATE 50). In the same year they also produced *Chinese and Gothic Architecture, properly Ornamented*, and *Rural Architecture in the Chinese Taste*. Gothick could be seen as an alternative to *Chinoiserie*, and was exotic, Rococo, and slightly strange, although it had a claim to be rather more rooted in the native soil than was *Chinoiserie*. William Halfpenny seems to have resided in Richmond, Surrey, and in London, during the early-Georgian period, and also carried out works in the West Country, including the Redland Chapel, Bristol. Interestingly, William Halfpenny carried out designs for Viscount Hillsborough at Hillsborough, Co Down, in 1732: could the Halfpennys have been in any way responsible for the Parish church of St Malachy at Hillsborough, completed in 1772, and one of the loveliest of all Georgian Gothick churches? (PLATE 51) Sir Albert Richardson suggested George Richardson (*ob* 1813), architect of the Gothick churches of Stapleford, Leicestershire (1783) (PLATE 52) and Teigh, Rutland (1782), as the architect of St Malachy's. Robert William Furze Brettingham (*c* 1740–1820) also carried out several works in Co Down, including the choir of the Cathedral Church of the Holy Trinity, Downpatrick, of 1795, Downpatrick Gaol (1789), and enlargements of Hillsborough House, Co Down (1790s). He was then clearly well entrenched in Ulster, and his delightful Gothick in Down Cathedral deserves comparison with the interior of Hillsborough church, although he would have been very young if he had worked on the latter.

Thomas Wright (1711–1786) visited Ireland in 1746–47, and published a work on Irish antiquities. He published *Six Original Designs of Arbours* and *Six Original Designs of Grottos* in 1755 and 1758 respectively, but he had considerable success

PLATE 50 *The Orangery at Frampton Court, Frampton-on-Severn, Gloucestershire, of c 1750, probably by William or John Halfpenny, a charming example of Georgian Gothick* (JSC).

as a designer of landscaped gardens, and many of his designs for garden-buildings survive in the Avery Architectural and Fine Arts Library, Columbia University, New York, including proposals for various Gothick buildings at Tollymore Park, Co Down (PLATE 53). Wright stayed with Lord Limerick, who laid out Tollymore, and the designs appear to date from *c* 1740, although the Gothick works at Tollymore were still being built in the 1780s. Wright appears to have been responsible for the curious, melancholy, and touching 'Shepherd's Grave' or 'Monument' at Shugborough in Staffordshire of *c* 1758 with which James 'Athenian' Stuart (1713–88) was probably involved: it consists of two primitivist Greek Doric columns, with the flutes only partially carved, carrying a primitive Doric entablature above which are shell-like antefixae; this ensemble forms an aedicule framing a grotto-like arch

PLATE 52 *The church of St Mary Magdalene, Stapleford, Leicestershire, by George Richardson, of 1783 (JSC).*

PLATE 51 *St Malachy's Parish church, Hillsborough, Co Down, completed in 1772 (JSC).*

PLATE 53 *Gothick arch at Tollymore Park, Co Down, by Thomas Wright (JSC).*

PLATE 54 *The Shepherd's Grave at Shugborough, Staffordshire, by Thomas Wright and James Stuart (JSC).*

taken straight from Wright's *Grottos* within which is a carved relief by Peter Scheemakers derived from Pouissin's celebrated *Et in Arcadia Ego*. The altar-like pedestal on which the relief stands is inscribed with the mysterious letters

O . U . O . S . V . A . V . V
D   M

which some have suggested may be Masonic. The D M probably stands for DIS MANIBUS or DI MANES, a term given to the Roman dead as a sort of title. *Et in Arcadia Ego* is usually given to mean 'And I too (the occupant of the tomb) was in Arcady', but it can also mean 'I too (the tomb, itself) am in Arcady', or 'Even in Arcady there am I', meaning Death. The tomb in the landscape is, of course, in Arcadia, and suggests loss, longing, and an unattainable ideal. The Shepherd's Tomb is a fascinating instance in which Neo-Classicism (of which more anon), Primitivism, Rustick (related to Gothick), and Antique allusions merge (PLATE 54). Capitals with dots between them signify the first letters of a sentence, perhaps a line from Virgil, or they may represent initials.

Paul Decker, about whom little is know at present, published *Chinese Architecture, Civil and Ornamental, adapted to this Climate*, and *Gothic Architecture Decorated, consisting of a large collection of Temples, Banqueting, Summer and Green Houses, etc.,...Being a Taste entirely new, likewise Designs of the Gothic Orders, and Rules for Drawing Them*, both in 1759, and in 1767 William Wrighte brought out his charming *Grotesque Architecture or Rural Amusement, consisting of Plans, Elevations and Sections for Huts, Retreats, Summer and Winter Hermitages, Terminaries, Chinese, Gothic and Natural Grottos, Cascades, Mosques, Moresque Pavilions, Grotesque and Rustic Seats, Greenhouses, etc., many of which may be executed with Flints, Irregular Stones, Rude Branches and Roots of Trees*, a second edition of which appeared in 1790. There were thus plenty of illustrated books from which enchanting and varied designs could be taken.

Another pattern-book, perhaps the prettiest and most Rococo of all, was Charles Over's *Ornamental Architecture in the Gothic, Chinese and Modern Taste, being above fifty entire new designs...etc* of 1758, and this was followed by Thomas Collins Overton's *The Temple Builder's Most Useful Companion, being fifty entire new original designs for pleasure...in the Greek, Roman and Gothic taste* in 1766. There were others, too, including Robert Manwaring's *The Carpenter's Complete Guide to the Whole System of Gothic Railing*, of 1765, which includes designs by Johann Heinrich Müntz (1727–98), who worked for Horace Walpole for four years from 1758, designed the 'Gothic Cathedral' for Kew Gardens in 1759,[16] and was probably the originator of the Moorish 'Alhambra' as well. Gothick and Chinese were clearly regarded very much in the same light, for Müntz provided designs for frets in both styles. Even

Flitcroft designed a tower at Stourhead in 1762, while Kent added a Gothick gable with buttresses to the Cuttle Mill at Rousham in *c* 1740. There is a strange Gothic gateway of *c* 1760 at Auckland Castle, Bishop Auckland, Co Durham, by Sir Thomas Robinson (*c* 1702–77), while Isaac Ware produced some Gothick designs, and there is a whole series by Richard Bentley (1708–82).[17]

However, Gothick came of age as a fashionable style with Horace Walpole's Strawberry Hill (PLATE 55). John Chute (1701–76) played a very great role in the design of this extraordinary house: Walpole described Chute as his 'oracle in taste, the standard to whom I submitted my trifles, and the genius who presided over poor Strawberry!' Walpole announced in 1750 that he was going to build a little Gothic castle, and that it would be asymmetrical, the very antithesis of Palladianism. By 1753 Walpole determined to give himself a 'Burlington-air': as Chiswick was a model of Classicism, Strawberry would be so of Gothic. Yet the labels and quatrefoils are straight from Langley, and William Kent's Gothick at Esher Place, Surrey, of *c* 1733, was close at hand for study: significantly, Esher Place was greatly admired by Gray, Walpole's close friend and mentor. Richard Bentley, J. H. Müntz, John Chute, Thomas Pitt (1737–93), Robert Adam (1728–92), and James Essex (1722–84) all contributed to this fabulous, asymmetrical, Gothic villa, parts of which were genuinely based on closely observed real bits of Medieval architecture, but, in spite of his good intentions, Strawberry is overwhelmingly Gothic in the Georgian Rococo sense, rather

PLATE 55 *Strawberry Hill, Twickenham, by John Chute and others. The Beauclerk Tower by Essex is on the left* (JSC).

than truly archaeological in flavour. Professor Michael McCarthy holds that it is absurd to place Strawberry Hill in the stylistic category of 'Rococo' or what he described as the 'nonsense category' of Rococo Gothick. He holds that because Rococo is asymmetrical, but linear and confined to two dimensions, this makes it impossible for Strawberry to be Rococo because the plan and the volumes are three-dimensional and asymmetrical, so are quite different. He holds that Rococo is free from historical association, but that Strawberry is 'characterised by faithful adherence to historical precedent'. But, in objection, there is very little in Strawberry Hill that really looks 'faithful to historical precedent', and the overwhelming impression is of whimsical Georgian Gothic, light, frothy, and elegant, so the present writer begs to differ from Professor McCarthy on this point.

Kent's use of asymmetry in gardens had led to the asymmetrical architecture of the Picturesque.[18] When the Beauclerk Tower (PLATE 55) at Strawberry Hill was finished in 1776 (to designs by Essex), Walpole felt the effect was very pretty, breaking the long line of the house picturesquely and looking very 'ancient'. Strawberry had a very great effect on taste, and, because of its asymmetry and its archaeological pretensions, influenced much that was to follow. Yet eventually Walpole was to note, wryly, that 'every true Goth must perceive' that the rooms of Strawberry were 'more the works of fancy than imitation'.[19]

James Essex also designed a tower at Wimpole, Cambridgeshire, in 1768, with Y-tracery and a lot of windows. One of the most perfect little Gothick churches was Hartwell church in Buckinghamshire of 1753–55 by Henry Keene (1726–76): it was built to an octagonal plan with an elaborate fan-vaulted ceiling, and pretty towers attached to the east and west parts of the octagon (PLATES 56-57). From the 1750s Keene worked on drawings for Trinity College, Dublin, and in 1761 he was appointed Architect to the Kingdom of Ireland for His Majesty's Works, and he remained in Ireland for most of the 1760s. He had worked with Sanderson Miller on drawings for Hagley in 1749, and in 1749–50 he vaulted and fitted out Hartlebury Castle Chapel, Worcestershire (PLATE 58), in a Gothic style that looks like an early run for Hillsborough Parish church. From 1761 he prepared drawings for Arbury Hall, Warwickshire, where the enchanting dining-room appears to be partly his work, and partly that of Sir Roger Newdigate, Bart (PLATE 49).

Arbury Hall is probably the most beautiful of all Gothick

PLATE 56 *Church at Hartwell, Buckinghamshire, by Henry Keene, of 1753–55* (RCHME BB71/3607).

PLATE 57 *Interior of Hartwell church, Buckinghamshire, showing the beautiful fan-vaulting* (RCHME C44/438).

PLATE 58 *Interior of Hartlebury Castle chapel, Worcestershire, of 1749–50, by Henry Keene* (RCHME BB83/5036).

The Castle Style

In the 1760s the first signs of a revival of a 'castle' style, as opposed to building follies, could be detected. Mention has been made of 'Castle Airs' in Vanbrugh's works, but Roger Morris also designed in the Castle manner, notably at Clearwell Castle, Gloucestershire, of *c* 1728, a castellated mock-Medieval symmetrical composition with the centre flanked by huge towers. In 1745, however, Morris designed the first major castellated Gothic house since Vanbrugh's time: this was Inveraray Castle, seat of the Third Duke of Argyll. It has a Palladian plan, but window-openings are pointed, and there are four circular towers at each corner. The central hall was illuminated from a mighty crenellated clerestory and in this respect we are back in the world of Wollaton Hall, and more immediately at Eastbury, Dorset, Vanbrugh's great house which was published in *Vitruvius Britannicus*.[20] Inveraray was also one of the earliest planned towns of the period. Many mock castles were built after this, and, like Inveraray, had Classical interiors. Robert Adam's castellated Mellerstain with Neo-Classical interior was a fine example, but his greatest essay in the Castle style is unquestionably Culzean, Ayrshire (PLATE 59) perched high above the sea on the west coast within sight of Ailsa Craig. It is a symmetrical composition of 1777–92, with crenellations, turrets, bartisans, and loopholes, but the windows are sashes and the interior is deliciously light and Classical. Adam's Seton Castle, of 1790 and after (PLATE 60), owes even more, perhaps, to Vanbrugh, and recalls a mix of the latter's own house at Greenwich with Seaton Delaval.[21]

interiors of the period, and Castle Ward the most unusual, with one side of the house Gothic and the other Palladian (inside and out) (PLATES 37–38). From about 1762, however, the light frothy Rococo Gothic began to fail, except in Ireland where Hillsborough church (1770s) and Down Cathedral (1790s) are two outstanding examples. Taste moved more towards castellated extensions and a refined Gothic or Classicism for interiors. Tetbury church, Gloucestershire, of 1771–81 by Francis Hiorne (1744–89), the son of William Hiorne (*c* 1712–76) who had carried out works from 1748 at Arbury Hall, is a beautiful example of the late, slender, refined Gothic manner, now partly archaeologically correct, with the main style Perpendicular (PLATE 156). He (Francis Hiorne) also designed the Classical parish church of St Anne, Belfast, of 1776, a date which could also link him with Hillsborough, for stylistically Tetbury and Hillsborough have similarities.

PLATE 59 *Culzean Castle, Ayrshire, by Robert Adam* (RCAHMS AY/925).

Unlike the spectacular Adam castles in Scotland, however, Richard Payne Knight's Downton Castle in Herefordshire, begun in 1772 (PLATE 61) is completely asymmetrical, and has Gothic windows. It is crenellated and provided with machicolations. The massive 'keep' has a miniature Pantheon inside (the dining-room), and the dominant flavour of the interiors is Neo-Classical (PLATE 62). However, the exterior asymmetrical composition is Picturesque, but Culzean, high above the sea, verges on the Sublime (PLATE 59) Knight justi-

fied the mixture by stating that the best style for irregular and Picturesque houses *was* a mixture, alluding to buildings in paintings by Claude and Poussin, rough masonry, buttresses, and perfectly formed Classical Orders. Ireland also acquired symmetrical 'castle' houses, and, later, asymmetrical Picturesque types. John Nash's beautiful Caerhayes Castle, Cornwall, of *c* 1808, is a charming example of the Picturesque asymmetrical manner. Nash also applied his asymmetrical Picturesque compositional techniques to castellated forms: his Killymoon Castle, Cookstown, Co Tyrone, of *c* 1801–03 (PLATE 63), has turrets, towers, and semicircular-headed somewhat Norman windows, but with Y-tracery, while Childwall Hall, Lancashire, of 1806–13, was more Tudor, as was West Grinstead Park, Surrey, of *c* 1809.

PLATE 60 *Seton Castle, East Lothian, by Robert Adam* (RCAHMS EL/45).

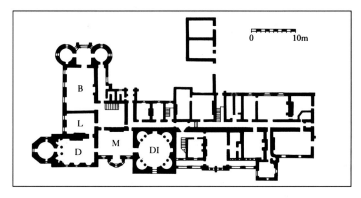

PLATE 62 *Plan of Downton Castle, Herefordshire, from 1772, by Richard Payne Knight. B Ballroom; L Library; D Drawing-Room; M Morning-Room; DI Dining-Room (Pantheon)* (JSC).

PLATE 61 *Downton Castle, Herefordshire, by Richard Payne Knight, started 1772* (RCHME BB77/5128).

PLATE 63 *Killymoon Castle, Cookstown, Co Tyrone, by John Nash, of c 1801–03* (JSC).

Chinoiserie and Orientalism

The evocation of Cathay had been fashionable for interior decoration and furnishings from the latter part of the seventeenth century, and Chinese porcelain, Japanese lacquer, and Indian textiles had been prized by the rich in the reign of James I and VI. Pseudo-oriental furniture was being made in the second decade of the seventeenth century. The drinking of tea, after all, was an oriental custom, and from about 1700 tea was the national drink in England. This encouraged the manufacture of all the impedimenta concerned with tea (pots, cups, saucers, caddies, and so on) in an oriental style. Genuine Chinese porcelain was preferred, but by 1700 the Potteries in Staffordshire were producing cups and teapots in the Chinese Taste.

The *Trianon de Porcelaine* by Louis Le Vau (1612–70) which was built at Versailles in 1670 was the first of many garden-buildings in the Chinese Taste which were to become so popular throughout Europe. Chinese pagodas, lattice-work tea-houses, and temples were built from Scandinavia to Italy, and from Russia to the Atlantic. *Chinoiserie* was enthusiastically embraced in Germany too, and in England and the Netherlands it was well entrenched by the time of William and Mary.

By the Georgian period there were plenty of Chinese artefacts and objects in the Chinese style about. There was a Chinese Bridge of *c* 1738 at Stowe which aroused little inter-

PLATE 64 *The Chinese Pavilion of 1747 at Shugborough, Staffordshire* (JSC).

est because there was so much 'Chinese-work' everywhere, and there is a charming survival of around 1747 at Shugborough, Staffordshire, in the Chinese pavilion, a square building with concave roof and wide-spreading eaves, deliciously painted in red, green, and gold (PLATE 64). *Chinoiserie* reached the heights of popularity around 1750, and so coincided with the craze for Rococo Gothick. Chinese frets occurred in chair-backs and trellises, bridges, and staircases. Fields were fenced with Chinese palings, and exotic Chinese pagodas graced many a park. Many hipped roofs acquired horned corners and little bells under the eaves (PLATE 72). Bedragoned robes and silk Chinese-gowns were assumed at

PLATE 65 *Sir William Chambers's Pagoda at Kew Gardens, of 1761–62* (JSC).

routs; painted panels, lacquers, tapestries, and wallpapers adorned the walls of rooms; and in 1769 Claydon House, Buckinghamshire, acquired its amazing Rococo-Chinese plasterwork by Luke Lightfoot. Thomas Chippendale published many designs in the Chinese Taste in his *Gentleman and Cabinet-maker's Directory* of 1754.

A vogue for *Chinoiserie* pieces in the Rococo style continued until virtually the end of the eighteenth century, but the Classicists and the Goths opposed such taste. Early in the century *Chinoiserie* was well established indoors, but as Horace Walpole remarked, and has been mentioned previously, Gothick forced the pagodas to 'take the veil' outside. Then Rococo arrived from France, enthusiastically embraced by Chippendale and others, and styles became confused. A 'happy mixture' of Chinese and Gothick Taste was pronounced an 'improvement' in architecture.[22] Many of the pattern-books mentioned above contained 'Chinese' designs, including those of William Halfpenny.

The English landscape-garden was known as *le jardin anglo-chinois*, and it frequently contained Chinese bridges with fretwork railings and vermilion-painted pagodas, shaded by Chinese-looking weeping willows. It was, however, called 'Chinese' not just because of these obvious visual allusions, but because it was irregular, Picturesque, and not laid out on rigid geometrical patterns. Sir William Temple (1628–99), in his essay, *Upon the Gardens of Epicurus* of 1685, praised the Chinese way of planting in an apparently haphazard manner 'without any Order of Disposition of Parts', and noted that the English had 'hardly any Notion of this sort of Beauty'. This irregularity, he declared, the Chinese called *Sharawadgi*. The word is also called *Sharawaggi*, which may be a corruption of *Sa-ro-kwai-chi* (meaning the quality of being surprising through graceful disorder), or *San-lan* or *So-lu-wai-chi* (meaning widely scattered or disorderly arrangement in short spaces enlivened tastefully by disorder), according to the *Quarterly Bulletin of Chinese Bibliography*, New Series, I, 4, for December 1940. Pope also referred to *Sharawaggis* of China, and complained he had little or no idea of what they were, while Walpole, in his letter to Mann (25 February 1750), said he was almost as 'fond of the *Sharawaggi*, or Chinese want of symmetry, in buildings, as in grounds or gardens'.

So irregular gardens began to be regarded as Chinese, as Joseph Addison (1672–1719) reminds us. Kew Gardens acquired the House of Confucius, complete with fretwork, bells, and upturned horned hips, in *c* 1745 to designs by J. Goupy, and Sir William Chambers was to add the Pagoda (1761–62) (PLATE 65) and many other exotic structures. Chambers published his *Plans, Elevations, Sections and Perspective Views of the Gardens and Buildings at Kew in Surrey* in 1763, and in 1757 he had published *Designs of Chinese Buildings, Furniture, Dresses, etc.* The Kew volume, a lavish folio, included the pagoda, aviary, and bridge in the Chinese Taste, a Moorish-Gothic 'Mosque', and several Classical buildings. The pagoda had painted dragons, with the inevitable bells in their mouths, on each of the storeys, and, when erected, was the most scholarly in Europe, though not, apparently, modelled on a particular real precedent in China. It soon became one of the sights of London. Chambers's *Designs of Chinese Buildings* and the Kew book were important because they revived interest in *Chinoiserie* and provided the pattern-books for many buildings in the Chinese Taste in Germany, Russia, Scandinavia, and the United States: they also, as Hugh Honour has written,[23] mark a 'new attitude to oriental art which was to prevail in the later years of the century and which demanded free but essentially accurate imitations, rather than amusing parodies, of Chinese objects'.

'Capability' Brown supplanted Chambers as the architect for Claremont Park, Surrey, in 1770, so Chambers worked off his rage in an attack on Brown in his *A Dissertation on Oriental Gardening* of 1772: garden-scenery, he wrote, should differ as much from 'common nature as an heroic poem doth from a prose relation', and he argued that nature was incapable of giving pleasure without the assistance of art. Chambers observed that an ideal garden-design was quite unlike anything produced by Brown. But Chambers's book, dressed up in its exotic Chinese garb, was only literary camouflage for his attack on the bare landscapes created by Brown. It was too subtle, and Chambers's book was assumed by the public to propose the Chinese garden as an exemplar, for imitation: he was therefore obliged to publish an 'Explanatory Discourse' in the second edition of 1773 in which he made it clear that his attack on Brown had been 'put into the mouth of a Chinese', but not before William Mason, egged on by Horace Walpole, published his satire *An Heroic Epistle to Sir William Chambers* (1773) which ridiculed 'the scattered glories of Chinese Virtù', and embarrassed Chambers, although it helped sell several hundred more copies of the *Dissertation*.

The uproar which the *Dissertation* and the *Heroic Epistle* stirred up spelled the expulsion of some 'Chinee-pagodas' from the garden: William Shenstone, among others, had always sniffed at 'China's vain alcoves', and Walpole was never keen on the 'fallaballas' of 'Chinee-work'. Nevertheless, Chinese bridges, fishing-houses, and some minor pagodas were built, and another edition of William Wrighte's *Grotesque Architecture ... consisting of Plans, etc, ... for Chinese ... Rustic Seats ... etc*, came out as late as 1790. Henry Holland's (1745–1806) large Chinese Dairy at Woburn Abbey, Bedfordshire, of *c* 1787 has lots of fretted woodwork, bamboo supports, and other 'Chinee'-motifs. At Carlton House, Pall Mall, Holland designed the Chinese drawing-room of the 1780s for the Prince of Wales (later George IV), the details of which derived from Chambers.[24]

PLATE 66 *Sezincote, Gloucestershire, by S.P.Cockerell, of the early 1800s. An example of the Indian Taste* (JSC).

After the death of Brown, Humphry Repton, 'Capability's' prolific successor as designer of landskips, viewed Chinese bridges, fences, and fripperies with a more kindly eye, and 'Chinee-pieces' rose on the ruins of rock-works, plantations, and wildernesses. Repton also demonstrated a more scholarly attitude to appropriate planting to surround various buildings, and proposed plants imported from China to set off Holland's Dairy at Woburn. Later, from 1797 to 1802, he was consulted about suitable plants to show off Sezincote, that extraordinary house in the 'Indian Taste', near Moreton-in-the-Marsh, Gloucestershire, designed in the early 1800s by S. P. Cockerell (1753–1827) and Thomas Daniell (1749–1840). Sezincote is exotic, oriental and Picturesque, with its onion-domes, multifoil arches, and *chattra*-topped pinnacles (PLATE 66).

Now Repton became enthusiastic about 'Hindoo' taste, and prophesied that England was on the verge of a great change in architecture and landscape gardening because of the illustrations of the scenery and buildings of India published by artists such as Daniell and Hodges. Daniell's *Oriental Scenery* (1808) and his published views of Calcutta based on drawings of his own and those of his nephew, William Daniell (1769–1837), made from 1784, helped to popularise the Indian style. William Hodges (1744–97), who went to India under the aegis of Warren Hastings in 1778, published many views of India in 1786 which were very influential: Friedrich Heinrich Alexander von Humboldt (1769–1859) stated that it

was Hodges's views of India which led him to become a traveller with a taste for the exotic. Hodges published his *Travels in India* embellished with plates from his own drawings in 1780–83, and a French edition came out later. Hodges also wrote a *Dissertation on the Prototypes of Architecture, Hindoo, Moorish and Gothic* in 1787 to introduce a series of large aquatints, and much of the material in the *Dissertation* appears in *Travels in India*. Hodges realised that non-Classical architecture could not be judged by Classical rules, and proposed that Egyptian, Hindu, Moorish, and Gothic all derived from a common visual memory of stalactite and rock formations. His theory suggests the longing for the primitive and the natural which was a feature of late eighteenth-century Romantic sensibility. Repton, in turn, felt that Indian arches derived from subterranean caves and grottoes. Hodges praised the Taj Mahal as the 'most perfect pearl', and his *Select Views in India* (1785–88) revealed the 'Barbaric Splendour' of Asiatic buildings to the West; and Sir Joshua Reynolds (1723–92) felt the pictures would 'furnish an architect with models to copy'. One of the first fruits of the linking of Indian and Gothic forms was George Dance's (1741–1825) south façade of Guildhall, City of London, of 1788–89 (PLATE 67).

Both *Chinoiserie* and Hindoo tastes were combined at the Royal Pavilion, Brighton. William Porden (*c* 1755–1822)

produced designs for a 'Chinee-pavilion' in 1803, and in the next year he introduced the Indian style into the stables, riding-school and coach-house of 1804–08 (he had worked under Cockerell at Sezincote) (PLATE 68). Repton then suggested a Hindoo design for the Pavilion itself, which delighted the Prince of Wales, and was published in 1808. When, in 1815, the Prince commissioned John Nash to design an 'Indian' Pavilion, Repton was, not unnaturally, upset, but the building, finished in 1821, had an exotic interior to end all exotic interiors, the dominant theme being *Chinoiserie* inside but Hindoo without (PLATES 69–70).

Brighton Pavilion has cast-iron staircases with balustrades in the form of bamboo lattice, while the music-room (Plate 72), one of the most exotic interiors of all, may be based on Marco Polo's description of the pavilion of Kublai Khan. Thus *Chinoiserie* and the 'Hindoo' styles were often mixed, and can, in a sense, be regarded, like aspects of Gothic, as facets of European Rococo (PLATE 71). Yet there were other aspects to all this, and these were the Moresque and *Turquerie* styles. Müntz designed an 'Alhambra' for Kew Gardens in 1750, and

PLATE 67 *Indian-Gothick façade of Guildhall, City of London, of 1788–89, by George Dance the Younger* (GLCL).

PLATE 68 *Stables and Riding-School at Brighton by William Porden, from* VRP *of 1826, Vol II, No 26* (SM).

PLATE 69 *Steyne Front Geometrical Elevation of the Royal Pavilion, Brighton, from* VRP, *Vol II, No 4* (SM).

PLATE 70 *The Kitchens of the Royal Pavilion, Brighton, showing the palm-leaf capitals, from* VRP, *Vol II, No 24* (SM).

PLATE 71 (RIGHT) *'Chinese Architecture' from Peter Nicholson's* Architectural and Engineering Dictionary *of 1835. Note the bells hanging from the turned-up eaves, the frets, and other characteristic features* (JSC).

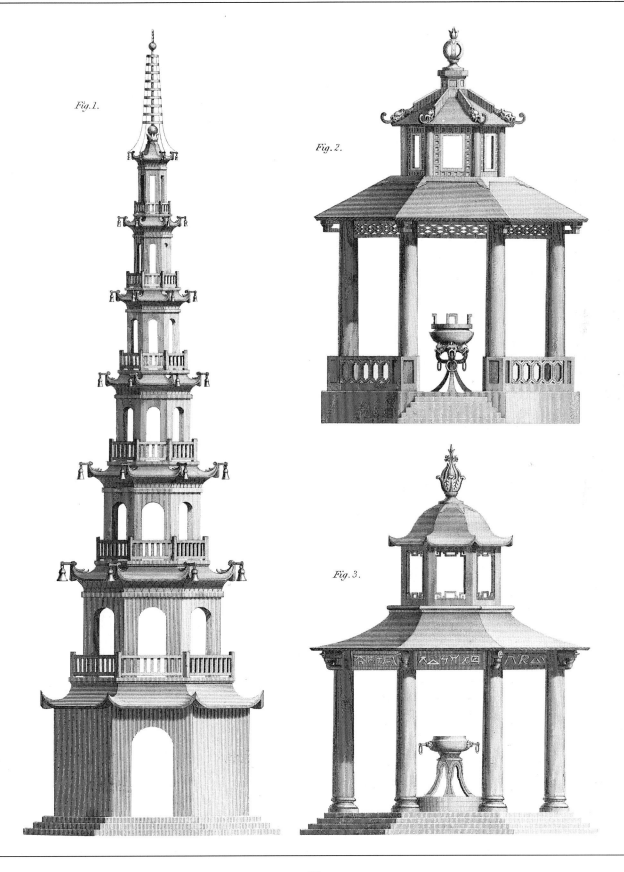

Fig.1.

Fig.2.

Fig.3.

PLATE 72 *The exotic Chinese Music-Room at the Royal Pavilion, Brighton, from* VRP, *Vol II, No 16 (SM).*

Chambers designed a 'Mosque' of 1761 and an 'Alhambra' of 1758. It must not be forgotten that the cradle of Classical civilisation, Greece, was part of the Ottoman Empire, and so many views of Greek buildings show turbanned Turks, especially those depicting the discovery of important sites and artefacts of Antiquity.

Thomas Hope (1769–1831) created from 1799, in his house in Duchess Street, Portland Place, rooms to suggest India, Egypt (PLATE 73), and Greece, and looked eastwards for qualities of style, not necessarily from a purely archaeological point of view, but in order to capture essentials. This is fully and ably discussed by Doctor David Watkin in *Thomas Hope 1769–1831 and the Neo-Classical Idea*, of 1968. Daniell produced a Capriccio of Hindu and Moslem architecture for Hope's 'Indian' Room at Duchess Street and this Capriccio was placed opposite a Pannini view of the Roman Forum. Hope was painted by Sir William Beechey (1753–1839) in 1798 on the Grand Tour, but in sumptuous Turkish clothes, and standing in front of a Mosque. William Beckford (1759–1844), the author of *Vathek: an Arabian Tale* (1782, but not published until 1786), was not only fascinated by Orientalism, but was particularly keen on Arabic and Mughal works. He built his Sublime Gothic fantasy, Fonthill, Wiltshire, to designs by James Wyatt (1746–1813), in 1796–1812, the most outrageous monument of the Romantic period in the Gothic style, but he also built in 1825 a 'Moorish' summer-house in his garden at 20 Lansdown Crescent, Bath. The Islamic inspiration in British architecture is discussed in John Sweetman's *The Oriental Obsession* (1988) and in Patrick Conner's *Oriental Architecture in the West* (1979).

Egypt[25] was to play its part too, but the Inspiration of Egypt was only partly of the Rococo-Exotic type, as it was closely connected with the rediscovery of Antiquity and with the search for Primitivism and purity in architecture. It is to this phase that we now turn.

PLATE 73 *'Egyptian Room' at Thomas Hope's house in Duchess Street, London, from his* Household Furniture and Interior Decoration *of 1807, Plate VIII. Note the chairs with seated Piranesian-Egyptian figures on arm-rests, the Canopic jars on stumpy pedestals, and figures of Antinoüs (JSC).*

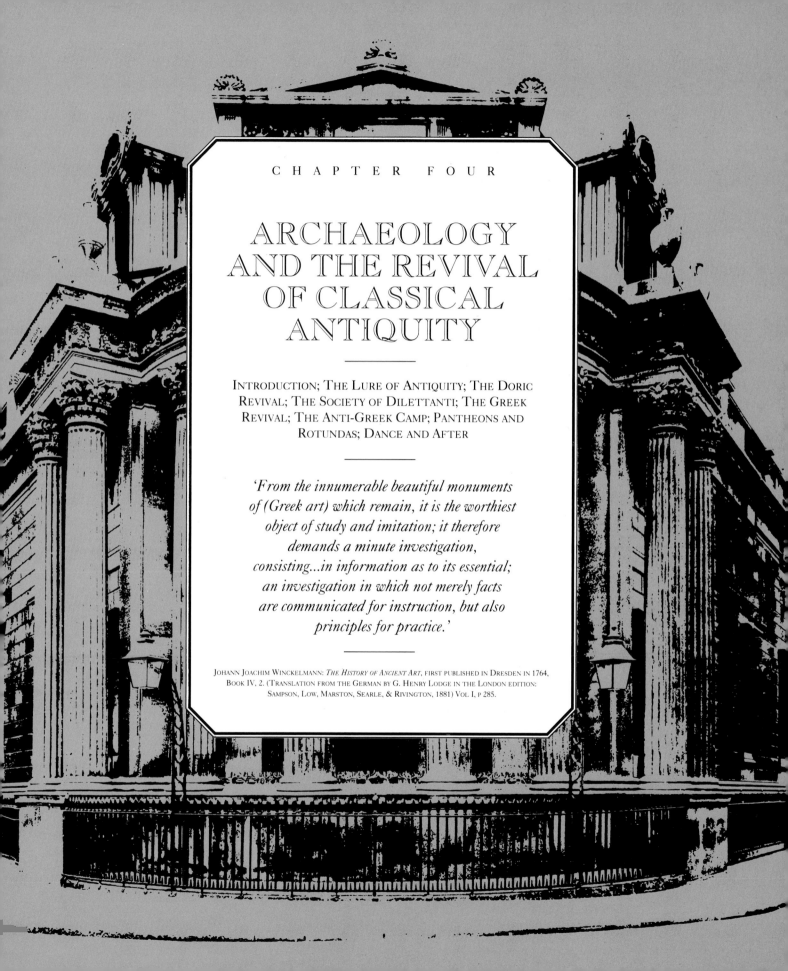

CHAPTER FOUR

ARCHAEOLOGY AND THE REVIVAL OF CLASSICAL ANTIQUITY

INTRODUCTION; THE LURE OF ANTIQUITY; THE DORIC
REVIVAL; THE SOCIETY OF DILETTANTI; THE GREEK
REVIVAL; THE ANTI-GREEK CAMP; PANTHEONS AND
ROTUNDAS; DANCE AND AFTER

*'From the innumerable beautiful monuments
of (Greek art) which remain, it is the worthiest
object of study and imitation; it therefore
demands a minute investigation,
consisting...in information as to its essential;
an investigation in which not merely facts
are communicated for instruction, but also
principles for practice.'*

JOHANN JOACHIM WINCKELMANN: *THE HISTORY OF ANCIENT ART*, FIRST PUBLISHED IN DRESDEN IN 1764,
BOOK IV, 2. (TRANSLATION FROM THE GERMAN BY G. HENRY LODGE IN THE LONDON EDITION:
SAMPSON, LOW, MARSTON, SEARLE, & RIVINGTON, 1881) VOL I, P 285.

Introduction

The supremacy of Palladianism in matters of Taste, as we have seen, was being undermined by the Cult of the Picturesque during the 1740s, and by around 1750 it was merely an option among several architectural styles. One of the problems of understanding architecture and architectural history is that there has long been a tendency to 'compartment' styles. This tendency has been encouraged by biased writing: to read certain architectural works published over the last half-century or so, one would imagine that no buildings erected since, say, 1936, were worthy of note unless they conformed to the tyranny of the International Modern style. Great masters of Classical Architecture, such as Sir Edwin Lutyens (1869–1944), Sir Reginald Blomfield (1856–1942), and Sir Albert Richardson (1880-1964), were often ignored or sneered at. This matter is ably discussed by Doctor David Watkin in his *Morality and Architecture*.[1]

As has (hopefully) been made clear, Palladianism, Gothick, and *Chinoiserie* were all being used at the same time, and during the second half of the eighteenth century, the options expanded to include Hindoo, Greek, Egyptian, and other styles. To the simple-minded, Medieval Gothic architecture suddenly stopped when the first Renaissance works appeared in England. Yet Pietro Torrigiano (1472–1528) was commissioned to make the tomb-chest and effigies for King Henry VII and his Queen in 1512. The choir-stalls and pulpitum in King's College Chapel, Cambridge, have the monograms HR and AR, suggesting a date of 1533–36, the period when Anne Boleyn was Queen of King Henry VIII.[2] Even thereafter, everything built was *not* in the Renaissance style, for Gothic continued to be used well into the seventeenth century, including the spectacular Hall Staircase at Christ Church, Oxford, dating from *c* 1640, and made by a London mason called Smith. There appear to have been several groups of masons in the seventeenth and early eighteenth centuries still working in ways that had not changed much since the Reformation, and therefore the Gothic tradition survived. Places like Chipping Campden had local craftsmen still skilled in Gothic design,[3] and it seems fairly clear that by the time Wren was building in the Gothic style (St Mary Aldermary, Bow Lane, London, and Tom Tower, Oxford), part, at least, of a Medieval tradition survived. We refer to post-Renaissance examples of Gothic (like the Hall Staircase at Oxford) as Gothic Survival, while buildings consciously designed by architects in a Gothic style are called Gothic Revival.[4]

Similarly, Traditional and Classical architecture did not end suddenly, although to read the architectural magazines of the 1940s and 1950s one would have little inkling that this was the case, for there is no doubt that the arguments for Modernism were being actively and exclusively published. Yet history, true history, involves the recovery of facts from our past, and those facts provide evidence to enable the historian to retrieve the past: the truth serves as the basic material from which the historian can fashion his story, and it is not the business of the historian to be a judge of morality, a prophet, or an arbiter of taste.

The Lure of Antiquity

Palladian Classicism had pretensions to link contemporary design with the Architecture of Roman Antiquity. Palladio himself had studied extant Roman remains and had prepared illustrations based on accurate measured drawings. But Palladio, as a source for true Antique architecture, it began to be realised, was a filter through which Antiquity was perceived. Gradually, the argument went, antiquarians should study real Antique remains rather than get their ideas and sources through a Palladian filter.

The published works of Giovanni Battista Piranesi attracted attention to the architecture of Roman Antiquity, for this architecture was revered anyway, and the superiority of Antique architecture over that of the moderns was accepted as an eighteenth-century article of faith. Piranesi's *Le Vedute di Roma* was published from 1745, and showed etched views of ruins and of the architecture of ancient and modern Rome. These etchings were greatly admired, and had a significant influence on the formation of a Romantic idea of Roman magnificence. In *c* 1745 Piranesi began work on a series of imaginary views of prison interiors: these obsessive, dark, brooding vistas, terrible and powerful images, and, above all, the gigantic scale of the architecture, struck chords. Here was Sublime Terror indeed. Now this tendency in Piranesi to exploit scale, and suggest vastness, was also present in his views of Rome, and was evident in his *Antichità Romane* of 1756, in which Roman architecture and antiquities were inflated to appear gigantic. The result was that visitors to Rome on the Grand Tour, who had previously been excited by Piranesi's images, tended to be disappointed by the reality, for the buildings were smaller than Piranesi suggested. Even Piranesi's views of vases and ash-chests had a tendency to a megalomaniac scale. Thus images by Piranesi reinforced attitudes which regarded Antiquity as superior, grander, more noble, and overwhelming than anything the eighteenth century could produce. Later, in 1761, Piranesi was to produce his controversial *Della Magnificenza ed Architettura de' Romani*, which was essentially a visual polemic extolling

PLATE 77 *Cairness House, Aberdeenshire, of 1789–97. The end of the service-wing showing the stumpy Doric Order and lintel forming a primitive type of Diocletian or Thermal window* (RCAHMS AB1300).

from the Roman ritual to encompass Greece as well. Horace Walpole waspishly declared that the nominal qualification for membership of the Society was having been to Italy, but the real one was to get drunk. There was some truth in this, as some members, like Sir Francis Dashwood, Bart (1708–81), were rarely sober when they made the Grand Tour, and embraced dissipation as a way of life. The Dilettanti, like many clubbable types of the Georgian period, enjoyed gluttony and learning, large quantities of drink and Antiquarian collecting, civilised conversation and indecent ribaldry. To the Dilettanti travel and antiquarianism, especially the study of Classical antiquities, were both agreeable and worthy. The Society made it its business to study Roman, Greek, and Graeco-Roman architecture and artefacts. It was opposed to the political cult of Sir Robert Walpole, and was therefore unenthusiastic about the Palladianism espoused by the Whig Oligarchy: it was sympathetic to the exotic, the Gothick, and the Antique. And if it could be a new sort of Antique, then so much the better.

The word *Dilettanti* deserves some more explanation. A *dilettante* meant a lover of fine arts; one who cultivates them for love of them rather than professionally. A *dilettante* was therefore an educated amateur. Gradually, the term became slightly pejorative, meaning one interested in an art or a science merely as a pastime, without a serious aim or study. The Society could boast several members who were important collectors of antiquities, and it did not lack men or taste, learning, and discernment. Sir William Hamilton (1730-1803), for example, made famous collections of antiquities, including

the celebrated Greek vases: the priapic nature of many of the vase decorations encouraged publication. Hamilton's first collection was published in 1766, and the second, by W. Tischbein, as *Collections of Engravings of Ancient Vases...etc* (Naples 1791-95). In 1786 Payne Knight published his *An Account of the Remains of the Worship of Priapus*, which incorporated material derived from Hamilton's collections, but, apart from the phallic aspects, the collections influenced designs, notably Adam and Wedgwood, and Hamilton himself deserves respect as a great antiquary, collector, and scholar, whose work formed a key part of the British Museum's displays, rather than attracting curiosity as the husband of Nelson's mistress.

The Society had many members who were interested in Classical archaeology and topography, and it was to encourage a systematic exploration of the Greek Classical sites. Robert Wood (*c* 1717–71), who was to become a member of the Society, toured the Greek Islands in 1742–43, and in 1749 James Caulfeild, Fourth Viscount and First Earl of Charlemont (1728–99), visited a number of sites in the company of Richard Dalton (*c* 1715–91),who made detailed drawings of Greek antiquities. Places visited included Chios, Cnidos, Corinth, Delos, Halicarnassus, and Lesbos. Charlemont knew Burke, Oliver Goldsmith (*c* 1730–74), William Hogarth, and Samuel Johnson (1709–84), and became Chairman of the Committee of the Dilettanti appointed to superintend research into the Classical antiquities of Asia Minor and Greece under the aegis of the Society. Dalton's drawings stimulated further interest, and in 1748 James Stuart and Nicholas Revett (1720–1804) determined on a project which would establish an archaeological approach to Greek antiquities on the lines of Antoine Desgodetz's (1653–1728) *Édifices de Rome* of 1682. It was decided to organise and finance an expedition that was to make Greek architecture, Greek Orders, and Greek details as familiar as those of Rome, and the Society of Dilettanti helped to fund the travels and work of Stuart and Revett from 1751 to 1754. If Stuart and Revett had thought up the project, the proposal was supported by, and may even have been partly conceived by, Matthew Brettingham, Junior (1725–1803), who visited Italy and Greece with Stuart and Revett in 1747, and remained in Rome until 1754 buying statues and paintings for Lord Leicester and his great house at Holkham, Norfolk (PLATES 25–27). Also involved was Gavin Hamilton (1723–98), the Scottish archaeologist, art-dealer, and painter, who was a leading member of the Neo-Classical Circle of Mengs and Winckelmann. Hamilton carried out many important excavations near Rome, and he was an influence on the great sculptor Antonio Canova (1757–1822).

The work of surveying, measuring, and drawing the remains of Greek buildings was slow, painstaking, and often fraught with danger, but eventually the first volume of *The Antiquities of Athens measured and delineated by James Stuart, F.R.S. and F.S.A., and Nicholas Revett, Painters and Architects* appeared in 1762. This was a major event in the history of Classical archaeology, and the book was recognised as a work of significant architectural scholarship: it became the principal source-book for the Greek Revival. The rest of the work was slow in appearing: Volume II came out in 1789 (although the imprint says 1787), and the third, fourth, and fifth volumes were published in 1794, 1814, and 1830 respectively, largely the work of younger men. So this great work of scholarship took eighty-two years to appear complete, and its impact in architecture was spasmodic. Volume I only had one example

PLATE 79 *The Tower of the Winds (Horologium of Andronikos Cyrrhestes), Athens, from* AA, *Vol I, Chapter III, Plate III* (SM).

PLATE 78 *The Choragic Monument of Lysicrates, Athens, from* AA, *Vol I, Chapter IV, Plate III* (SM).

of Doric, and also depicted the temple on the Ilissus, the Choragic Monument of Lysicrates (PLATE 78), the Tower of the Winds (PLATE 79), and the Stoa, all in Athens. Volume II (1789) contained the major buildings of Acropolis, including the Parthenon, the Erechtheion (PLATE 80), the Propylaea, the Thrasyllus Choragic Monument (PLATE 87), and the Temple of Zeus Olympios. By the time the publication of *The Antiquities...* was completed in 1830 (Volume V), all the major buildings of Athens, Delos, Bassae, and other centres had been illustrated, but from the 1789 volume (edited by William Newton), the contribution of Stuart and Revett was interpreted and expanded by the works of Willey Reveley (1760–99) (Volume III), Joseph Woods (1776–1864) (Volume IV), and Charles Robert Cockerell (1788–1863), Thomas Leverton Donaldson (1795–1885), William Wesley Jenkins

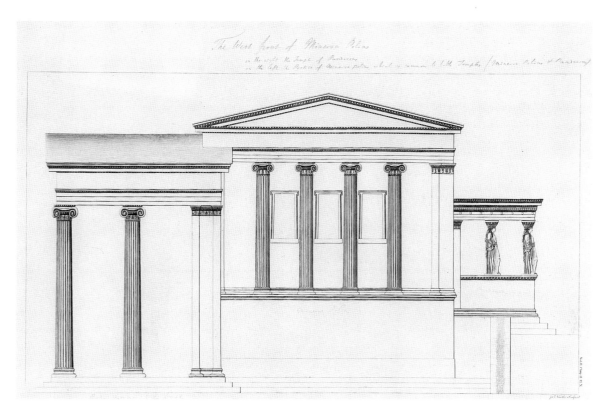

PLATE 80 *The Erechtheion, Athens, showing the Caryatide porch and the very beautiful Ionic Order with an anthemion collar under the capitals. From* AA, *Vol II, Plate X* (SM).

(*ob* 1864), William Kinnard (*c* 1788-1839) and William Railton (*c* 1801–77) (Volume V).

Even before the publication of Volume I of Stuart and Revett's book, however, there were other less accurate, but nevertheless important, publications on Classical architecture. Julien-David Le Roy (1724-1803) brought out his *Les Ruines des plus beaux monuments de la Grèce* in 1758, and Robert Sayer published his *Ruins of Athens and other valuable Antiquities in Greece* in 1759. Robert Wood's *Ruins of Palmyra* appeared in 1753, and his *Ruins of Baalbec* in 1757, all of which added to the store of knowledge of buildings of Classical Antiquity, while Robert Adam's *Ruins of the Palace of the Emperor Diocletian, at Spalatro, in Dalmatia*, was published in 1764. So, in the middle of the eighteenth century the Primitive had been extolled, Greek architecture was being discovered, and Antique architecture seemed to offer more real, purer exemplars than did the second- or third-hand works of the Italian Renaissance, even where there was a strong dose of Roman Antiquity, as in Palladio's *oeuvres*. There were attempts to show how Greek details could be adapted to Palladianism, notably by Stephen Riou (1720–80) in his *The Grecian Orders of Architecture delineated and explained from the Antiquities of Athens* in 1768, which was intended to publicise Greek Antique architecture, to promote the work of Stuart and Revett, and to demonstrate how Greek Orders could be treated.

The Greek Revival

James Stuart's Doric 'temple' at Hagley of 1758 is recognised as the first Doric Revival building in Europe, and this was followed by the Doric Temple (1764), the Triumphal Arch (a copy of the 'Arch of Hadrian' in Athens of 1764–67), the Tower of the Winds (1764) (PLATE 81), and the Lanthorn of Demosthenes (PLATE 82), a copy of the Choragic Monument of Lysicrates in Athens (1770), all at Shugborough, Staffordshire, where, it will be recalled, there is also a *Chinoiserie* pavilion (PLATE 64) and the curious Shepherd's Grave (PLATE 54). Stuart also designed the Tower of the Winds, a charming belvedere overlooking Strangford Lough, Co Down, at Mountstewart (*c* 1780) (PLATE 83). These archaeologically correct Greek Revival buildings were all derived from the surveys carried out for *The Antiquities of Athens*. The Choragic Monument of Lysicrates, for example, was illustrated in Vol I (1762) Ch IV, plate 3, but the 'Arch of Hadrian' (PLATE 84) was not published until 1794 (Vol III, Ch 3, plate 4).

Nicholas Revett's church at Ayot St Lawrence in Hertfordshire (PLATES 85–86) of 1778–9 is a bare brick box with an apse at one end and a tetrastyle Doric portico at the other. It has two colonnades on either side linking it to two

PLATE 81 *Tower of the Winds at Shugborough, Staffordshire, of 1764, by James Stuart* (JSC).

PLATE 82 *Lanthorn of Demosthenes by James Stuart, based on the Choragic Monument of Lysicrates, Athens, at Shugborough, Staffordshire* (JSC).

PLATE 83 *The Tower of the Winds at Mountstewart, Co Down, of c 1780, by James Stuart* (JSC).

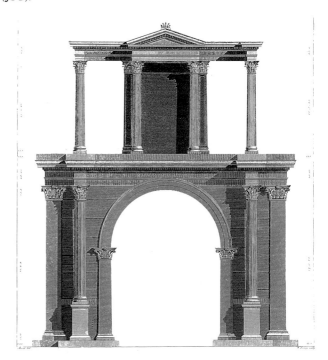

PLATE 84 *The 'Arch of Theseus' or 'Arch of Hadrian', from* AA, *Vol III, Chapter III, Plate IV* (SM).

Plate XXVIII.

WEST ELEVATION

PLATE 90 *St Pancras church of 1819–22, showing the eclectic use of Greek motifs, from Richardson* (BTB/SH).

of late-Georgian Greek Revival churches: it is an eclectic mix of elements from the Erechtheion (the Caryatide porches, and the Order of the portico), the Tower of the Winds and the Choragic Monument of Lysicrates (the ingenious tower), and other Athenian buildings culled from *The Antiquities of Athens* and other source-books. The invention of the tower applied to a temple with two rows of windows (one above and one below the gallery) on its long sides was ingenious, for congregational worship and side windows were not features of Greek temples, yet the overall composition owes much to the precedent of St Martin-in-the-Fields of a century before (PLATES 89–90).

(Sir) Robert Smirke visited the Greek sites early in the century, and became one of the most successful practitioners of the Greek Revival style: his Royal College of Physicians, Trafalgar Square, of 1822–25, is a chaste example of his style, using an Ionic Order, while his British Museum (1823–46)

combines a composition based on English Palladianism (and especially reminiscent of Sir Edward Lovett Pearce's Parliament House in Dublin [started in 1728], with its central pedimented portico, flanking colonnades, and projecting wings [PLATE 32]), with scholarly quotations for the Ionic Order itself (PLATES 91–93). Smirke's capitals are based on the Temple of Athena Polias at Priene (published in *Ionian Antiquities* in 1769), but his bases are derived from the Temple of Dionysus at Teos, as is his entablature. Even before these, though, Smirke had designed the old Covent Garden Theatre (1808–09), burnt down in the 1850s: it had a severe and plain exterior, and a huge tetrastyle Greek Doric portico with pediment.

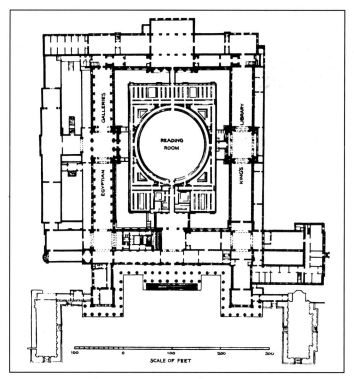

PLATE 91 *Plan of the British Museum from Richardson. The circular reading-room was added later* (BTB/SH).

Decimus Burton's (1800–81) Colosseum at Regent's Park combined the Roman Pantheon and a mighty hexastyle Greek Doric portico (1823–27), while his beautiful Ionic Screen at Hyde Park Corner (1824–30) and his Athenæum Club, Waterloo Place (1827–30) (PLATE 94), put the Greek Revival style firmly before the public. Other notable monuments of the Greek Revival are the chilly but magnificent Greek Doric High School in Edinburgh (1825–29) by Thomas Hamilton (1784–1858) (PLATE 95); Belsay Hall, Northumberland (1810–17), with its mightily severe and plain

PLATE 92 *The front of the British Museum by Sir Robert Smirke, from Richardson* (BTB/SH).

PLATE 93 *The King's Library, the British Museum, one of the finest rooms ever created in the Greek Revival style. From Richardson* (BTB/SH).

PLATE 94 *The Athenæum Club, Waterloo Place, London, of 1827–30, by Decimus Burton. From Richardson* (BTB/SH).

PLATE 95 *The High School in Edinburgh of 1825–29 by Thomas Hamilton. From Richardson* (BTB/SH).

PLATE 96 *Belsay Hall, Northumberland. One of the most severe of Greek Revival exteriors* (RCHME BB78/6768).

PLATE 97 *Attingham Park, Shropshire, by George Steuart, of 1783–85* (JSC).

exterior (with distyle *in antis* Doric portico) (PLATE 96), and serenely beautiful Hall of superimposed Ionic and Roman Doric Orders by Sir Charles Monck (1779–1867), Sir William Gell, and John Dobson – the plan recalls that of a Graeco-Roman villa, the whole design has a Classical authority and a noble simplicity which make it one of the great buildings of the Greek Revival, and the stable block has a belfry based on the Tower of the Winds; and the Royal Institution (1822-26) and National Monument on Calton Hill (with C. R. Cockerell, 1824–29), both in Edinburgh, and both by William Henry Playfair (1790–1857).

The severe, primitive Doric from Paestum was used by Soane at 936 Warwick Road, Solihull (his 'Barn à la Paestum' [PLATE 74]), and by Benjamin Henry Latrobe (1764–1820) at Hammerwood Lodge, Sussex, of *c* 1793, an advanced design inspired by Continental Neo-Classicism (Latrobe studied at the Moravian College in Saxony). In 1796 Latrobe emigrated to America where he designed a number of important buildings in the Greek Revival manner. Latrobe's tough, primitive work of the 1790s should be contrasted with George Steuart's

(*c* 1730–1806) attenuated, elegant, and delicate designs, including Attingham Park, Shropshire, of 1783–85 (PLATE 97), and the church of St Chad, Shrewsbury, of 1790–92, where the elements are broken up into body, vestibule, and tower (PLATE 98).

Charles Robert Cockerell set off on the Grand Tour in 1810, then, with the young Liverpool architect, John Foster (*c* 1787–1846), he left for Greece. In Athens he met the congenial Germans, Baron Johann Carl Christopher Joachim Haller von Hallerstein (1774–1817) – a former pupil of David Gilly – and J. Linckh. The group discovered the celebrated sculptures from the Temple of Aphaia at Aegina which are extremely vigorous and primitive (they are now in the Glyptothek in Munich), and surveyed the Temple of Apollo Epicurius at Bassae, which was unusual in that it had Doric, Ionic, and Corinthian Orders all in the one building. Cockerell and Haller were the first to notice and study the

PLATE 98 *Church of St Chad, Shrewsbury, Shropshire, by George Steuart, of 1790–92* (JSC).

entasis on Greek columns. Cockerell was to use the interesting and somewhat surprised-looking Ionic 'Bassae' Order at his University Library, Cambridge, 1837–40, and Ashmolean Museum and Taylorian Institution, Oxford, of 1841–45.

'Athenian' Stuart's posthumous fame rose as the Greek Revival triumphed after 1815. He was credited with the introduction of chaste and pure styles. The Greek Revival was hailed as a revolution, no less. Of course the style was not associated with Absolutism, nor was it in any way connected with Palladianism and Whiggery (rather the opposite), and its very freshness made it ideal for a new start. The post-Waterloo period saw a great number of public and institutional buildings go up, including University College, London (the 'Godless College'), libraries, museums, schools, and clubs. The times were moving towards a greater franchise, culminating in the Reform Bill of 1832, and the Greek style, severe, serious, high-minded, archaeological, and 'purer' than anything derived from Rome or the Italian Renaissance, seemed ideal to express both the times and the aspirations of a growing, educated, mercantile, professional, and middle class.

Joseph Gwilt (1784–1863) in his *An Encyclopaedia of Architecture, Historical, Theoretical, & Practical*, of 1842, with

PLATE 99 *Section through the hall and rotunda of Paine's design for Kedleston, from his* Noblemen and Gentlemen's Houses, *Plate LII* (SM).

subsequent revisions, stated (paragraphs 516 and 517) that the 'public taste was purified by a corrected knowledge of the buildings of Greece'. He also noted that the 'chasteness and purity which' Stuart and Revett 'had, with some success, endeavoured to introduce into the buildings of England, and in which their zeal had enlisted many artists, had to contend against the opposite and vicious taste of Robert Adam, a fashionable architect, whose eye had been ruined by the corruptions of the worst period of Roman art. It can scarcely be believed, the ornaments of Diocletian's palace at Spalatro should have loaded our dwellings contemporaneously with the use among the more refined few of the exquisite exemplars of Greece, and even of Rome, in its better days. Yet such is the fact; the depraved compositions of Adam were not only tolerated but had their admirers'.

The Anti-Greek Camp

As has been intimated, the Grecians did not have it all their own way, and indeed the opposition was vitriolic. Adam professed to loathe Greek architecture (he may have been jealous of Stuart), and Chambers, in his *Treatise on Civil Architecture*, made his opposition to 'Attic Deformity' clear. 'How distant the Grecians were from perfection in proportions', he wrote. He felt that 'none of the

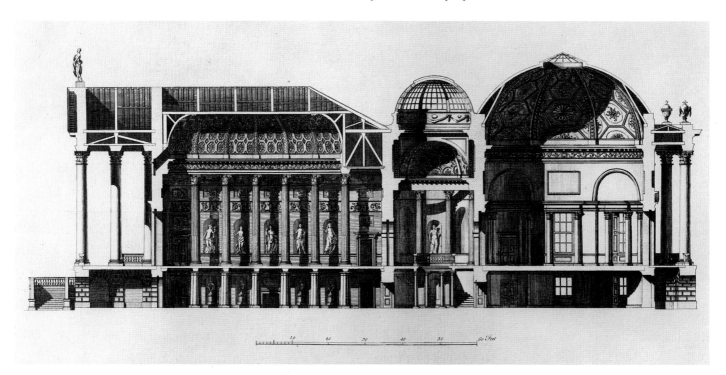

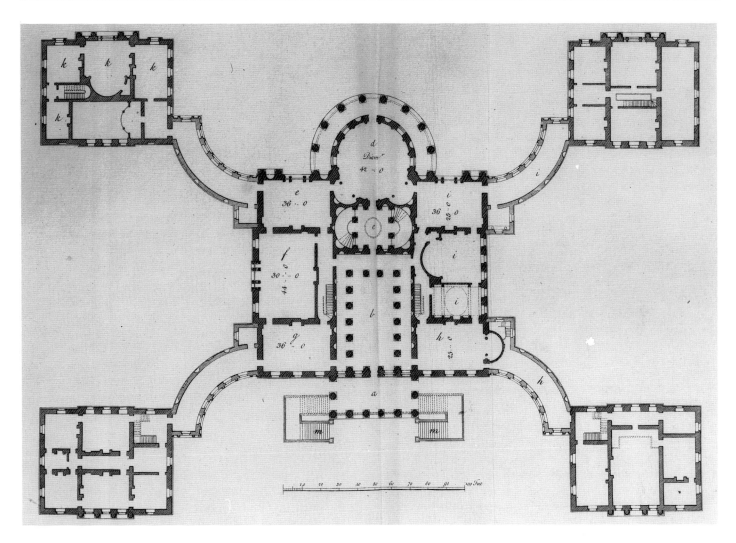

PLATE 100 *Plan of the main floor of Kedleston, Derbyshire, by James Paine.*
It is derived from Palladio's Villa Mocenigo. Note the rotunda. From
James Paine's Plans, Elevations, and Sections of Noblemen and
Gentlemen's Houses, *Plates XLIV and XLV* (SM).

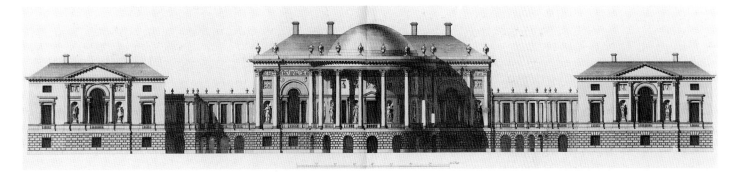

PLATE 101 *The south front of Kedleston, as designed by Paine, from his*
Noblemen and Gentlemen's Houses, *Plates L and LI* (SM).

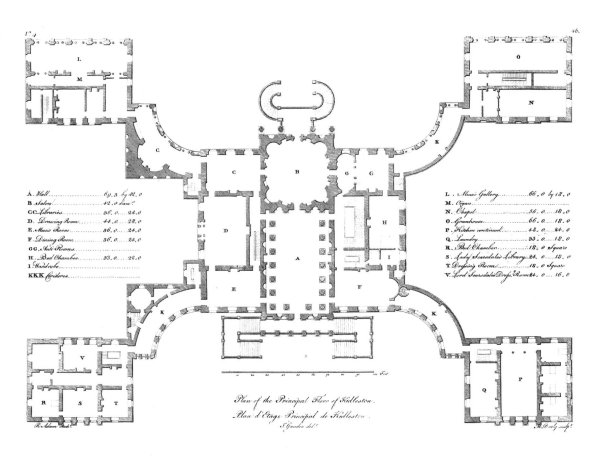

few things' remaining of Greek architecture 'seem to deserve great notice, either for dimensions, grandeur of style, rich fancy, or elegant taste of design'.[10] He had virtually nothing good to say about Greek architecture, and compared the Parthenon unfavourably with Gibbs's St Martin-in-the-Fields. Some of Chambers's and James Adam's intemperate comments have been quoted above.

James Paine was no Greek either, and considered that Greek architecture was merely 'despicable ruins'. Paine produced a design for Kedleston Hall in Derbyshire (1757–59) which had a central block linked to wings by means of quadrants (PLATES 99–100): this was derived from Palladio's Villa Mocenigo. But Paine did not start with a blank sheet, for Matthew Brettingham the Elder had already built the north-east wing. After Paine completed the north-west wing, Robert and James Adam were brought in. Kedleston is really a late-Palladian mansion, but Paine had proposed a reconstruction of a Vitruvian 'Egyptian' colonnaded Hall behind the Corinthian hexastyle portico which would lead to a symmetrically disposed staircase, beyond which was a circular Saloon or drawing-room projecting from the garden-front like a Roman circular temple (PLATES 100–101). The overall disposition of parts at Kedleston is derived from Holkham,

while the columned hall also recalls that noble room at the Norfolk house. The great portico at *piano-nobile* level derives from Wanstead.[11]

The Adam intervention (PLATES 102–104) made a reference to Roman Antiquity more powerful, for they put the circular Saloon into a square block, creating a Pantheon-like interior, and attaching an elegant Triumphal Arch, complete with Attic storey and inscription with date (1765), to the garden-front (PLATE 105). This Triumphal Arch was again at *piano-nobile* level, and was approached by a symmetrical *perron*: the exemplar was the Arch of Constantine, and there are four detached Corinthian columns close to the wall, each carrying a projecting part of the entablature. Paine had proposed Serlianas on either side of his Rotunda, flanked by end-features with niches themselves flanked by engaged columns, but Adam treated the front on either side of the Triumphal Arch quite plainly, with pedimented windows at *piano-nobile* level and plain rectangular windows above. The Hall at Kedleston, with its fluted Corinthian columns of alabaster and its coved ceiling with stucco decoration, is one of the grandest rooms of the Georgian period. The plain niches contain casts of Antique statuary by Matthew Brettingham Junior, and above are *grisaille* panels of Classical

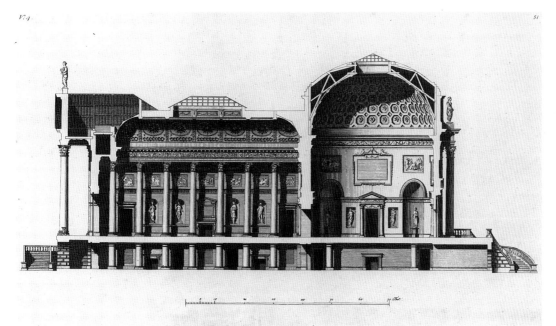

PLATE 103 *The north front of Kedleston, Derbyshire, by Paine, as amended by Adam, from VB, Vol IV, Plates 47–48* (BAL/RIBA).

PLATE 104 *Section through the centre of Kedleston, Derbyshire, showing Adam's great interiors with the triumphal arch and* perron *on the right. From VB, Vol IV, Plate 51* (SM).

PLATE 105 *The south front of Kedleston, Derbyshire, as designed by Adam. In the centre is the triumphal arch and* perron. *Note the attic storey over the triumphal arch. From VB, Vol IV, Plates 49–50* (BAL/RIBA).

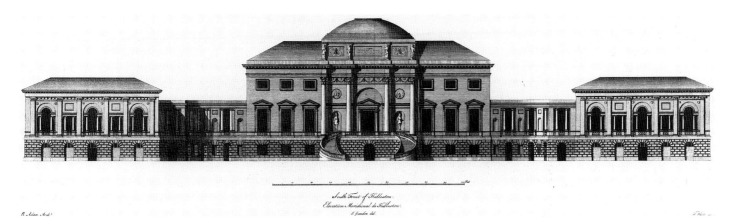

PLATE 106 *The south elevation of the Register Office in Edinburgh, by Robert Adam. Note the rusticated ground floor and Serlianas in the corner pavilions. From* Works in Architecture, *Vol I, No IV Plate 6* (SM).

subjects derived from Homer. The relationship of the Hall and the Rotunda is a reference to the atrium and vestibulum which Robert Adam described in his *Ruins of the Palace of the Emperor Diocletian at Spalatro* of 1764. The other beautiful interiors of the house were designed by Adam and his team, among whom may be mentioned Joseph Rose, George Richardson, Joseph Bonomi, and Antonio Zucchi.

Robert Adam had started the Grand Tour in 1754, and derived much from Piranesi and from Charles-Louis Clérisseau (1721–1820), but he never visited Greece, and the opinion of the Paestum temples by James Adam has been quoted above. In spite of his knowing Clérisseau, Adam does not appear to have been interested in French Classicism either. Instead, his architectural treatments are gay, light, and display a range of motifs culled from various sources. He particularly favoured 'Grotesque' decorations, such as those in the Vatican *Loggie*, and he adapted the newly discovered 'Etruscan' and Pompeian schemes of décor derived from excavations at Herculaneum and Pompeii and from the so-called 'Etruscan' vases (which were actually Greek). Adam used columned screens, hemi-domes, apses, and rooms based on the circle or on polygonal forms in order to suggest interest and create complexity, but his sources for these are *Thermae* and palatial buildings of Ancient Rome. At Syon House (1762–69) Adam actually used Greek Ionic detached columns

based on those of the Erechtheion in Athens (which suggests that his antipathy towards Greek architecture was more based on dislike of Stuart than on a dismissal of everything Greek).

Adam was eclectic, and his repertoire of ornament ranged from Antiquity to the *Cinquecento*. His greatest successes were in the field of interior design, and his planning was imaginative using a variety of shapes for his rooms instead of the plain early-Georgian rectangles. Walls, ceilings, floors, chimney-pieces, furniture, and details were designed as part of elegant and highly organised schemes, and incorporated Renaissance and Neo-Classical motifs such as sphinxes, batswing ornament, urns, altars, and gryphons. Plasterwork was exquisite, and patterns were highly refined, with painted panels of the highest quality by artists of the calibre of Rebecca, Zucchi, and Cipriani. Colour-schemes were the height of refinement, with delicate blues, greens, pinks, and other hues.

Certainly the south front of Kedleston is monumental, with references to Roman Antiquity, but Adam's Register House (1774–92) (PLATES 106–108) and University (1789–93) in Edinburgh are monumental in a different way, showing Adam as an imaginative composer of late-Palladian buildings, yet he was capable of designing Romantic piles, notably in his 'Adam-Castle' style, influenced not a little by Vanbrugh. His long ranges of terrace-houses, designed to look like uniform palaces (and so derived from the work of the Woods in Bath) were most successful at Charlotte Square, Edinburgh (designed 1791) (PLATE 109), and the south and east sides of Fitzroy Square, London (1790–94). His mausoleum of David Hume in Calton Old Cemetery, Edinburgh, of 1778 is based

Plan of the first Story of the Office for the public Records of Scotland

Plan du premier Etage du Bureau pour les Registres publics d'Ecosse.

PLATE 107 *The spectacular plan of the Register Office in Edinburgh, from* Adam's Works in Architecture, *Vol I, No IV, Plate 5. Note the circular central part, and the corner elements* (SM).

PLATE 108 *Section through Adam's Register Office in Edinburgh, from his* Works in Architecture, *Vol I, No IV, Plate 7* (SM).

PLATE 109 *The north side of Charlotte Square, Edinburgh, by Adam, of 1791* (RCAHMS B38827/21).

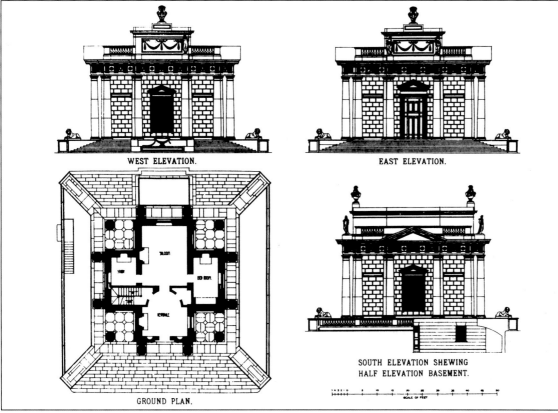

WEST ELEVATION.

EAST ELEVATION.

GROUND PLAN.

SOUTH ELEVATION SHEWING
HALF ELEVATION BASEMENT.

SCALE OF FEET

PLATE 110 *The Upton Mausoleum, Castle Upton, Co Antrim, by Robert Adam* (JSC).

PLATE 111 *Sir William Chambers's Casino at Marino, near Dublin, from Richardson* (BTB/SH).

PLATE 112 *Somerset House, London, by Sir William Chambers. Plan from Richardson (BTB/SH).*

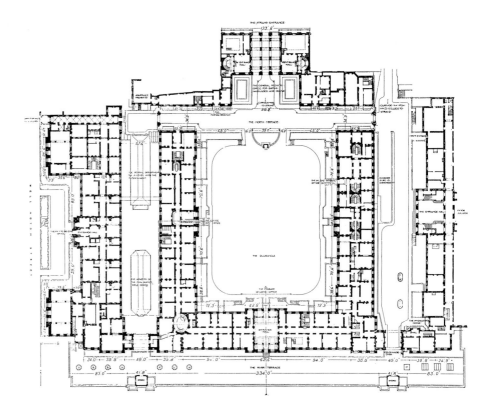

PLATE 113 *Elevations and sections of Chambers's Somerset House, London, from Richardson (BTB/SH)*

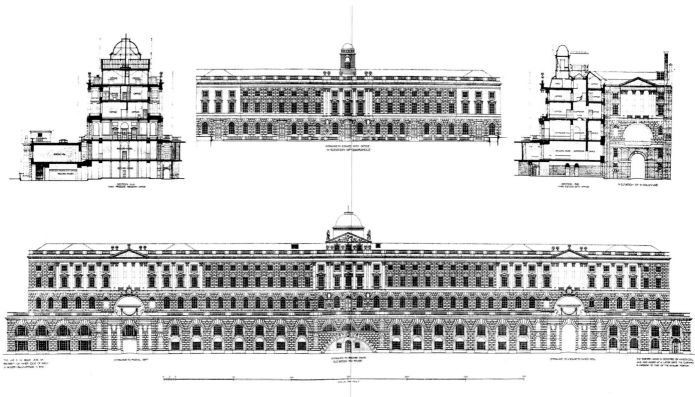

on Roman prototypes, notably the tomb of Caecilia Metella, and his elegant Upton mausoleum at Castle Upton, Co Antrim, dates from 1789 (PLATE 110).

Sir William Chambers studied in Paris with Blondel, and he knew Peyre, de Wailly, and Jacques-Germain Soufflot, who was to design the church of St Geneviève in Paris (1757) on a Greek-Cross plan, with Antique Corinthian prostyle portico, and a great dome over the crossing. Laugier hailed this building as the first model of a perfect architecture, for the geometry was clear, and the columns were expressed as such, carrying straight entablatures, and gave a completely different effect from that of earlier Baroque interiors with their engaged columns, pilasters, and mighty piers. Chambers also went to Rome, and met Clérisseau and Piranesi, so the Roman and French influences were strong.

When he returned to England, Chambers realised the charming Casino at Marino near Dublin for Lord Charlemont: it is an elegant essay using an Order of unfluted Roman Doric and is primarily French in its Neo-Classicism. It combines a Greek Cross on plan with scholarly attention to Classical detail (PLATE 111). His Somerset House, London, of 1776–86, probably the grandest official building ever erected in the capital, combines Palladian and French Classicism, and uses a Giant Composite Order (PLATES 112–113). The vestibule, with its severe unfluted Roman Doric paired columns, bucrania, and vaulted roof, has a grandeur that is both Roman and French.

Chambers published his *Treatise...*in 1759 which argues for the use of the Roman Orders in ways tried in Antiquity and during the Italian Renaissance: the book became a standard and influential work on Classical architecture. His pupil, James Gandon (1743–1823), also combined Palladian compositional methods with scholarly Roman Classical detail, as in the Custom House in Dublin (1781–91) (where elements of Wren's Chelsea and Greenwich Hospitals are also quoted, with parts of Chambers's Somerset House [PLATE 114]), and the Four Courts in Dublin (with Thomas Cooley [1786–1802]), which unites a severe Neo-Classical drum and dome, antique hexastyle pedimented portico, and three relatively plain blocks (PLATE 115). Gandon published, with J. Woolfe, two further supplements to *Vitruvius Britannicus* in 1769 and 1771. His work is probably more eclectically Classical than purely Palladian, although his compositional method owes much to English Palladianism.

Adam's success, carefully publicised from 1773 when the first volume of the *Works in Architecture of Robert and James Adam* came out, was undeniable. The judicious mixture of

PLATE 114 *The Custom House, Dublin, by James Gandon, from Richardson* (BTB/SH).

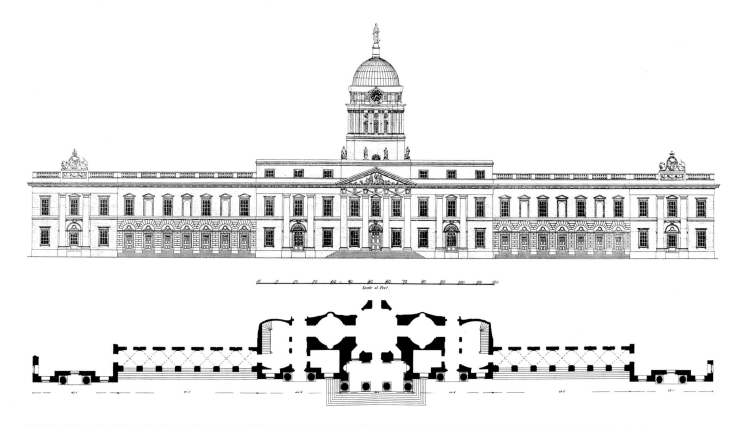

PLATE 115 *The Four Courts, Dublin, by James Gandon and Thomas Cooley* (JSC).

PLATE 116 *Heaton Hall, Lancashire, by James Wyatt, begun in 1772. Note the influence of Paine's design for the south front of Kedleston, but note the end pavilions are treated as canted bays with Serlianas. Note also that at Heaton the Orders rise from a plinth rather than a basement storey* (AFK G20181).

PLATE 117 *Plan of Castle Coole, Co Fermanagh, by James Wyatt, of 1790–98. Note the elliptical Saloon and columns defining the Hall and passage. S Saloon; H Hall* (JSC).

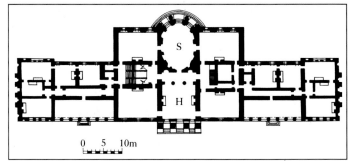

Roman Antique grandeur and delicate, even feminine décor (itself an amalgam of motifs from Antiquity to the Renaissance), struck chords. However, there was rather a lot of it, and there was the inevitable reaction. Chambers called the Adam style full of boyish conceits, and the syncretic method of décor 'trifling complicated ornaments'. Horace Walpole, having seen some of the younger architects at work, began to develop a taste for simplicity, and professed himself sick of Adam's 'ginger-bread and snippets of embroidery'.

James Wyatt was one of the most successful architects after Adam, and was remarkably undoctrinaire in matters of style. His Heaton Hall, near Manchester (*c* 1772) (PLATE 116), with its beautiful interiors influenced by Pompeii and Herculaneum, and the very fine Castle Coole, Co Fermanagh (1790–98), incorporating Gandon's *in antis* arrangement of columns in the corner pavilions, long ranges of colonnades, and a Roman Ionic temple-front to emphasise that the main rooms are on the ground floor, are two of his best houses. Castle Coole also incorporates the very Irish feature of an elliptical saloon expressed externally as a bow, embellished with engaged Roman Ionic columns (PLATE 117).

From the 1770s, indeed, architects like Henry Holland and Robert Mylne reacted against the complicated polychromatic-syncretic decoration invented by Adam, and looked to

PLATE 119 *Belle Isle, Windermere* (JSC).

France and French Neo-Classicism. Holland rebuilt Carlton House for the Prince of Wales (1783–96), with its superb Corinthian portico (now attached to the National Gallery) and a series of stunning interiors which Walpole found perfect. One of Holland's most exquisite houses is Berrington Hall, Herefordshire, of 1778–81, especially the charming top-lit staircase. Mylne redecorated Inveraray Castle in 1782–89 in a restrained Classical style.

Pantheons and Rotundas

We have seen the Antique Rotunda based on the Pantheon recur at Kedleston, the Dublin Four Courts, and the Burton building at Regent's Park. It was also used by John Plaw (*c* 1745–1820) for an ingeniously planned house at Belle Isle, Windermere, Westmorland, of 1774–75, published in his *Rural Architecture: or Designs from the Simple Cottage to the Decorative Villa* of 1785 (PLATES 118–119). This was probably one of the models for the great palace at

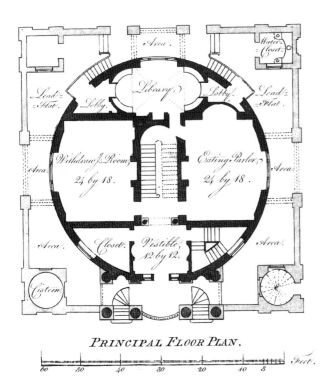

PLATE 118 *Plan of Belle Isle, Windermere, by John Plaw, from his* Rural Architecture, *Plate XXVI* (SM).

PLATE 120 *Ickworth, Suffolk, by Mario Asprucci and Francis Sandys* (JSC).

Ballyscullion on the shores of Lough Beg, in Ulster, consisting of an elliptical central block of two storeys and an attic, with a Pantheon dome, to which was attached a tetrastyle Corinthian portico (now the front of the Parish church of St George, Belfast). Two large plain single-storey quadrants joined the central building to pavilions and the various offices. This remarkable palace of Frederick Hervey, Fourth Earl of Bristol and Anglican Bishop of Derry (1730–1803), was probably designed by Francis Sandys of Kilrea, Co Londonderry (who had been on the Grand Tour to Rome in 1791), and Michael Shanahan. The Bishop's other great elliptical house, Ickworth in Suffolk (begun 1796), was designed by Mario Asprucci, and executed with modifications by Sandys (PLATE 120). The Ickworth central 'Pantheon' is, like Belle Isle and Ballyscullion, subdivided, but the exterior has two superimposed Orders (the lower Ionic, the upper

Corinthian), with a bas-relief frieze all around the crowning entablature, and panels of bas-reliefs between the engaged Ionic columns, executed by the Carabelli Brothers after Flaxman's illustrations of Homer.[12]

At Downhill, Co Londonderry, the Earl-Bishop also erected a huge palace sublimely sited above the sea, with the views of Inishowen in Co Donegal. James Wyatt may have been involved in the early designs, but the superintending architect was Michael Shanahan. Certainly the coupled elongated pilasters of Downhill recall those of Wyatt's Heaton Hall (PLATE 116) and the Radcliffe Observatory, Oxford (PLATE 121). Mr Peter Rankin also suggests Charles Cameron (*c* 1743–1812) as a possible author. The castle-like crenellated entrance recalls the Vanbrugh-Adam Castle Style. Perched on the cliffs above the sea is the Mussenden Temple, a delightful circular belvedere with an engaged Order of Corinthian columns carrying an entablature over which rises a dome capped by an urn (PLATE 122). It is loosely based on the Temples of Vesta at Tivoli and Rome, and Shanahan was the

PLATE 121 *The Radcliffe Observatory, Oxford, by Wyatt. Note the paired Greek Ionic pilasters and, in the upper storey, the reference to the Tower of the Winds, Athens, with Wyatt Windows (tripartite openings with straight central opening instead of semicircular Serliana)* (RCR).

PLATE 122 *Mussenden Temple, Downhill, Co Londonderry, by Michael Shanahan* (JSC).

architect: he also designed the Mausoleum (based on the tomb of the Julii at St Rémy, Provence), which looks somewhat Wyattesque.

Of other Pantheons, Thomas Harrison's (1744–1829) visionary schemes for a National Valhalla (*c* 1815) would have been supremely grand, with their Pantheon-domes and Greek Doric porticoes and colonnades. However, Harrison did succeed in creating a Pantheon-like interior at Shire Hall, Chester Castle (1791–1801), where he also built a severe Doric propylaeum (1810–14) with attic, a sort of trabeated version in Doric of a Triumphal Arch. John Kent (flourished 1800–30) and Charles Heathcote Tatham (1772–1842) built the circular Hall at Paultons, near Romsey, Hampshire, with its severe unfluted Greek Doric columns supporting an Ionic superimposed Order, in 1805 and *c* 1828. Robert Adam's sculpture gallery at Newby Hall, Yorkshire, of *c* 1767 is circular, and suitably Antique in flavour to set off the splendid collection of sculptures. Nash and Payne Knight designed a Pantheon-like dining-room for Downton Castle in 1782, complete with coffered ceiling, and the ceiling at Caledon House, Co Tyrone, by Nash, of 1812, suggests a floating Pantheon-dome. Perhaps one of the finest Pantheon interiors was the Pantheon Room attached to Ince Blundell Hall, Lancashire, of 1802, by John Hope (1734–1808); it was intended as a sculpture-gallery for Antique objects. Thomas Harrison's Lycæum Club of 1800–02 in Liverpool also had a fine domed room inside.

There were circular mausolea, of course. Hawksmoor's mighty Castle Howard mausoleum (1728–42) has an unfluted Order of Roman Doric as a peristyle around the drum with

PLATE 123 *The Mausoleum at Castle Howard, Yorkshire, designed by Nicholas Hawksmoor, 1728–29, and built 1731–42. The fortress-like base was designed by Daniel Garrett. The tall Tuscan columns have only one triglyph over each intercolumniation, so the effect is severe, grave, and powerful* (AFK H8911).

clerestory, but the intercolumniation is only one triglyph, which gives the building an air of overpowering strength and sombre grandeur. Normally, Roman Doric would have two or more triglyphs to each intercolumniation. The fortress-like podium on which the mausoleum stands was designed by Daniel Garrett, and recalls Vanbrugh, while anticipating the 'Castle Style' (PLATE 123).

James Wyatt's Pelham Mausoleum at Brocklesby Park, Lincolnshire (1787–94), has a peristyle of Roman Doric columns around a drum in the walls of which sarcophagi are set in niches. The handsome interior contains Neo-Classical monuments arranged round the walls, and there is a figure by Nollekens in the centre, under the Pantheon-like coffered dome. Other circular temple-like mausolea include the Forbes Tomb, Callendar House, Stirlingshire (1816), by Archibald Elliott, and the Huskisson tomb, St James's Cemetery, Liverpool (1836), by John Foster.

Dance and After

One of the most remarkable buildings ever erected in Britain was Newgate Gaol by George Dance the Younger (PLATE 124), of 1770–80. It recalled Piranesi's visions of prisons, and, with its mighty, crushing rustication, and terrifying blank walls, suggested retribution, justice, and impregnability. Nobody would get out of there in a hurry. This *architecture parlante* derives from Franco-Italian Classicism, and has echoes of Vanbrugh, (especially in the Governor's House in the centre), Hawksmoor, and even some of the French Neo-Classicists illustrated by Peyre in his *Oeuvres d'Architecture* (1765). Dance experimented with concealed top-lighting, perhaps inspired by Piranesi's drawings (as at Lansdowne House, London, and Cranbury Park, Hampshire).

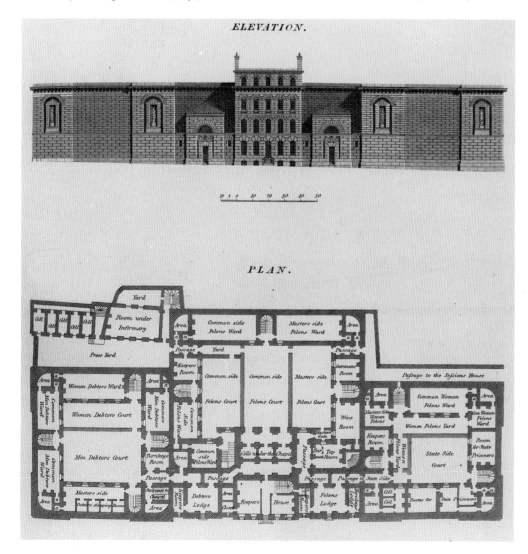

PLATE 124 *Newgate Gaol, London, by George Dance the Younger, from Peter Nicholson's* Architectural and Engineering Dictionary *(JSC).*

PLATE 125 *Interior of Soane's Consols Office of the Bank of England, showing his elemental architecture largely derived from Greek and Roman Antiquity, but stripped to the bare essence. From Richardson* (BTB/SH).

PLATE 126 *The Council Chamber at Freemasons' Hall, London, by Soane, of 1820* (SM).

PLATE 127 *The Lothbury Corner at the Bank of England, London, as designed by Sir John Soane, showing his extraordinary juxtaposition of Classical elements. The Order is that of the Temple of Vesta at Tivoli. From Richardson* (BTB/SH).

Dance was an architect who could create powerful effects by means of top-lit domes. His pupil, (Sir) John Soane was also concerned with the poetic aspects of architecture and with the *lumière mystérieuse* exploited by numerous French architects, notably Nicolas Le Camus de Mézières (1721-89), whose *Le génie de L'Architecture; ou, l'analogie de cet art avec nos sensations* came out in 1780 and contained the notion that architecture should please the senses and induce elevating impressions on the mind.

Soane, like Dance, was concerned to evolve an architecture based on Classicism, but freed from the stranglehold of Vitruvian and Palladian Taste. Soane's architectural language is stripped and bare, and his shallow saucer-domes seem to float over space, with light flooding down around them (PLATE 125). He also used segmental arches, sharp incised machine-like ornament, paterae, acroteria, and a large number of motifs culled from the architecture of death (including

PLATE 129 *Trentham Mausoleum, Staffordshire, by C.H.Tatham, 1807–08* (JSC).

cinerary chests, urns, and sarcophagi). His austere, even bleak, lodges at Tyringham, Buckinghamshire, of 1793, the primitive rustic Doric of the Dairy at Hamels, Hertfordshire (1781), and his remarkable Mausoleum and Gallery at Dulwich (1811–14) show how far he had moved from conventional Palladianism. His masterpieces were his own house at 12-13 Lincoln's Inn Fields (1792–1824), his Bank of England (1788–1833), and the beautiful Council Chamber of 1828 at Freemasons' Hall, Great Queen Street, London (PLATE 126), the last two destroyed, except for the altered screen-wall around the Bank (PLATE 127). It was at the Bank that Soane exploited his top-lit interiors to the full: in these destroyed interiors his reductionist architecture came into its own. However, the interiors at his private museum, office, and house at Lincoln's Inn Fields display his love of the interpenetrating space, lighting effects enhanced by coloured glass and mirrors, and floating shallow domed ceilings. Soane's idiosyncratic tomb for his wife and himself, in the overspill churchyard of St Giles-in-the-Fields at St Pancras, was designed from 1816, and incorporates segmental pediments, simplified square columns, a canopied aedicule within a canopy, and some very free detail (PLATE 128).

An even more powerful mausoleum, deliberately oversized, and with massive, stripped Graeco-Egyptian pylon-like piers, is the Trentham tomb of 1807–8 by C. H. Tatham. This design is clearly influenced by Franco-Italian ideas of the 1790s, when he was a student in Rome (PLATE 129).

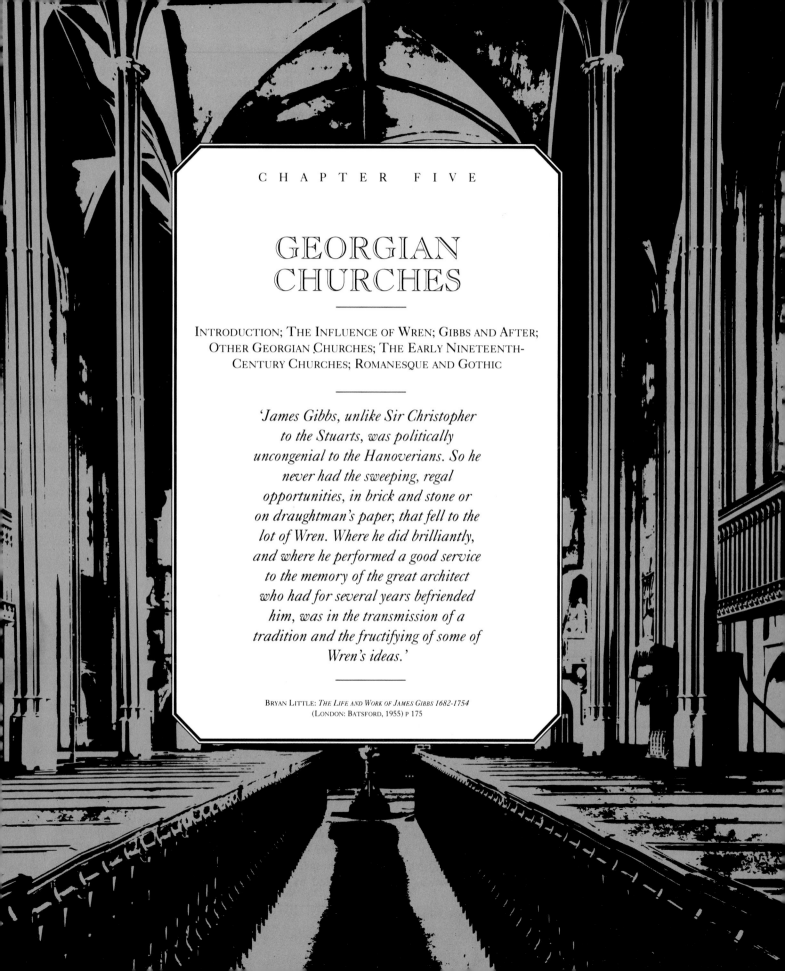

CHAPTER FIVE

GEORGIAN CHURCHES

INTRODUCTION; THE INFLUENCE OF WREN; GIBBS AND AFTER;
OTHER GEORGIAN CHURCHES; THE EARLY NINETEENTH-
CENTURY CHURCHES; ROMANESQUE AND GOTHIC

---

*'James Gibbs, unlike Sir Christopher
to the Stuarts, was politically
uncongenial to the Hanoverians. So he
never had the sweeping, regal
opportunities, in brick and stone or
on draughtman's paper, that fell to the
lot of Wren. Where he did brilliantly,
and where he performed a good service
to the memory of the great architect
who had for several years befriended
him, was in the transmission of a
tradition and the fructifying of some of
Wren's ideas.'*

BRYAN LITTLE: *THE LIFE AND WORK OF JAMES GIBBS 1682-1754*
(LONDON: BATSFORD, 1955) P 175

Introduction

After the Georgian period England experienced the rise of Ecclesiology, the Gothic and religious Revivals, and a spate of church-building on an enormous scale. Thanks to Tractarians, Ecclesiology, and Pugin, among other factors, attitudes to the church-building achievements of Georgian times were hostile. According to nineteenth-century opinion from the 1830s onwards, Georgian churches were pagan and un-Christian, and ought to be pulled down and rebuilt in a 'Gothic' Christian style. All Georgian additions to Medieval churches should be ripped out, for white Classical belfries and cupolas, Classical porticoes, box-pews, Baroque organ-cases, three-decker pulpits, Classically-based altar-rails, Royal Arms, painted and lettered reredoses (usually with the Ten Commandments), benefaction-boards, hatchments, and – perhaps most loathed of all – galleries, were hated by the Ecclesiologists.[1]

A.W.N. Pugin (1812–52) held that Vitruvius would 'spew' if he saw the works by those who had regarded the Augustan Roman as their master, while the intemperate John Ruskin (1819–1900) described the Renaissance as a 'foul torrent' and as 'base, unnatural, unenjoyable and impious'. Especial loathing was reserved for Georgian Gothick, which was, horrors of horrors, 'frivolous'. Pugin, of course, regarded Protestantism as a disaster because of its 'destructive principle' and the effects it had on 'Catholic art and architecture in England'[2] Pugin hated Dance's Guildhall in London, Nash's All Souls, Langham Place, the architecture of the Inwoods, all Neo-Classical sculpture (he illustrated a sculpture by Chantrey to make the point), and virtually everything by Smirke, Soane, Nash, Wilkins, or any of the great Neo-Classicists. As to the diversity of styles, he attacked 'Moorish Fish Markets, Egyptian Marine Villas, Castellated Turnpike Gates, Gin Temples in the Baronial style, Dissenting Chapels in Plain Styles, Monuments erected in Westminster Abbey with no regard to the locality', and all architecture not designed on the principles of Christian Gothic 'truth'. He was appalled by the 'restoration' of the great churches, and when Wyatt's refaced Palace of Westminster went up in flames in 1834, Pugin rejoiced in the 'glorious sight' as Wyatt's 'cement pinnacles and battlements' went 'flying and crackling'.[3] He was overjoyed when James Wyatt's gigantic Fonthill Abbey in Wiltshire (1796-1812) collapsed in 1825, for was not Wyatt the 'villain', 'the Destroyer', the 'monster of architectural depravity', and a 'pest of cathedral architecture'?[4] Strawberry Hill, like Fonthill, was disgusting to Pugin, and virtually all the Regency architecture was depraved, for it was merely a 'carnival', and its professors peddled Turkish, Christian, Egyptian, Greek, Swiss, and Hindoo styles indiscriminately, and even

put 'two or three costumes' on at the same time, creating a 'miserable degradation'[5]

Ruskin was also extremely rude about Classical architecture. T.L. Donaldson, in 1854, pointed to a fatal flaw in the Ruskinian approach, and noted that Ruskin, who praised the Doge's Palace in Venice and the Basilica of St Mark, was silent on the grandeur and nobility of Palladio's 'Basilica' at Vicenza, and ignored Brunelleschi, Bramante, Vignola, Inigo Jones, and Wren. 'The principles of sound construction and pure taste are set at defiance, and the mind of the student is directed more to the study of the ornamental...'[6]

Apart from the 'moral depravity' of the Georgians, with their wit, their scepticism, their rationality, their love of Augustan prose, landscapes, and architecture, their drinking habits, and their attitudes to sex, what worried the later nineteenth-century commentators was that the Georgians admired Gothic 'without the knowledge necessary for a proper adaptation of its features.'[7] Bits of real Medieval architecture were copied without any regard for the original purpose of the design. An altar-slab could be a hall-table, a piscina could be copied for a cupboard, and a tomb-chest could be the model for a chimney-piece. 'If in the history of British art there is one period more distinguished than another for its neglect of Gothic', wrote Eastlake,[8] 'it was certainly the middle of the eighteenth century.

The Influence of Wren

In spite of these strictures, Georgian churches can delight us today, and indeed offer considerable variety. The first point to remember about Georgian churches is that they were built, not for 'Catholic' ritual, with its processions, the Sacrifice of the Mass, veneration of the Virgin Mary, and all the other matters which absorbed the minds of those involved in the religious controversies of the 1830s, 1840s, and 1850s, but for static, Protestant, congregations. Every parishioner in England was, and is, entitled to a seat in a Parish church, and church-wardens would allot seats in the pews. During the Georgian period, too, the gentry could obtain faculties for building an 'aisle' which would be both a pew for the family, and also a burying-place. There are many examples of churches in which the charming Georgian box-pews still survive.

The Georgian church was essentially a large preaching-box, designed to hold the congregation, and was often fitted with galleries with benches, and sometimes with box-pews in the galleries as well. The model for early-Georgian churches was provided by the architecture of Sir Christopher Wren, who had built so many churches in London after the Fire of 1666. Wren's influence retained its hold even after the Palladians had begun to make Baroque unfashionable, probably because his churches were full of inventiveness and variety, evolving different types of plan, from the nave with aisles to the large unbroken space, either rectangular, or with a central circular space, as at St Stephen Walbrook. The ceilings and vaults could often vary considerably, while the tops of the towers were given different treatments. There were even forays into Gothic, as at St Mary Aldermary. Wren's churches had a large congregational space, with a Communion-Table at one end (usually at the east); a reredos; a wooden pulpit approached by steps, with a tester above, often elaborately carved and inlaid with different woods, and set in a commanding position; an organ-loft, usually with a fine Baroque organ-case; tall (usually semicircular-headed) windows filled with clear glass; and with a tower and inventive steeple. The whole was usually constructed with Portland stone. Chancels were unnecessary for Anglican worship then, so the Communion-Tables were placed against the east wall, or set in a slight recess or niche, far too small to be called a chancel, although the Communion-Rails were provided around the area in front of the Communion-Table and reredos. The latter were often given elaborate architectural treatment, with columns and panels on which were written the Ten Commandments, the Creed or the Lord's Prayer, or a combination of these. In Wren churches the richest decoration was usually 'concentrated on the reredos and pulpit'. 'The reredos presented an opportunity for an imposing Classical composition enlivened by elegant, but not unduly boisterous, carving'.[9]

The first significant barn-like space built for Protestant public worship in a Classical style in England was, of course, St Paul's, Covent Garden, of 1631-32, with its great Tuscan portico. Such grandeur was possible in the formal Piazza Jones created, but Wren's churches, tucked for the most part into narrow streets, or on to corners, were not treated with porticoes. Only occasionally, as at the east façade of his St Lawrence, Jewry, of 1671–77, did Wren create a grandly Roman elevation.

Wren, we must realise, however, was the 'creator of the modern Anglo-Saxon Protestant church'.[10] Wren designed places of worship that were 'primarily meeting-houses; his aim was to ensure hearing and seeing. Except in the smaller churches, the room was encircled on three sides by a gallery, with the choir and organ placed at the west end over the vestibule, according to the Continental custom. The choir stalls disappeared. The chancel was reduced as a result: sometimes it became a mere niche; often it was dispensed with. The altar, more commonly known during the eighteenth and early nineteenth centuries as the Communion-Table, retained its central position. In some cases the pulpit (height-ened to command the galleries) on one side of the altar was balanced by a conspicuous desk for the conduct of the service. But the tendency, followed widely during the eighteenth century, was to combine pulpit, reading desk, and clerk's desk, in a ponderous "three-decker". The font became a vase on a pedestal.

'Wren did not rest content with a bare meeting-house, however. He had the requirements of a meeting-house in mind, but satisfied those requirements by architectural treatment. In a typical church like St James's, Piccadilly, we find an oblong nave, separated from aisles of two storeys by square piers, from which rise single Corinthian columns; these support a barrel-vault of enriched plasterwork spanning the broad nave, and semicircular vaults over the aisles (separate for each bay), at right angles to the nave vault and supporting it. The gallery is not an intrusion but an integral part of the building. The pulpit, pew-ends, organ-case, and altarpiece were of fine oak elaborately carved.'[11]

The churches did not have much in the way of Christian symbolism, which did not worry the Georgians, but drove the Victorians to apoplexy. It must be remembered that even a Cross would have savoured of Romanism and Popery to a Georgian. Cherubs' heads were found a-plenty, however, but not the Madonna and Child into whose receptive ears the cherubs had once carolled so merrily. Instead of the Cross, with its promise of Eternal Life, mortality was evoked by the hour-glass. But pagan symbolism was, to a certain extent, deliberate, for it was a reaction against the religious 'Enthusiasm' of Restoration times, which had gained force during the eighteenth century. Classical architecture and symbolism were regarded as humanistic, and were the antitheses of the dark and superstitious art and architecture of the Middle Ages.

Later eighteenth-century architects tended to follow the Wren recipe. Before George I came to the throne, the Tories had passed an enactment for building fifty new churches in London; to be paid for by a tax levied on coal coming into the city. Not only were these to serve the suburbs, but they were to express the dignity and power of the Established Church. The Commissioners in charge of the building of these churches included the elderly Wren, as well as Vanbrugh and Archer, as previously noted. Ideally these churches were to be commodious, placed on island sites, and were to be monumental, with handsome porticoes on the most prominent elevations.

As it happens, twelve churches only were built, plus four subsidised by the Commission, and all were designed by architects who were masters of the Baroque, and who were strongly influenced by Wren. Hawksmoor's great churches of St Alphege (1712–14), St Anne, Limehouse (1714–30), St George-in-the-East (1714–29) (PLATE 130), Christ Church,

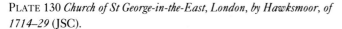

PLATE 130 *Church of St George-in-the-East, London, by Hawksmoor, of 1714–29* (JSC).

PLATE 131 *Christ Church, Spitalfields, London, by Hawksmoor* (JSC).

Spitalfields (1714–19), St Mary, Woolnoth (1716–24), and St George, Bloomsbury (1716–31) (PLATE 7), all combine a tremendous power of expression with reference to Antiquity, to Palladian motifs, to Baroque rhetoric, and to Medieval precedent. All, with the exception of St Alphege, were built during the Georgian period, and even St Alphege was being fitted up during the reign of George I, but all were the products of a Tory Act of Parliament, and all were alien to the incoming Whig Government. St Alphege has massive articulation and a huge Serliana at the east end; St Anne, Limehouse, has a delicate, almost Medieval, lantern; the Bloomsbury church has a spire derived from Pliny's account of the cele-

brated Mausoleum at Halicarnassus, and a massive prostyle hexastyle Antique Corinthian portico; while Christ Church, Spitalfields, has a broach spire, and a huge portico, again in the form of a Serliana (PLATE 131). St John, Horsleydown, Southwark, and St Luke, Old Street (both with John James) date from 1727–33. These splendid and original buildings, with Wren's City churches, provided the exemplars for late-Georgian churches. Instead of a spire, St Luke's sported a huge obelisk.

Thomas Archer's church of St Philip, Birmingham, of 1710–15, with Baroque tower of 1725, is an important provincial example, while his St Paul, Deptford (1713–30), and

Extends 55 .
a Scale of 30 Feet

PLATE 132 *Pavilion at Wrest Park, Bedfordshire, by Thomas Archer, from* VB, *Vol I, Plate 33* (SM).

PLATE 133 *Interior of St Paul's church, Deptford, London, by Archer, of 1713–30* (AFK H8137).

St John, Smith Square, London (1713–28), are excellent examples of a mature Baroque style, influenced by Italian models, and especially by Borromini: his pavilion at Wrest Park, Bedfordshire, of 1709-10, has an assurance and vigour about it that suggest an acquaintance with fine Continental work (Plate 132). Indeed, Archer brought a first-hand experience of Roman Baroque to England, which gives him a unique place in the annals of early-Georgian architecture. St Paul's is particularly interesting because it has an ingenious plan, and Archer resolved the tower-portico problem in an un-Gibbsian way. He made his tower circular and draped the semicircular portico around the tower (this portico probably derives from Wren's south transept at St Paul's Cathedral), and increased the effect by fanning out the steps from the Tuscan portico. Elaborate external *perrons* to the north and south also lead up to the podium on which the church stands. The almost square church is entered through a circular lobby in the tower, and there is a Giant Corinthian Order disposed in such a way that an illusion is created of an elliptical space, giving a very Roman Baroque impression. The altar is sited in an apse with a large attenuated Serliana illuminating the space (PLATE 133).

Gibbs and After

Edward Wing's church at Aynho, Northamptonshire, of 1723, is remarkable in that it represents an attempt to emulate the new London churches, while the church of St John the Baptist at Honiley, Warwickshire, of 1723, has quotations from both Archer and Hawksmoor. But, even more than Hawksmoor or Archer, Gibbs, of all the great Baroque architects, was the most important as an influence on church design for the rest of the century. The significance of his publications has been emphasised above, while his 'Gibbs Surround', a doorcase or window-architrave with plain blocks interrupting the verticality, can be found all over the British Isles, and is just one of the elements copied from his publications. His St Mary-le-Strand is a Georgian building, but it is also the most grandly Roman and Baroque of all such early-Georgian churches, with its two tiers of Orders and its semi-circular portico: the church of Sta Maria della Pace in Rome has certain affinities with the design of St Mary-le-Strand (PLATES 5–6). The semicircular porch at the west end is echoed by the semicircular apse at the east. Gibbs clearly drew on Wren's niches at St Paul's Cathedral, on Fontana's plans for the Lateran façade, and on Pietro da Cortona's Sta Maria della Pace. It was no wonder that the Whigs suspected Gibbs of Papist unsoundness. St Mary's is one of his loveliest works, and the steeple pays tribute to Wren. Indeed, in 1719 Gibbs was requested to add a spire to Wren's tower at St Clement Danes, further east down The Strand.

St Mary's was designed for the Commissioners, but Gibbs was removed from his post when the new régime of Hanoverians and Whigs came in. In spite of this, and Gibbs's difficulties as a possible Jacobite sympathiser, so successful was his design for St Mary's that his reputation as an architect was made. In 1720–26 he designed and built the church of St Martin-in-the-Fields in London which was one of great importance as a precedent for Georgian Anglican churches erected during the following century (PLATE 134). There is a huge prostyle hexastyle Corinthian portico with pediment, suggesting an Antique Roman temple-front, attached to a simple rectangular body of the church, the side elevations of which are pierced by two storeys of windows (one row above and the other below the gallery) dressed with Gibbs Surrounds. Above the church behind the portico is the two-stage tower with steeple rising in four stages terminating in a variety of spire, a concoction that translated a Gothic form into a Classical idiom: the transition from the simple square tower to the spire-like pierced cap with its concave sides on an octagonal plan was contrived in well defined stages. The juxtaposition of the rectangular preaching-box, temple-front, and steeple does not really work very well (St Mary-le-Strand is far more successful) because temple-fronts with steeples rising from behind are generally unrelated forms: nevertheless, the formula was repeated in churches for at least a century, and was exported to the colonies as a result of its publication in *A Book of Architecture*.

Now St Martin's was a replacement of an earlier church, and was not a Commission job, yet it seems in all respects to obey the criteria set down by the Commission: island site, grand portico, monumentality, and so on. However, the real surprise is the wonderful interior (PLATE 135), for Gibbs used a basilican form of nave with narrower aisles (but no clerestory), and created a chancel, emphasised by curving the ends of the nave inwards, illuminated at the east end by means of a large Serliana (PLATE 136). Because of the pews, the columns inside had to be placed on pedestals: this Corinthian Order carries blocks of entablature from which the ceiling-vaults spring, and the columns also support the galleries.

St Martin's was a far more important exemplar for churches in the English-speaking world than anything the great Baroque masters produced in Britain. Its success lay in the clean, clear, logical plan, combined with the basilican arrangement (and therefore connected with Antiquity), in the character of the architecture which suggested Antiquity and modernity without the brooding heaviness of Hawksmoor's work, and in the fact that this fashionable church, sited in a fashionable part of London Town, was published, together with different possible versions of the tower and steeple, in Gibbs's *A Book of Architecture* (PLATES 137a & b). Gibbs also employed the clerestory-less nave in his remarkable church of All Hallows, Derby (now the Cathedral), of 1725. Massive unfluted Roman Doric columns (like those of St Martin's, on pedestals) carry the fragmentary entablatures from which the elegant vaulting springs, and again, at the east end, is a Serliana. Gibbs retained the Perpendicular tower, and used vigorous Gibbs Surrounds on the outside walls around the window-openings. Derby Cathedral is therefore a variation on the St Martin's theme.

Gibbs used the Italian stuccoers Artari and Bagutti to decorate the vaults of St Martin-in-the-Fields, and he used them again in his exuberantly Baroque Orleans House at Twickenham (1720), and in the stupendous Saloon or Great Hall at Ragley, Warwickshire, of 1750–55. At Ragley, a house built in 1679–83 by Robert Hooke (1635–1703) in a somewhat heavy Restoration-Baroque style, Gibbs also carried out other works to the interior, but the handsome portico was added by James Wyatt around 1780.

St Martin's, as has been mentioned above, spawned several progeny, the first of which was Flitcroft's St Giles-in-the-Fields of 1731, sited only about half a mile north of St Martin's: it has a Gibbsian west door, an interior resembling that of St Martin's, but less Baroque and more Palladian, and

PLATE 134 *Church of St Martin-in-the-Fields, by James Gibbs. Plan and perspective, from* A Book of Architecture, *Plate I* (SM).

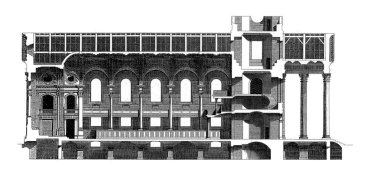

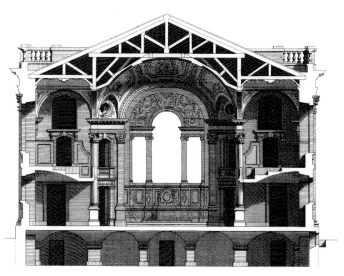

Section from South to North

PLATE 135 *Longitudinal section of St Martin-in-the-Fields, from* A Book of Architecture, *Plate 5. Note the relationship of the portico to tower and body of the church, the tall columns on pedestals, and elaborate vaulting* (SM).

a tower and steeple also based on St Martin's, but with a Palladian flavour. St Andrew-by-the-Green in Glasgow, of 1739, was the city's first new church erected since the Reformation, and was designed by Allan Dreghorn and Mungo Naismith: the hexastyle portico in this instance is not stuck on to the rectangular body of the church, but is the same width, and so appears to be more a part of the building than at St Martin's. The treatment of the side elevation is similar to that of St Martin's, and the steeple is derived from Gibbs's published designs for an alternative to the built steeple of that church.

It would be tedious to list *all* the churches derived wholly or in part from St Martin's, but there are a few which will be mentioned. North Leith church, Leith, Edinburgh, of 1814–16 by William Burn (1789–1870), and St George's church, Hardwicke Place, Dublin, of 1802–13, by Francis Johnston (1760–1829), both have steeples closely modelled on St Martin's, but the details are all Greek rather than Roman. Roger Eykyn (*c* 1725–95) designed St Paul's, Birmingham, of 1771–79, based on designs in Gibbs's *Book of Architecture*. William and David Hiorne designed Holy Cross church at Daventry, Northamptonshire, of 1752–58, the nave arrangements of which are drawn from Derby Cathedral and St Martin's, using a Doric Order, while the tower and steeple are derived from Flitcroft's St Giles-in-the-Fields and from a design published by Gibbs from which the Hiornes left out the octagonal stage. The steeple of St Lawrence's Mereworth, Kent, of 1744–46 (PLATES 138–9), is almost a direct quotation from St Martin's, while the western portico is semicircular on plan, and consists of Tuscan columns derived from Jones's St Paul's, Covent Garden, which was also the model for the wide mutuled eaves and pediment. Inside St Lawrence's, however, there is a basilican arrangement of

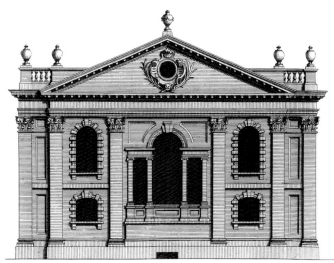

The East End

PLATE 136 *Section looking east, and east elevation, of St Martin-in-the-Fields, from* A Book of Architecture, *Plate 4. Note the Gibbs Surrounds framing the windows, and the large Serliana* (SM).

PLATE 137 *Various designs for towers and spires for St Martin-in-the-Fields, from* A Book of Architecture, *Plates 29 and 30. Architects working in the Classical idiom had to invent combinations of stages to Classicise what was essentially a Gothic form* (SM).

P. 30.

PLATE 138 *Church of St Lawrence at Mereworth, Kent. Note the resemblance to Gibbs's designs for the spire of St Martin-in-the-Fields, and the clear expression of the portico and body of the church (AFK G21029).*

PLATE 139 *Interior of the church of St Lawrence, Mereworth, Kent, showing the coffered barrel-vault, Diocletian window, and severe arrangement of the Roman unfluted Doric Order (AFK H22054).*

Tuscan columns carrying entablatures from which a barrel-vault springs to cover the nave, while the aisles are lower with ceilings divided into compartments by entablatures. At the end of the barrel-vault (which is painted to resemble coffering) is a Diocletian window. This is a very clever synthesis of Palladian/Gibbsian/Jonesian/Antique themes, and the design is attributed to Roger Morris, who carried out works at Mereworth Castle.

Given the basic basilican-temple-steeple arrangement of St Martin's as a model, it is surprising to find so many permutations in the treatment of the vaulting. At St Martin's and Derby the columns carry square blocks of entablature from which the vaults spring. Brunelleschi used square entablature-blocks at San Lorenzo and San Spirito in Florence from which the nave arcades spring. The arrangement at St Lawrence, Mereworth (with its barrel-vault springing from a continuous entablature, and lower aisles with flat ceilings divided into bays by means of entablatures), recurs in another version at All Saints' church at Gainsborough, Lincolnshire, of 1736–44, by Francis Smith (1672–1738): the exterior (PLATE 140) is based on St Martin's, complete with Gibbs Surrounds, but the interior is almost Neo-Classical, with tall unfluted Corinthian columns carrying straight entablatures over which there is a coved ceiling. All Saints' has an apse with a Venetian window. This is a similar arrangement to Holy Trinity church, Leeds, begun 1721 to designs by William Etty (*c* 1675–1734), except that at Holy Trinity the Venetian window in the apse is much bigger, the side windows have alternate segmental and triangular pediments, and there are no Gibbs Surrounds. The Leeds and Mereworth interiors are the most 'Palladian'-influenced of all Georgian church interiors. Etty did not design the tall steeple at Holy Trinity: it was rebuilt in 1839

PLATE 140 *All Saints' church, Gainsborough, Lincolnshire, by Francis Smith, showing the influence of Gibbs* (JSC).

to designs by Robert Dennis Chantrell (1793–1872) after Etty's work had been damaged in the Great Wind of that year. A further variation of ceiling is when the entablatures over the capitals are carried back to join the nave walls, and barrel-vaults spring from these entablatures, then stopping at the aisle walls at one end and at arcades when they stop at the nave. The nave ceiling can thus be raised to accommodate a clerestory, as at Christ Church, Spitalfields.

James Brydges, First Duke of Chandos (1673–1744), built a house and chapel at Cannons, near Edgware, to designs by Gibbs, 'done at vast Expence'. The house was demolished in 1747, but Lord Foley bought the pictures in the chapel and everything else which could be removed, and instructed Gibbs to install the material in the new chapel of 1735 at Great Witley, Worcestershire (PLATE 141). Glass is by Joshua Price, and the paintings are by Bellucci, now set in the chapel ceiling, but the pews are not original. This delightful interior, thoroughly Italian and just pre-Rococo, has a *papier-mâché* ceiling. Apparently the mouldings at Cannons were copied and adjusted to fit the new chapel of St Michael. Windows are semicircular-headed, and at the east is a Venetian window. The organ-case came from the chapel at Cannons, and it was for the Duke's pleasure that Händel composed his 'Chandos' anthems, spending two years at Cannons. St Michael's also contains a fine Baroque funerary monument to Lord Foley of

1732 by John Michael Rysbrack (1694–1770), who worked with Gibbs.

The most numerous American buildings derived from Gibbs are churches in the eastern seaboard States, and include Christ Church, Philadelphia (1727–54), St Michael's Charleston, South Carolina (1750s), Christ Church, Cambridge, Massachusetts (1760–61), First Baptist Meeting-House, Providence, Rhode Island (1775, and very close to the *Book of Architecture*), and the Center Church, New Haven, Connecticut (1812–15).[12]

One of the architectural puzzles is why Palladianism so signally failed to supplant the pattern established by the Baroque in church architecture. Baroque, after all, was a style associated with Popery, with Absolutism, with the Counter Reformation, and it was manifest in the reign of the Francophile Charles II (1660–85), whose devotion to Anglicanism was slight. Joseph Crouch, in his *Puritanism and Art: An Inquiry into a Popular Fallacy*,[13] noted that a study of the works of Hawksmoor, Gibbs, and Archer would 'suffice to show the taste that prevailed during the century immediately following the Restoration, and though the best work of the times was sound in construction, excellent as craftsmanship, and equal in its way to anything of similar character produced abroad during the same period, it is impossible to point to it with satisfaction as work that in any degree suggests the devotional character that the Catholic mind associates with the building and adornment of the House of Prayer.'[14] The puzzle cannot be answered: perhaps the answer lies in the curious position of Anglican theology itself.

Gibbs's positioning of the steeple on top of the vestibule of the body of the church, with the portico standing in front, as at St Martin's, was commonly followed during the next century. Wren, on the other hand, brought his towers down to the ground, and made little use of the portico. It has to be said again that the junction of steeple, rectangular box, and portico was extremely difficult to bring off, and resulted in uncomfortable compositions. The gigantic Serliana-portico set against the wide tower of Hawksmoor's Christ Church, Spitalfields, reads better, as the tower continues downwards as the front of the body of the church, and therefore the combination of portico-tower-rectangular box works better. Where porticoes were dispensed with, the tower often rose from the ground, and stood before the front of the church, with the main door punched on it. Examples are St John's Parish church, Moira, Co Down, of 1722 (PLATE 142), Knockbreda Parish church, Co Down, of 1747 by Richard Cassels (a Gibbs Surround on the door), and Holy Trinity, Ballycastle, Co Antrim, of 1756: all three of these Irish examples are basically Classical, but all have octagonal spires.[15] Less ambitious Georgian churches followed the Gibbs arrangement, but much simplified: plain rectangular

PLATE 142 *St John's church, Moira, Co Down, of 1722* (JSC).

PLATE 143 *Randalstown Presbyterian church, Randalstown, Co Antrim, of c 1790. The plan is elliptical, and the church is shown before the roof was raised and a new row of windows was added in c 1926* (RHB).

preaching-boxes, with doorcase or simple porch, short belfry over the gable, tall box-pews, and three-decker pulpit, were usual. The church of St Katharine, Chislehampton, Oxfordshire, is a modest and charming example of a Georgian country church of 1762: it is a plain box with gables terminating at urns over the string-course, with scrolls at the top between which rises a very simple belfry. The doorcase is a dignified architrave over which is a cornice.

The architecture of such cellular boxes is symptomatic of the easy latitudinarianism of the time, as Anglicanism moved away from the grandeur of the Baroque, and the last vestiges of seventeenth-century observance and tradition were abandoned. Evangelicalism was gaining ground, and was even

PLATE 141 (LEFT) *The church at Great Witley, Worcestershire* (RCHME BB88/6584).

more unfavourable to fine artistic expression than had been Puritanism. Worldliness and rationalism were gradually abandoned for bleak Evangelicalism with a narrow bigotry, and churches that had interiors more like utilitarian meeting-halls than places of Anglican worship were symptomatic of this new trend.

Dissent also gained ground in the Georgian period, and spawned large numbers of non-liturgical meeting-houses, many of which were domestic in character, with a square or rectangular plan and a double row of windows above and below the gallery. If square, there were often columns or piers in the centre, carrying the roof. The central feature of such buildings was the pulpit, below which was the Table. Pews consisted of the box type and plain benches, for social hierarchies prevailed in Nonconformity as well. Gradually, however, during the Georgian period, Dissent became more the religion of the lower-middle and artisan classes, and Nonconformist gentry often returned to Anglicanism. Even in America, long before the Revolution, pews were assigned according to social position in both Anglican and Nonconformist places of worship.

Many Georgian Nonconformist meeting-houses are simple and charming. The symmetrical centrally planned arrangements demanded by the static congregation and a dominant pulpit from which the Word and long sermons could be dispensed created a move towards polygonal or circular buildings, but such examples, strangely, are rare. The Octagon

PLATE 144 *Dunmurry Non-Subscribing (Unitarian) Presbyterian church, Co Antrim, probably by Roger Mulholland. Note the Gibbs Surrounds* (JSC).

Presbyterian Chapel in Norwich (1754), Octagon Chapel, Milsom Street, Bath, (1767), and the spectacular elliptical Presbyterian church at Randalstown, Co Antrim (*c* 1798) with Gothic pointed windows, are examples (PLATE 143). One of the most perfect elliptical Georgian churches is the Non-Subscribing Presbyterian church in Rosemary Street, Belfast, by Roger Mulholland (1740–1818).[16] It consists of a pure elliptical body with a rectangular portion containing the two staircases to the gallery, the vestibule, and the vestry attached to the street front. The galleries, carried on Composite columns, have fronts which sway backwards and forwards with convex and concave curves, and the transition from walls to ceiling is enlivened by a complex system of pointed vaults rising from corbels: the overall effect is as though a Bavarian or Bohemian Baroque church by a Dientzenhofer or a Zimmermann had been translated from Catholicism into Ulster Presbyterianism, giving an enchanting and beautiful effect. The window above the pulpit was of the Serliana type, and the organ was in the gallery above the entrance. In spite of injudicious alterations, the basic elements of this charming building survive. Mulholland was probably responsible for the Non-Subscribing (Unitarian) Presbyterian church at Dunmurry, Co Antrim, of 1779, a rectangular box with hipped roof, and Gibbs Surrounds to windows and doors (PLATE 144).

Most Nonconformist churches of the late-eighteenth and early-nineteenth centuries, however, were rectangular boxes: usually very plain, with a pedimented front, unadorned or with pilasters or columns. There are many outstanding examples in Ulster.[17]

Other Georgian Churches

St Paul's, Covent Garden, was a large single-cell space, with Tuscan portico. Many smaller Georgian churches owed more to Jones's other ecclesiastical building, the Queen's Chapel at Marlborough Gate, Pall Mall, Westminster (another single-cell space, but much smaller): this has a large Serliana or Venetian window at the east end, probably the first in England. The ceiling is coffered, and has a segmental section, which is rather inconsistent with Italian precedent.

An example of a church directly influenced by the Queen's Chapel is St Mary's at Glynde, East Sussex, by Sir Thomas Robinson of 1763–65: it has a projecting pedimented ashlar porch, an ashlar pediment and bellcote, and a Serliana at the east end. More Baroque is St Lawrence's church, Little Stanmore, Middlesex, of 1715–20, built for the Duke of Chandos: it is again of the single-cell type, but the east end is treated theatrically with the altar visible behind a segmentally arched opening flanked by a Corinthian Order. The entire interior is aglow with painted walls and ceilings by Laguerre, and there are also paintings by Bellucci, who also carried out the designs now at Great Witley, mentioned above. The architect was not Gibbs, but John James, whose St George's, Hanover Square, is his best known church, with its big hexastyle Corinthian pedimented portico, short tower on the west end of the church behind the portico (in the Gibbs manner), and heavily rusticated exterior. St George's has a nave with semi-elliptical tunnel-vault, and aisles with vaults in compartments separated by architraves joining the straight nave entablature to the aisle walls. The galleries are carried on square piers above which are Corinthian columns, a variant on the types we have encountered so far, while the east window is an elaborate Serliana with pairs of Corinthian columns and a semi-elliptical arch over instead of the usual semi-circle (PLATE 145). The great Corinthian porticoes of Gibbs's St Martin's and Hawksmoor's St George's, Bloomsbury, date from the same period as James's church of St George, which is, of course, a variant on the basilican type, of which St Martin-in-the-Fields is the pre-eminent example.

George Dance Junior's church of All Hallows, London Wall, of 1765–67, is a simple and severe brick box on the outside, but the Neo-Classical interior, with its engaged Ionic columns, hemi-dome over the apse, and large high-level lunettes breaking into the barrel-vault of the ceiling, is an impressive early example of the search for Antiquity, strongly flavoured with Greek detail (PLATE 146).

Neo-Classicism, influenced by the fashion for Greek detailing, did not influence plan forms much at first. John Pitt (*c* 1706–87) was the probable architect of the church of St Mary

PLATE 145 *Interior of St George's church, Hanover Square, London, by John James, showing the tunnel-vault, with individually vaulted compartments over the aisles separated by architraves* (AFK H218).

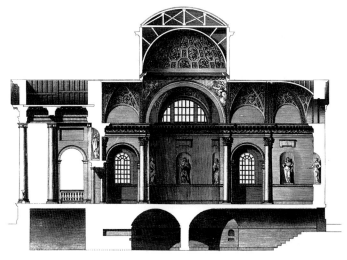

PLATE 147 *Section through Gibside Chapel, Co Durham, from Paine's* Noblemen and Gentlemen's Houses, *Plate LXIX. Note the burial-vault underneath* (SM).

PLATE 146 *Interior of the church of All Hallows, London Wall, by Dance* (AFK H133).

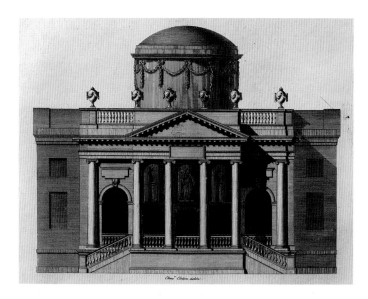

PLATE 148 *Gibside Chapel, Co Durham, by Paine, from his* Noblemen and Gentlemen's Houses, *Plate LXVIII* (SM).

at Stratfield Saye, Hampshire, an exception to the rule, which has a Greek Cross plan with an octagonal lantern and dome over the crossing, erected 1754–58. Even more splendid is Gibside Chapel, Co Durham, by James Paine, begun in 1760, which contains a burial-vault underneath (PLATE 147). The plan is a Greek Cross, over which is a drum with dome, and the angles are filled with small domed spaces. A handsome Ionic portico gives access to the chapel. Paine's chapel is Vitruvian-Roman, with a strong Palladian flavour (PLATE 148). Far more severe and Neo-Classical is James Stuart's remarkable church of All Saints at Nuneham Courtenay, Oxfordshire, partly designed by Lord Harcourt, and dating from 1764. Yet the details are more Roman than Greek, for the hexastyle portico has unfluted Ionic columns, and the plain drum, like the walls, is pierced by Diocletian windows. The building doubles as a 'temple' in the park. Stuart's associate for *The Antiquities of Athens*, as has been mentioned above, designed the severe Neo-Classical church at Ayot St Lawrence, Hertfordshire, with its Doric Order based on that of the Temple of Apollo at Delos, but even that has a Diocletian window, and the building serves as a mausoleum and eyecatcher (PLATES 85–86). Greek Crosses recur at St James's, Great Packington, mentioned above, in which Paestum Doric is used, with lunettes and Diocletian windows (PLATES 75–76). Plaw's St Mary's, Paddington, is also a Greek Cross, and there are other examples in the British Isles.

Of Robert Adam's interesting Neo-Classical church at Mistley (PLATE 149) in Essex, only the twin towers with cupolas and attenuated columns survive. One tower contained the altar and the other a stair and offices, and the church was a rectangle with a secondary axis running across it terminating in shallow apses screened by pairs of columns. It must have been a charming building, and dated from 1776. Another remarkably secular-looking church was St Mary's, East Lulworth, Dorset, of 1786, by John Tasker (*c* 1738–1816), a building for the Roman Catholic rites, designed to look like a garden-temple, with a quatrefoil plan, Tuscan porch, and dome over the crossing. Inside, the language is entirely Neo-Classical, and the plan is centralised.

In the 1780s the centralised plan became moderately fashionable. The elliptical church of St Andrew, Edinburgh, went up in 1782–84 to designs by Andrew Frazer (*ob* 1792), and All Saints, Newcastle-upon-Tyne, by David Stephenson (1757–1819), in 1786–89. At All Saints the tower projects in front of the church, and a detached portico stands before the tower: the body of the church is elliptical. The Belfast and Randalstown ellipses have been mentioned above. St Chad's, Shrewsbury, has also been recorded: it has the elongated Adamesque detail which was going out of fashion in the 1790s (PLATE 98).

Strangely enough, the Wren Baroque style in the form of St Stephen, Walbrook, was revived in the 1790s by Samuel Pepys Cockerell at St Mary's, Banbury, Oxfordshire, where the nave is formed of a circular dome over a square plan defined by twelve columns from which arches and pendentives spring to carry the low saucer-dome. The exterior is powerful and tough, and does not suggest the Wren Revival within.

The Early Nineteenth-Century Churches

The French Revolution and the Napoleonic period put the Fear of God into Society generally, and it was decided to put paid to experimental churches. Under the Church Building Act of 1818 the aim was to bring the Established Church to the expanding suburbs and new industrial areas. Unlike the previous Queen Anne Act, however, quantity and economy rather than grandeur were to be the main criteria. The Commissioners required simple rectangular preaching-boxes with a row of columns or piers supporting galleries, with a vestigial chancel, and some kind of font with architectural pretensions. Of course by 1818 the Greek Revival was in full swing, and many architects experimented with the problem of converting the Gibbsian/Wrenian steeple form to comply with Greek details, often providing handsome Greek Revival porticoes as well (PLATES 150–151). Among

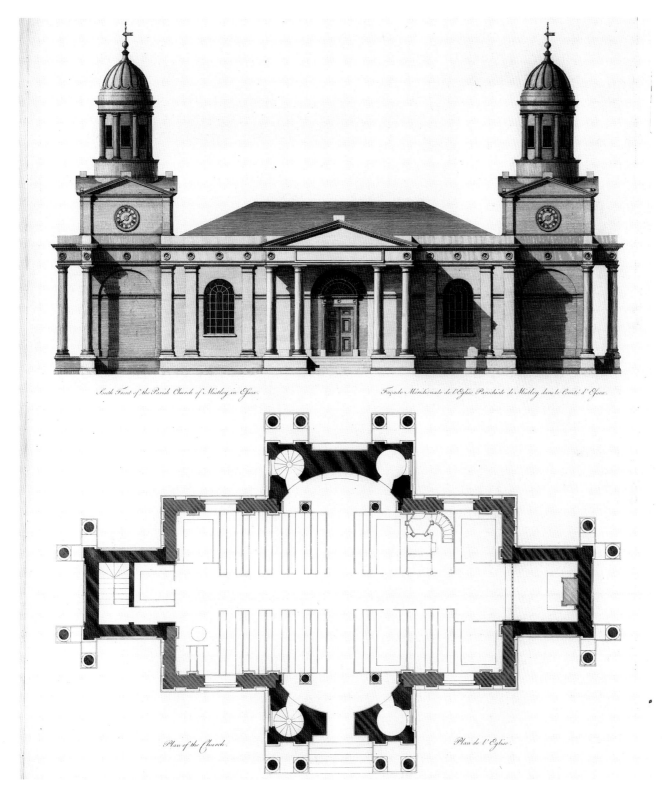

South Front of the Parish Church of Mistley in Essex.   *Façade Méridionale de l'Eglise Paroissiale de Mistley dans le Comté d'Essex.*

Plan of the Church.   *Plan de l'Eglise.*

PLATE 149 *Church of St Mary, Mistley, Essex, designed by Robert Adam,*
from Works in Architecture, *Vol II, No V, Plate I* (SM).

PLATE 150 *Design for a chapel by M.A. Nicholson, from Peter Nicholson's* The New Practical Builder *(1823), Plate XXIII* (JSC).

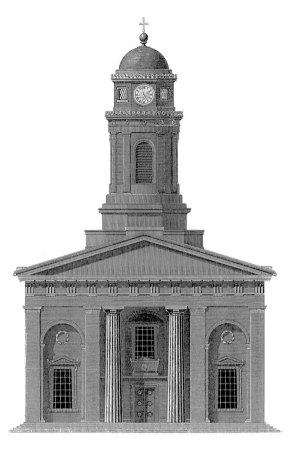

PLATE 151 *Longitudinal section of M.A. Nicholson's design for a Greek Revival chapel, from Peter Nicholson's* The New Practical Builder, *Plate XXV* (JSC).

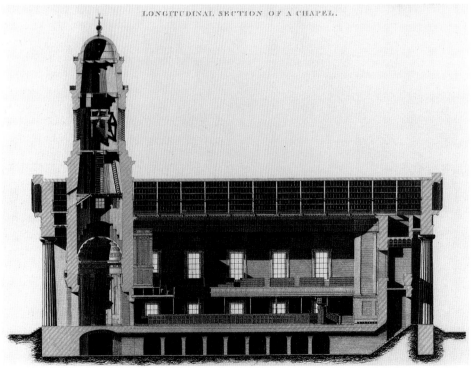

LONGITUDINAL SECTION OF A CHAPEL.

Plate 152 *Porden's church of St Matthew, Brixton* (AFK H8670).

the churches erected as a result of the Act are Nash's All Souls, Langham Place (1822), Francis Bedford's St John's, Waterloo Road (1823) – with its Greek Doric portico with Greek Tower behind, an interpretation of the Gibbsian arrangement derived from St Martin's – and Charles Ferdinand Porden's (1790–1863) tremendous Greek Doric church of St Matthew, Brixton, of 1822–24, which resolved the portico-tower problem by moving the tower to the east end (PLATE 152).

The Gibbs formula was successfully translated into Greek by the Inwoods at their fine church of St Pancras, London, mentioned earlier (PLATES 89–90): the Caryatide porches, Erechtheion portico, and octagonal tower with palm-capitals from the Tower of the Winds and elements from the Choragic Monument of Lysicrates were ingeniously quoted in this splendid building. But St Pancras, if archaeologically correct and ingeniously, even beautifully, formed, was far too expensive at over £70,000 to be a model, although Archibald Simpson's church of St Giles, Elgin, of 1827 uses pure Greek quotations too, and was cheaper.

However, it has to be said that the Commissioners' churches were often rather mean in appearance. There were occasional essays in church-building of note, however, including Thomas Rickman's (1776–1841) church of St George, Everton, Liverpool, of 1813–17, built in collaboration with John Cragg, ironmaster: it has a slender and elegant cast-iron

structure and tracery, and the style is Perpendicular Gothic.

Rickman, curiously, was a Quaker, yet he was among the first to give Gothic proper attention, and his *An Attempt to discriminate the Styles of English Architecture from the Conquest to the Reformation* appeared in 1817: it was the first systematic treatise on Gothic in England, and Rickman's nomenclature entered into general use as Early English, Decorated, and Perpendicular. James Savage (1779–1852) designed St Luke's church, Chelsea, in 1820–24, with a spire based on Wren's St Dunstan's-in-the-East, and is remarkable for the fact that the body of the church has a stone vaulted roof supported by flying buttresses. Most Georgian Gothick churches had ceilings of plaster or wood (even Wren's St Mary Aldermary had a plaster vault) and so St Luke's is therefore recognised as an important building in the history of the Gothic Revival. Savage's St James, Thurland Road, Bermondsey (1827–29), with which George Allen (1787–1847) was also involved, was, at £22,900, the third most expensive of the Commissioners' churches, the other two being Savage's St Luke's and Soane's Holy Trinity, Marylebone Road. St James's is a fine essay in the Greek Revival style, with a prostyle tetrastyle Ionic portico and tall steeple rising from a mass of masonry to which the portico is attached, so it is a well resolved variant of the Gibbs St Martin's theme.

Romanesque and Gothic

The Norman Revival was very short, and produced few masterpieces. Thomas Hopper (1776–1856) designed a Gothic Conservatory at Carlton House in 1807, but his remarkable Gosford Castle, Co Armagh (*c* 1820) and Penrhyn Castle, Caernarvonshire, of *c* 1825– *c* 1844, are both aggressive and hard essays in the Norman Picturesque style. In church architecture only a few 'Norman' examples may be mentioned: Wolverton church, Buckinghamshire, of 1810–15, by Henry Hakewill (1771–1830); London Colney church, Hertfordshire, of 1825–26, by George Smith(1783–1869), who was later to design Kilrea Church, Co Londonderry, in a Romanesque style for the Mercers' Company;[18] and St Clement's church, St Clement's, Oxford, of 1827–28, by Daniel Robertson, who was given to drink, and had to be driven about on Lord Powerscourt's estates in a wheelbarrow,

clutching his bottle of sherry. Robertson may also have designed the 'Norman' church at Kennington, Berkshire, of 1828, shortly before he suddenly left Oxford for Ireland. Perhaps the most delightful, if batty, Romanesque Revival church is the work of S. P. Cockerell at the church of St Peter and St Paul, Tickencote, Rutland, of 1792: these are additions to the stupendous Romanesque church of *c* 1160 (PLATE 153).

Gothic, and especially Gothick, however, played a far greater part than Romanesque. As we have seen, Wren used Gothic occasionally, there was a Gothic Survival at Oxford and elsewhere, and Hawksmoor designed a Gothic tower for St Michael, Cornhill (1718), the Gothic west towers of Westminster Abbey (1734), and the Gothic All Souls, Oxford.

In Ireland, Queen Anne's Bounty of First Fruits and Twentieth Parts was granted to the Anglican Church in Ireland in 1711, and the Board of First Fruits, with income derived from the first annual revenue of a Bishopric or Benefice, was empowered to build churches and carry out repairs. The result, even after the Irish Government made an annual grant to the Board after 1777, was rather too often a

PLATE 153 *The church of SS Peter and Paul, Tickencote, Rutland* (JSC).

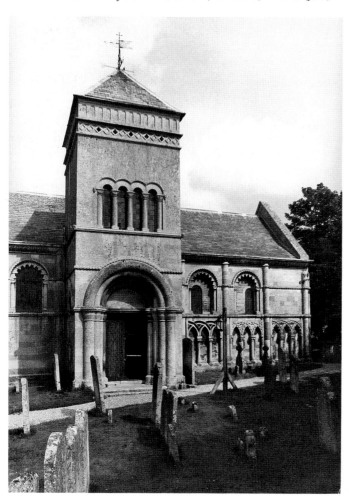

PLATE 154 *The church of St John the Baptist, King's Norton, Leicestershire, by John Wing the Younger, of 1757–75* (JSC).

simple box with pointed windows. Where the Bishop of Derry was involved, though, several simple Georgian Gothic preaching-boxes acquired handsome towers and spires, notably at Tamlaghtfinlagen, Ballyscullion, and Banagher, all in Co Londonderry, while great landowners, such as Lord Hillsborough, were responsible for charming Gothick churches such as St Malachy's at Hillsborough, Co Down, completed 1773. (Possible architects have been suggested above, to which should be added Doctor Maurice Craig's suggestion of Sanderson Miller,[19] on the grounds that Miller was also involved at Hillsborough Fort.)

John Wing (1728–94) designed two fine Gothick churches at King's Norton (1760–75), Leicestershire (PLATE 154), and East Carlton church (1788), in Northamptonshire. His father, also John (*ob* 1752), designed Galby church in Leicestershire in an amusing Rococo Gothic. The delightful Rococo Gothick of St John's at Shobdon, Herefordshire has previously been mentioned (1753) (PLATE 155), as has the noble church of St Mary at Tetbury, Gloucestershire (1771–81), although the nave piers in the latter church are excessively

PLATE 155 *The Rococo Gothick church at Shobdon, Herefordshire* (JSC).

PLATE 157 *Church of St Peter, Brighton, by Barry* (AFK H265).

PLATE 156 (LEFT) *Church of St Mary, Tetbury, Gloucestershire, of 1777–81, by Francis Hiorne of Warwick* (RCHME BB493005).

PLATE 158 *Interior of the church of St Peter, Brighton, a fine essay in the Perpendicular style of Gothic* (AFK H266).

style: the church is particularly remarkable for having cast-iron tracery made at Coalbrookedale. Henry Keene's lovely church at Hartwell, Buckinghamshire (1753–55) and his enchanting Hartlebury Castle chapel (*c* 1750) have both been cited as very fine examples of Georgian Gothick (PLATES 56–58). Also charming for its mid-eighteenth-century Gothick style is the church of St Mary Magdalene at Croome d'Abitot, Worcestershire, of 1758–63, by Lancelot 'Capability' Brown, with interior decorations by Robert Adam in his daintiest manner. The Commandment- and Creed-boards have ogee heads.

We cannot leave Georgian Gothic church architecture without mentioning the contribution of (Sir) Charles Barry (1795–1860), whose lovely church of St Peter, Brighton, of 1824–48 (an inventive composition made before Gothic was based on archaeological correctness [PLATES 157–158]), and the Perpendicular Holy Trinity, Cloudesley Square, Islington, of 1826 are delicate examples. With Barry and Savage, Gothic church architecture started to look more serious and less whimsical, although Hiorne had done well at Tetbury too. Barry designed a number of Gothic churches, but none, perhaps, was as successful as Holy Trinity or St Peter, while Savage's interior at St Luke's was undeniably impressive, and even fairly correct in its Perpendicular detail.

With the end of the Georgian period and the accession of King William IV things changed. Tractarianism, Pugin's rabid Catholicism, Ecclesiology, the religious revival, Reform, moral earnestness, censoriousness, and Evangelical versus High Church all contributed to a new climate. Suddenly Gothic was taken very seriously, and instead of being a mere style, was endowed with moral meaning. In the process its archaeology was studied, and 'correctness' in Gothic was earnestly sought: if an architect failed to convince the arbiters of Ecclesiology, woe betide! Gothic was no longer Gothick, Rococo, even Chinee-Gothick, but was a deadly serious matter: a style of a Christian country, dogmatic, powerful, tough, and soaring, and sometimes that of a mighty citadel of faith or dogma in a hostile environment of dirt and squalor. The prettiness of Georgian Gothick, the power of Georgian Baroque, the elegance of Georgian Neo-Classicism, or the dainty delights of Georgian Rococo, were consigned to the dustbin of contempt: Georgian architecture, like the easy-going Georgian religion, the limpid clarity of Georgian prose, and the magisterial style of Georgian historians such as Gibbon, were all viewed with suspicion. The eighteenth century began to be seen as morally depraved, and its architecture was denounced and undervalued by those who were left such a rich legacy.

slender, a structure made possible because they are stiffened by means of cast-iron members in the centres (PLATE 156). At Wroxton in Oxfordshire, not far from Edge Hill, Sanderson Miller built a tower with flimsy Gothick details in the 1740s, and there are pretty Gothick churches by George Richardson at Teigh in Rutland (1782) and Stapleford in Leicestershire (1789). The delightful Georgian Gothick fittings in Downpatrick Cathedral have also been mentioned (Doctor Craig suggests that Charles Lilley of Dublin could have been the architect). Also Rococo Gothic is Sir Robert Taylor's elegant spire of 1776 at St Peter's church, Wallingford, Oxfordshire. John Carline (1761–1835) designed and built the church of St Alkmund, Shrewsbury, of 1794–95, in a Gothic

CHAPTER SIX

INDUSTRIAL, COMMERCIAL, INSTITUTIONAL, & MARKET-BUILDINGS

INTRODUCTION; IRON STRUCTURES; MARKET-BUILDINGS;
COURT-HOUSES; COMMERCIAL ARCHITECTURE
APART FROM MARKET-BUILDINGS; PRISONS AND HOSPITALS;
BUILDINGS FOR MILITARY USE; EDUCATIONAL BUILDINGS
AND CHARITY SCHOOLS; BUILDINGS FOR PROFESSIONAL
ORGANISATIONS; CONCLUSION

*'If we could capture the spirit of Georgian
architecture, how should we set about our task? Not
by the blind imitation of form, not by the mere
revival of the phases of the style; for continuity does
not flourish in this way. On the contrary we should
try to understand its realism, its refined austerity, its
clarity and its logic.'*

A. E. RICHARDSON: *AN INTRODUCTION TO GEORGIAN ARCHITECTURE* (LONDON: ART & TECHNICS,
1949) P 127

PLATE 159 (Top) *Plan, Section, and Elevation of the Iron Bridge at Coalbrookdale, Shropshire, by T.F. Pritchard and Abraham Darby III. (Bottom) Iron Bridge built over the river at Sunderland (1793–96), projected by Rowland Burdon, cast by Walker of Rotherham, and erected under the direction of Thomas Wilson. From Peter Nicholson's* Architectural and Engineering Dictionary, *Vol I, Plate I (JSC).*

Introduction

As has been mentioned earlier, the Georgian period saw the Industrial and Agrarian Revolutions, and with them the development of new building types, structures, and landscapes.

Generally, the Georgians concealed structure, or hid it beneath an ornamental envelope. Georgian Gothick vaults, for example, were usually of plaster, and the forms were used decoratively, whereas Medieval Gothic vaults of stone did have some structural logic, even though their prime purpose was also decorative. James Savage's vaults at St Luke's church, Chelsea, of 1824, were, however, of stone. Curiously, the Georgian period was one in which the Primitive Hut, as an origin of Classical architecture, was extolled, and the Doric details of triglyphs, mutules, and guttae were said to represent beam-ends and dowels. So there was an eighteenth-century belief in the logic of a structural system as the basis for the Classical style. Yet a deliberate expression of structure only seems to have occurred when expense was to be kept to the minimum, and the buildings concerned were factories, warehouses, mills, farms, stores, and other utilitarian structures. Bridges, too, were often treated very simply, and yet the beauty and purity of the forms derived primarily from the structures.

Iron Structures

Once the Industrial Revolution had got under way, however, the possibilities of exploiting structure and technology in architecture began to be realised. The smelting of iron had traditionally been carried out with charcoal made from wood, but as timber became scarce, an alternative had to be found. When it was discovered by Abraham Darby (1677–1717) that coke could be used instead, probably around 1713, the production of iron was revolutionised. Dud Dudley (1599–1684), however, was one of the first to produce iron using coal. In 1665 he published *Metallum Martis, or Iron Made with Pit-Coale, Sea-Coale*, etc, and had gained a patent for making iron using coal as early as 1638. Even before that, in 1613, John Rovenson had made iron using coal as his fuel.

The second Abraham Darby (1711–1763), around 1738, perfected the process of smelting iron-ore in blast-furnaces, and greatly expanded the operations of producing iron at the Coalbrookdale Ironworks in Shropshire. His son, Abraham Darby III (1750–91), is remembered as the builder of the first iron bridge in the world, the foundation-stone of which was laid in 1769 (PLATE 159). Pevsner, in *The Buildings of England*,[1] attributes the design to Darby, but it is quite clear that Thomas Farnolls Pritchard (1723–77) designed the bridge in 1775, which was of completely iron construction, and which was built by Darby (with a few modifications) in 1777–79. Pritchard's designs are illustrated in *The Philosophical Magazine and Annals of Philosophy*,[2] and also in John White's *On Cementitious Architecture as applicable to the Construction of Bridges, with a Prefatory Notice of the First Introduction of Iron as the Constituent Material for Arches of Large Span, by Thomas Farnolls Pritchard in 1773*.[3] White was Pritchard's grandson. The bridge consists of a semicircular arch spanning the Severn, with two concentric arches above connected with a series of iron members. In the spandrels are a circlet and an ogee arch, and the composition is capped by a thin railing. There are two smaller arches on the south bank. In nearby Madeley churchyard are several cast-iron funerary monuments, including the handsome pedestal with columns in the corners commemorating William Baldwin (*ob* 1822).

Thomas Paine (1737–1809), author of *The Rights of Man*, was interested in the possibilities of iron as a structural material, and, in consultation with Benjamin Franklin (1706–90), proposed a bridge of iron over the Shuylkill in Pennsylvania in 1786, later presenting his ideas to the Academy of Sciences in Paris (where Soufflot and Victor Louis had used iron in architecture in the 1780s). The Shuylkill was eventually spanned by a suspension-bridge in 1809 designed by James Finley. In 1789 Paine designed an iron bridge based on the principles of a spider's web, and the parts were made by Messrs Walker of Rotherham: it was erected at Leasing (now Paddington) Green in 1790, and its main arch was based on a catenary curve. The bridge was demolished in 1791, but Paine's designs were adopted, slightly modified, for the great bridge over the River Wear in Sunderland, of 1793-96, and, according to Samuel Smiles, in his *Lives of the Engineers* (1861), parts from Paine's bridge were used in its construction. The Wear bridge had centring for the great central arch designed by Jonathan Pickernell Junior, but the overall design seems to have been by Rowland Burdon, and Pickernell was undoubtedly involved as well. However, the structure had to be strengthened in 1805, and was rebuilt in 1896.

The most handsome and daring Georgian bridges were those designed by Thomas Telford (1757–1834): his Buildwas Bridge of 1795–96 was his first iron bridge, with a segmental arch (now destroyed) (PLATE 160), and this was followed by the Craigellachie, Banffshire (1812–15), Waterloo Bridge, Betws-y-Coed, Caernarvonshire (1815), Menai Suspension (1819–26), and Conway Suspension (1821–26) Bridges. These elegant structures are incredibly timeless, and demonstrate the possibilities offered by iron to a designer of genius. Telford also designed the Tern Aqueduct, Longdon,

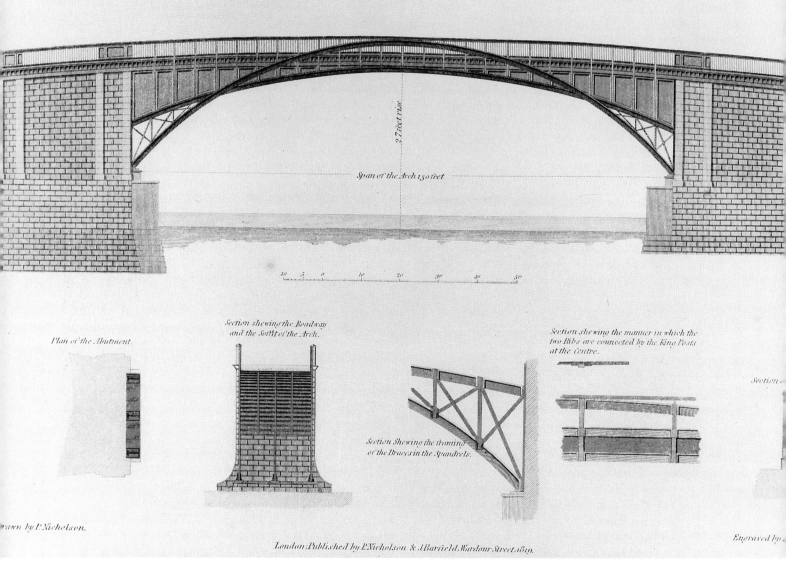

IRON BRIDGE.

PLAN, ELEVATION and SECTIONS of the IRON BRIDGE built over the RIVER SEVERN, at BUILDWAS in the COUNTY of SALOP, in the Years 1795 and 179

2 Feet rise.

Span of the Arch 130 feet

Plan of the Abutment.

Section shewing the Roadway and the Soffit of the Arch.

Section shewing the manner in which the two Ribs are connected by the King Posts at the Centre.

Section Shewing the framing of the Braces in the Spandrels.

Drawn by P. Nicholson.

Engraved by

London; Published by P. Nicholson & J. Barfield, Wardour Street, 1819.

PLATE 160 *Buildwas Bridge, Shropshire, of 1795–96, by Telford, from Nicholson's* Architectural and Engineering Dictionary, *Vol I, Plate II* (JSC).

Shropshire (1793–94), carrying the Shropshire Union Canal, and the great aqueducts at Chirk, Denbighshire (1796–1801), and Pont-y-Cysyllte (1795–1805) when Engineer and Architect to the Ellesmere Canal. At the end of the Georgian period, in 1829 (revised 1831), Isambard Kingdom Brunel (1806–59) designed the Clifton Suspension Bridge, with its Egyptian pylons, great chains, suspension-rods, and sarcophagi-like anchoring-blocks. Before that, in 1823, Captain (later Sir) Samuel Brown (1776–1852) had used the pylon form for the four iron towers from which the Brighton Chain Pier was suspended.[4] Brown had invented an improved method of manufacturing links for chain-cables which he patented jointly with Philip Thomas in 1816, and in the following year he patented improvements in suspension bridges, the patent including a special sort of link which allowed such bridges to be constructed on a larger scale than had been possible before. The first such large suspension bridge in England was the Union (1820) over the Tweed near Berwick at Loan End, and Brown's inventions also made the Telford suspension bridges, such as the Menai and Conway, possible.

From the beginning of the Georgian period large mills were constructed, one of the earliest being T. & J. Lombe's Derby Silk Mill of 1717: this was a long structure, five storeys high, with as many windows as possible piercing the walls to illuminate the interior. Power was supplied by a large water-wheel. Normally, most workshops or weaving-sheds in the eighteenth century were domestic in scale, often on top of the living quarters (examples survive in Spitalfields and elsewhere), and the new large-scale mills must have seemed awesome compared with the small buildings associated with cottage industries.

The problem with the large factory, several storeys high, was fire. Warehouses, too, could be very tall, but could be a lot wider on plan because they were stores, and so good light was less necessary than where goods were being manufactured. However, both factories and warehouses usually had outer walls of brick or stone, with timber posts inside carrying beams over which floors were laid, all of timber. In the 1780s segmental brick arches spanning between beams were introduced to try to lessen the risk of fire, but in 1792 William Strutt (1756–1830) designed a fireproof mill at Derby which included cast-iron columns and floors carried on segmental brick arches spanning between the beams. In 1796 Charles Bage of Shrewsbury designed the flour-mill for Messrs Marshall, Benyon, & Bage, at Spring Gardens, Ditherington, Shrewsbury, Shropshire: the cast-iron columns have cruciform sections and support iron beams from which the twenty bays of segmental brick vaults spring. Window-frames were of iron too, set in the load-bearing brick walls. This appears to be the first multi-storey and iron-framed building ever erected

PLATE 161 *Marshall, Benyon, & Bage Mill, Shrewsbury, Shropshire, of 1796* (AFK G6292).

(although the outer walls were not framed) (PLATE 161). After this the system of iron columns, iron beams, segmental brick vaults (or hollow-pot construction), with outer walls of brick or stone, became fairly common for factories and warehouses, although timber was still widely used.

In 1796 Daniel Asher Alexander (1768–1846) was appointed Surveyor to the London Dock Company, for which he designed extensive ranges of capacious warehouses: his Skin Floor, London Docks, Wapping (1811–13), was designed with cast-iron cruciform columns from which struts branched to carry the great wooden roof-structure, giving the appearance of a series of trees. The reason was to allow a large floor area, interrupted by as few columns as possible. George Dance in the 1770s also attempted to create a large clear floor area at his Porter Tun Room in Chiswell Street, London, by improving the king-posts with cast-iron shoes and a system of straps. Of course iron could enable thinner members to be used, permit greater spans, and, above all, ensure speed of erection.

Many of these Georgian warehouses and factories were monumental, severe, plain, and unadorned. When Schinkel visited England in 1826 he took note of the cast-iron structures, the 'thousands of smoking obelisks' that were chimneys, and the vast factories of Lancashire, seven or eight storeys high, and as many as forty bays long. He also visited the London Docks, where there were already impressive Georgian warehouses, and later those at St Katherine Dock by Philip Hardwick (1792–1870) of 1827–29, with their severe unfluted Doric columns and plain brick walls. Interestingly, Schinkel also made a charming sketch of the Gasworks at Tanfield, Canonmills, Edinburgh, built 1824 to designs by William Burn, which had only just been completed. It was a wonderful, symmetrical, stripped Italianate *Rundbogenstil*

composition, worthy of Ledoux at his boldest,[5] and even slightly reminiscent of Schinkel's own *Rundbogenstil* work in Potsdam.

Cast iron was also used to provide the structural girders for the staircase of 1805 at Sezincote, Gloucestershire, designed by S. P. Cockerell, and John Nash designed the charming cast-iron staircases at Brighton Pavilion of 1815-21, with their balustrades in the forms of bamboo *Chinoiserie*, and with pierced risers. Nash also produced the designs for the cast-iron columns with copper palm-leaf capitals in the kitchen of the Pavilion (PLATE 70). Nash was responsible for the iron bridge at Stanford-on-Teme, Worcestershire, of 1795, the Gothick cast-iron balustrades and brackets for the Grand Hall at Corsham, Wiltshire, of 1797–98, and the Gothick balustrade of cast iron at Longner Hall, Shropshire, of *c* 1805. Thomas Hopper's Gothic cast-iron conservatory at Carlton House (1807) was designed with pierced fan-vaulting to admit light through coloured glass, and was one of the first large complete cast-iron structures used in a house, as opposed to an engineering structure.

Iron was first used for conservatories in the Georgian period. The glass dome, erected in 1827 at Bretton Hall, Yorkshire, was constructed of cast and wrought iron and glass:

PLATE 162 *Hillsborough Tholsel, Co Down* (JSC).

all vertical structure was of cast iron, and all the sash-bars for the roof-ribs were of wrought iron. The contractors were Messrs W. and D. Bailey, of Holborn, and this system of construction, including the carved bendable sash-bars, was designed by John Claudius Loudon (1783–1843).

Market-Buildings

Many market-halls were in the same buildings as exchanges or court-houses: often the court-house was in a room above the arcaded or colonnaded lower area. Robert Adam's elegant Market-Hall at Bury St Edmunds in Suffolk (1774–80) contained a theatre, and was rusticated and arcaded on the ground floor, with the upper floor embellished with niches, Serlianas, and attenuated columns carrying pediments. Hillsborough, Co Down (c 1790), has a large market-house combined with a court-house and the Downshire Estate Office: the entire ensemble was referred to as a Tholsel, and is very Palladian in manner (PLATE 162). The architects appear to have been W. Forsyth and James McBlain, whose father built the spire of Hillsborough Parish church in the 1770s (PLATE 51). The building at Lisburn, Co Antrim, with its handsome cupola designed by the McBlains in 1808, had an assembly-room, as did Ferdinando Stratford's Newtownards Market-House of 1765 in Co Down. Antrim, of 1726, had an arcaded market-hall above which was the court-room: C. R. Cockerell, in 1823, admired and drew it, describing it as 'Florentine'.

Very large market-buildings, such as Charles Fowler's (1792–1867) Covent Garden Market of 1828–30, had glass-roofed arcades and ranges of colonnades. Smaller market-buildings would have the open colonnaded or arcaded ground floor over which would be the court-room or assembly-room, as noted above, so the larger market-buildings were an extension of the basic form. One of the most spectacular of the larger market-buildings to survive is the stunning Piece Hall in Halifax, Yorkshire, of 1774–79, designed as a cloth market: it consists of an arcaded ground floor over which is a range of piers, and the top floor has a colonnade of widely-spread columns (PLATE 163). Behind the arcade and colonnades are small shops and offices. The Piece Hall surrounds a huge open square which is entered through a severe pedimented gateway, set in a plain, almost windowless, stone wall. The architect was probably John Hope (1734–1808), although Mr Cruickshank[6] suggests Thomas Bradley was responsible: whoever actually was the architect, it is clear he was trying to create a Roman Forum, for it is one of the grandest Classical sights in England.

The Exchange and Market, Bristol, of 1741–43, and the Exchange of 1749–54, Liverpool, both by John Wood the Elder, looked like a town mansion and a Palladian country-house respectively. Liverpool acquired a dome in 1802 to designs by John Foster (c 1759–1827) and James Wyatt, and a portico in 1811. Grandly Classical were Thomas Cooley's Royal Exchange in Dublin (1768–79) and David Hamilton's (1768–1843) Royal Exchange in Glasgow (1827–29). There are plenty of pleasing and refined market-halls and exchanges dotted throughout the British Isles, and it would be both superfluous and impossible to list them all here. From the ultra-simple and refined court- and market-house at Eglinton, Co Londonderry, of 1823–26, by James Bridger, perhaps based on a design of 1822 by Michael Angelo Nicholson (1796–1842), to John Adam's (1721–92) Royal Exchange in Edinburgh (1753–61), which also contained a Custom House, the market-house-cum-exchange-cum-court-house offered distinctive and dignified additions to the Georgian town.

PLATE 163 *The Piece Hall, Halifax, Yorkshire* (JSC).

PLATE 164 *The White Linen Hall, Belfast (demolished), probably by Roger Mulholland. Note the Gibbs Surrounds* (UM Local History Collection W10/21/60).

One of the finest of all exchanges was Belfast's White Linen Hall of 1785, probably by Roger Mulholland, where the sale and distribution of bleached linen was organised. It contained the offices of the linen drapers as well as the Linen Hall Library, opened in 1802. The building was laid out around a large courtyard, and contained many of Mulholland's favourite features such as Gibbs Surrounds: it had a main façade forty-three windows wide (PLATE 164).

Court-Houses

As has been mentioned above, court-houses were often set within market-halls. The Hillsborough Tholsel (PLATE 162) is an excellent example of this type. Thomas Rogers (*n* 1744) designed the Palladian Middlesex County Sessions House in Clerkenwell Green, London, of 1779–82, with its fine pedimented front and reliefs by Nollekens. Palladian too is John Carr's Assize Courts at York 1773–77, which is balanced across the square by the same architect's Prison for Females, an almost identical façade: the composition has a central tetrastyle pedimented portico set

PLATE 165 *The Assize Courts, York, of 1773–77, by John Carr. From Richardson* (BTB/SH).

between pilasters, with three-window-wide elements on either side terminating in end-pavilions with Ionic columns again set between pilasters (PLATE 165).

Ireland contains several fine court-houses, including the splendid Four Courts by Gandon of 1786–1802 (PLATE 115). Severe Greek Revival court-houses can be found at Dundalk (by Edward Park and John Bowden of 1813-18) and Londonderry (John Bowden, 1813–17). Francis Johnston's Court-House of 1809 in Armagh has a curiously thin Roman Doric pediment carried on very attenuated Tuscan columns. Enniskillen has a court-house of 1785 with a severe unfluted Greek Doric portico by Isaac Farrell of 1822; Omagh, Co Tyrone, has a handsome court-house of 1820, with prostyle tetrastyle Tuscan portico by John Hargrave; while Caledon, Co Tyrone, was embellished with a severe stripped Neo-Classical court-house of *c* 1822, possibly by Francis Johnston. All are buildings with a distinctive presence and architectural quality.

Powerful, too, in its severe Greek Doric toughness, was William Stark's (1770–1813) Glasgow Court-House of 1810. Many courts were provided in Shire Halls (as at Gandon's Nottingham Shire Hall) or in larger complexes such as Thomas Harrison's Chester Castle (1788–1822). In Ireland the function of court-house often overlapped that of town-hall, for local government was partly the responsibility of the Grand Jury which was housed in the court-house. So the court-house, often associated with local government, with commerce, and even with estate management (as at Hillsborough), had a position of civic importance reflected in the architecture.

PLATE 166 *The Sessions-House in Bourne, Lincolnshire, of 1821, by Bryan Browning* (JSC).

One of the most remarkable buildings of the court-house type is the Sessions House in Bourne, Lincolnshire, of 1821 by Bryan Browning (1773–1856): the front has an ingeniously arranged stair behind a columnar screen carrying a segmental arch (PLATE 166). The composition is one of the most interesting of any court-house in the British Isles.

Commercial Architecture apart from Market-Buildings

As outlined above, the development of technology, notably cast-iron structure, was closely connected with the growth of communications, especially bridges and aqueducts. It was also associated with the building of factories and warehouses. However, such innovations were not generally evident in the architecture of banks, exchanges, or shops.

In the Georgian period most business activity (other than markets or exchanges) was carried out from buildings that were either private houses or looked like domestic structures. Even banks were generally in buildings that did not differ greatly from private houses. A separate office-building type was not a feature of the Georgian period, although the County Fire Office in Lower Regent Street of 1819 by Robert Abraham (1774–1850) has been identified by Pevsner as the first purpose-built office in England.[7] The first building erected for office use by different firms seems to have been in Clement's Lane at the Lombard Street end, of around 1823, designed by Annesley Voysey (*c* 1794–1829), who was a partner of Richard Suter (*ob* 1883), Surveyor to the Fishmongers' Company, in the 1830s. The Voysey building is generally regarded as the first building in London designed exclusively for offices to be let out, and those offices would have been for different types of business, in contrast to the tobacco-merchants of Glasgow (who acquired a specially built office-block in Virginia Street in 1819, with a charming galleried court inside), and Sir Robert Taylor's Six Clerks' and Enrolment Office, Lincoln's Inn Fields, of 1774–80, with its tall semicircular-headed windows at first-floor level to illuminate the Writers' rooms (PLATE 203).

The Bank of England, designed by Soane from 1788 to 1833, in London, was indeed purpose-built. Its most remarkable features were the surrounding wall (embellished with columns using the Order from the Temple of Vesta at Tivoli [PLATE 127], blank panels, rusticated masonry, and urns and sarcophagi), and the series of impressive vaulted top-lit spaces, all constructed of brick. The Bank was designed as a

PLATE 167 *Shop-fronts from Nicholson's* The New Practical Builder *of 1823* (JSC).

fortress, to protect the offices and contents from the gin-soaked London Mob, which could be a frighteningly destructive phenomenon, and indeed burned down part of Newgate Gaol. Soane's use of segmental arches, his saucer-domes, and simple stripped incised detailing, gave the Bank interiors a severe and no-nonsense quality (PLATE 125): one could feel that sobriety and security were well to the fore. Most other Georgian banks, however, did not look distinctive as banks, but more like grander domestic buildings: examples include Carr's central block at George Street, Halifax, of 1766. Archibald Elliott Junior's (*ob* 1843) handsome Royal Bank of Scotland in Glasgow of 1827, with its fine hexastyle Greek Ionic portico, does actually begin to look like a building of unusual gravity, but not necessarily like a bank as such: it could be a court-house, club, or exchange. Banks as distinctive types were to emerge after the 1830s.

With regard to shops the usual eighteenth-century arrangement was to have a couple of bow-windows with a door in the centre, the whole with an entablature, and with a door at the side giving access to the rooms above (which were usually

lived in or let out for offices): a good example of this type is at Artillery Lane, Spitalfields, of about 1757. Bow-windows were designed to gain space inside, and often encroached on the street or pavement. gradually the bows became flattened, and segmental on plan, while the detailing became refined, as at 46 Stonegate, York. The bows themselves had glazing-bars, thick at the beginning of the period, and very thin by the 1790s. When the Neo-Classical taste dictated greater simplicity, shop-fronts became flat, divided by means of pilasters or columns, with a fascia over (PLATE 167): when plate-glass became cheap and available from around 1825, glazing-bars were taken out and display became more startling. Uniform groups of shop-fronts (as in arcades, or in streets such as Woburn Walk in Bloomsbury [1820s]) were unusual, because the tendency has always been to allow the Nation of Shopkeepers to do what it likes at the expense of architectural order. At Regent Street there was a brave try at the imposition of such order, but it gradually gave way to a free-for-all, and at other sites, such as d'Olier Street, Dublin (*c* 1800) and Reform Street, Dundee (from 1824), frightful mayhem has replaced the order intended by the original designers.

Where covered top-lit arcades were built, attempts to impose uniformity on the shop-fronts were usually more successful, probably because of the covenants imposed by the ground-landlords. The Royal Opera Arcade by Nash and Repton of 1816–18 survives, as does Burlington Arcade of 1818–19 by Samuel Ware (1781–1860), although Beresford Pite altered the Piccadilly entrance in 1929–31. John Baird (1798–1859) designed the Argyle Arcade, Glasgow, of 1827–28, with exposed iron roof-structure, one of the finest of provincial arcades, among which can be mentioned James Foster's (*c* 1748–1823) Upper and Lower Arcades of 1824–25 in Bristol, and Henry Edmund Goodridge's (1797–1864) The Corridor in Bath of 1825.

Prisons and Hospitals

The odd thing about early-Georgian prisons is that they were either of the lock-up type tucked away in a town gate or placed under a market- or court-house, or remarkably un-prison-like, as at Carr's Prison for Females in York, which looks like a Palladian mansion. The Gaol at King's Lynn, Norfolk, of 1784, by William Tuck, appears to be a three-storey five-window-wide Georgian house: what gives it away is the narrow rusticated pedimented element in which are chains and shackles (PLATE 168). These symbols of incarceration, restriction, and punishment were used again at

PLATE 168 *The former Gaol in King's Lynn, Norfolk, showing the chains and shackles over the door* (JSC).

PLATE 169 *Downpatrick Gaol, Co Down* (JSC).

Kilmainham Gaol, Dublin, of 1796, by John Trail, who embellished the pediment on a heavily rusticated wall with chained serpents and disagreeable-looking maggots.

Some of the greatest and most powerful of Georgian Architecture was to be found in Gaols, or Houses of Correction. Inspired by the theories emanating from France, and by the images of prisons by Piranesi, the drama of retribution was expressed in the awe and terror suggested by blank walls, massive rustication, terrifying chains and fetters, and crushing weights of masonry over tiny doors. George Dance the Younger's Newgate Gaol of 1770–80 was a monumental and terrible (in the true sense) building of the first rank, with forbidding walls featuring blind niches, heavy rustication, and chain-festooned openings. Here was Sublime Terror indeed (PLATE 124). Thomas Cooley's Newgate in Dublin of 1773 was clearly inspired by Dance's London Gaol, and like the London Newgate, had features derived from Piranesi and Giulio Romano. Blank walls and rustication are also found at the handsome frontispiece to Downpatrick Gaol, Co Down,

which may be the work of Robert William Brettingham of 1789, although Robert Reid (1774–1856) has also been credited with the alterations of 1824–30 (PLATE 169).

While the grimness of prisons and the ghastliness of incarceration were expressed in such structures, there was another type of architectural treatment given to gaols in which the Primitive Doric or Tuscan Orders featured. Thomas Johnson's (*ob* 1800) County Gaol in Warwick of 1778–82 has a severe unfluted Doric Order of engaged columns all along the façade carrying a mighty Doric entablature. Heaviness, massiveness, and overpowering weight were also features of Bury St Edmunds Gaol by George Byfield (*c* 1756–1813) of 1803, while Bryan Browning gave the House of Correction at Folkingham, Lincolnshire, of 1823–25, a dramatically mighty front reminiscent of Vanbrugh and Ledoux at their best (PLATE 170). Browning, in fact, was one of the most interesting of Regency architects, having designed the Sessions House at Bourne: he was to go on to produce the powerful Institution in Stamford, an essay in Graeco-Egyptian synthesis. Cork Prison for Males of 1818–23 was designed with a severe Greek Doric portico set against blank walls embellished with tough blind openings having stripped detail. Inside, the plan was an octagon with radiating cell-blocks several storeys high. It was designed by James (*c* 1779–1877) and George Richard Pain (*c* 1793–1838) (PLATE 171).

George Moneypenny's (*n* 1768) Sessions House and House of Correction at Knutsford, Cheshire, of 1817–19, had

PLATE 170 *The House of Correction, Folkingham, Lincolnshire, of 1823–25, by Bryan Browning* (JSC).

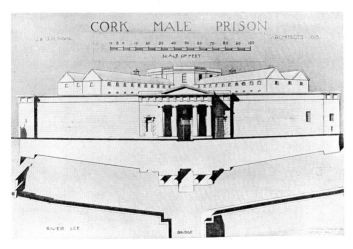

PLATE 171 *Cork Prison for Males by the appropriately named J. and G.R. Pain. From Richardson* (BTB/SH).

massive rusticated door-surrounds, while Francis Goodwin's (1784–1835) County Gaol, Derby, of 1823–27, had a Doric Order of Sublime Primitiveness which C. R. Cockerell saw as 'powerful', claiming Goodwin could beat anything for 'raciness, invention, resource, and... grandeur'. Towards the end of the Georgian period the castellated style was occasionally invoked for Gaols: Leicester County Gaol of 1825–28 by William Parsons (1796–1857) is an example (PLATE 172), with its curiously feeble crenellated towers and bogus portcullis, but the blank brick walls of the perimeter with their simple buttresses are Sublimely Aweful.

From 1778 prison planning underwent a great change as a result of legislation passed after the publication of John Howard's (*c* 1726–90) *State of the Prisons in England and Wales* (Warrington, 1777). Howard was well acquainted with developments in design on the Continent, and he proposed building prisons out of towns, segregation of prisoners, good heating and ventilation, plans to facilitate supervision, and cell-blocks. French Neo-Classical designs inspired Jeremy Bentham's (1748–1832) ideas for his Panopticon of 1791, with storeys of cells around the periphery of a drum and an observation-post in the centre. Sir Samuel Bentham (1757–1831) had produced a proposal for an 'Inspection House' in *c* 1785 which was the principle of the Panopticon, and, it was argued, could be applied to schools, factories, hospitals, and prisons. This pattern was used by William Blackburn (1750–90) for the House of Correction at Northleach, Gloucestershire, of 1787–91, and in 1785–97 Thomas Jefferson and Benjamin Latrobe designed a great Neo-Classical semicircular prison at Richmond, Virginia. The Edinburgh Bridewell was also based on a semicircle, and was built to designs by Robert and James Adam in 1791–95. A fully circular plan was adopted for Devizes Gaol in Wiltshire of 1808–17 by Richard Ingleman (1777–1838). Cell-blocks radiating like spokes from a central octagon were built at Cork Male Prison (as noted above), Ipswich Gaol of 1785–90, Liverpool Gaol of 1787–89, and Dorchester Gaol of 1789–95, all by Blackburn. Another example was the County Bridewell, Abingdon, Berkshire (now Oxfordshire), by (Sir) Jeffrey Wyatville (1766–1840) of 1805–11. A variant was Millbank Prison of 1813–21 by William Williams, Thomas Hardwick (1752–1829), John Harvey, and Robert Smirke, which had radii that were not straight cell-blocks but a block forming a pentagon.

Perhaps even more Sublimely Terrible than some of the English examples was the grim House of Correction in Belfast, designed by Roger Mulholland, begun in 1817, the contractor being James Boyd (PLATE 173). It consisted of a plain brick wall divided by means of buttresses, with the main block having a tall pedimented centre-piece, two wings, and two pedimented corner pavilions sitting in the court contained by the wall. The main entrance was a simple pediment set over a blind arch in which was the portal over which was inscribed the legend

WITHIN AMEND, WITHOUT BEWARE.

The building had a Vanbrughian starkness and grandeur: it is a pity it was so inadequately recorded before it was replaced by Lanyon's splendidly handsome Crumlin Road Gaol in 1843–45.

Such Georgian prisons, with individual cells, were an enormous improvement on previous gaols where corruption of every kind was evident. The Benthams argued that fireproof construction, using cast iron and masonry, good ventilation and heating, adequate control of solar glare, and *lavatories in each cell* should be provided. It is a sorry state of affairs that in the 1990s we are still talking about 'slopping out' because there are no lavatories in many prison-cells, which are over-occupied anyway.

The principles of prison design, as noted, also apply to hospitals. Again, the main ideas were Continental. However, early-Georgian hospitals looked like houses, and were usually often treated as long terraces. Purpose-built hospitals were very plain, like the London Hospital, Whitechapel, of

PLATE 172 *Leicester County Gaol, of 1825–28, by William Parsons* (JSC).

PLATE 173 *The House of Correction, Belfast, of 1817, by Roger Mulholland* (UM Local History Collection Ic/3c/Correction).

1752–77 by Boulton Mainwaring, the main façade based on a design for an infirmary attributed to Isaac Ware. Also involved in the building of the London Hospital was Joel Johnson (*c* 1721–99), but he appears to have been more a Clerk of Works and carpenter than an architect. Other simple Georgian infirmaries, often with a central pediment, and usually quite plain, with sash-windows punched into a brick or ashlar wall, include Worcester, Salisbury, Armagh, and others. Somewhat more pretentious were Gibbs's buildings for St Bartholomew's Hospital, Smithfield, London of 1730 and after, the Rotunda Hospital, Dublin, of 1751, a fine Palladian composition by Richard Cassels, and Guy's Hospital, London, begun 1722, but greatly improved by Richard Jupp (1728–99) from 1774 to 1778. The latter hospital was of the quadrangle type of plan, developed for naval hospitals such as the Haslar Royal Naval Hospital in Hampshire of 1746-61 by Theodore Jacobsen (*ob* 1772) and John Turner. James Lewis (*c* 1751–1820) was appointed Surveyor to the Bridewell and Bethlehem Hospitals in 1793, and he designed the new Bethlehem Hospital at St George's Fields, Southwark, 1811–15, a well planned barrack-like building with a large

portico and a low saucer-dome behind it. Sydney Smirke (1797–1877) created the loftier cupola in 1838–46, and the wings were truncated in 1930. The Hospital is now the Imperial War Museum.

However, these Georgian hospitals were not very satisfactory from the hygienic point of view. John Howard again drew attention to the planning of European hospitals in his *An Account of the Principal Lazarettos in Europe* of 1789, and compared them unfavourably with British examples. The London Hospital had no cisterns for water, the vaults were offensive, and the baths were seldom used. Guy's and St Bartholomew's were better, as the wards were clean and the windows were open, but there were no water-closets in St Thomas's. The Radcliffe Infirmary in Oxford (1759–70 by Leadbetter and Sanderson) had wards that were close and offensive. Haslar near Gosport was praised, as was the Royal Naval Hospital of 1758–64 at Stonehouse, near Plymouth, by Alexander Rouchead (*ob* 1776). The latter was designed on the novel plan of insulated but linked blocks, or pavilions, and was illustrated by J. R. Tenon in *Mémoires sur les hôpitaux de Paris* of 1788, and also illustrated in Durand's *Recueil et*

PLATE 174 *The Belfast Charitable Society's Clifton House, Belfast, of 1771-72, by Robert Joy, based on a design by Robert Mylne* (B/BCS/JHP).

Parallèle des Édifices Anciens et Modernes of 1800. Now Wren had prepared a design for the Royal Naval Hospital at Greenwich before 1702 on the pavilion principle, and it is curious this sensible system was not adopted earlier in the Georgian period, for it enabled light and air to penetrate the pavilions while lessening the possibilities of infection. The pavilion type of plan became usual around the 1850s.

Unfortunately such plan types involved very large sites, so infirmaries in towns tended to be of the large house or collegiate building type, but after about 1810 adopted a Grecian guise. Good examples are the Royal Salop Infirmary, Shrewsbury, of 1828–29 by Robert Smirke and Edward Haycock (1790–1870); St George's Hospital, Hyde Park Corner, London, of 1827, by William Wilkins; and the fine Carlisle Infirmary of 1830–32 by Richard Tattersall (*c* 1803–44). So most Georgian hospitals were Classical, usually quite simple buildings like the London Hospital (twenty-three windows wide with a pediment over the middle seven, and two slightly projecting end pavilions three windows wide), but sometimes Palladian, and latterly Greek. There were rare forays into Gothic such as John Peter Gandy-Deering's (formerly Gandy) Infirmary at Stamford, Lincolnshire, of 1827–28, in Tudor Gothic.

Finally, one of the prettiest of infirmaries should be mentioned: Clifton House, Belfast, the Charitable Society's combined Poor-House and Infirmary, opened in 1774. A design for a two-storey five-window-wide block with a pedimented centre-piece three windows wide, with five-bay single-storey wings and blind panels at the ends was produced by Robert Mylne. These proposals formed the basis of the realised building by Robert Joy of 1771–74, where the five-window-wide central building is flanked by four-window-wide wings with pedimented end-pavilions (PLATE 174). Over the middle of the central block is a charming octagonal tower and spire, converting what might be an Irish Palladian country house into an institutional building, something the Irish shared with the Scots, for Hutcheson's Hospital, Ingram Street, Glasgow, of 1802–05 by David Hamilton, also has a steeple perched on top of the roof, but the Glasgow building is far more grand, institutional, and urban than the delightful Belfast example.[8]

Buildings for Military Use

If Gaols were often among the most impressive examples of Georgian Architecture, the biggest buildings were those associated with the military. That grandeur was often well to the fore was due in no small part to the fact that Vanbrugh was Comptroller of the Works from 1702. Unquestionably one of the most remarkable military buildings was the Dockyard Gate at Chatham of around 1717, and probably by Vanbrugh, for it is in his 'Castle Style' and looks like a Roman gate (PLATE 175). Also probably by Vanbrugh is the Model Room of the Royal Arsenal at Woolwich of 1719: it is of brick, with massive rusticated piers carrying plain piers pierced with slit-windows, and carrying an open-based pediment. Windows are circular, semicircular-headed, or square-headed if of the slit type. The overall effect is tremendous, fortress-like, forbidding, and massive. The entire Royal Arsenal complex must have looked stunning when new.

Bareness, stripped Classicism, and bold massing characterise Georgian military buildings, of which one of the noblest and impressive structures must be Fort George, sited on a promontory opposite Fortrose and Rosemarkie Bay, where the Moray Firth narrows north-east of Inverness. It was begun in 1746 by William Adam, Mason to the Board of Ordnance in North Britain, and completed by John and Robert Adam after 1748. The mighty Ravelin Gate is very Vanbrughian.

The vast symmetrical ranges of three-storey brick buildings that comprise the Royal Artillery Barracks at Woolwich were erected 1775–1808: there is a triumphal arch in the central block, while flanking blocks (each twenty-one windows wide) have pediments. James Wyatt was responsible for the additional barracks and riding-school of 1802–08. The scale of these vast ranges of buildings has no parallel anywhere except in St Petersburg in Russia.

Another enormous military building was the Royal Military Academy at Sandhurst, Berkshire, of 1807–12, with its Giant Greek Doric hexastyle portico and plain nine-window-wide wings with projecting three-window-wide end-pavilions. The architect was John Sanders (1768–1826), who also designed the Royal Military Asylum (now the Duke of York's Barracks) at Chelsea, of 1801–03.

If the Jacobite Rebellions of 1715 and 1745 had created the catalyst for military fortifications and buildings such as Woolwich Arsenal, the new Barracks and Ordnance Buildings at Berwick-on-Tweed of 1717 (probably by Vanbrugh), and Fort George, the Napoleonic Wars also created the need for military buildings. Rathmullen Fort, Lough Swilly, Co Donegal, of 1810, is a fine example, with battered walls, glacis, and gun ports. More common are the so-called Martello towers constructed around the east and southern coasts as a precaution against invasion by the French. The term *Martello* is a corruption of *Mortella* in Corsica at which was a circular tower which the British fleet had some difficulty in capturing in 1794. Such towers were circular, with battered sides, and, with a small garrison, could be defended against a larger force: they were common around the Mediterranean. British military experts considered that they would be of great value in

PLATE 175 *The Dockyard Gate, Chatham, of* c *1717, probably by Sir John Vanbrugh, in his 'Castle' style* (AFK G25854).

defence, and the erection of 'martello' towers was urged on the Government, which authorised the construction of several from 1804. The towers are small circular or elliptical forts with massive walls containing vaulted rooms for the garrisons, and have platforms for the guns. Some of the finest examples can be seen on the Suffolk coast from Aldeburgh to Bawdsey. Their construction was carried out under the direction of General William Twiss (1745–1827), who was instructed in 1805 to build the system of defences, and most were in place by 1812. Twiss was assisted by Captain Ford, who seems to have been the supervising engineer on the spot.

Educational Buildings and Charity Schools

Clearly the finest buildings for educational purposes were those erected for the Universities, and at Oxford, especially, new ideas were exploited. Reference has already been made to the importance of Peckwater Quadrangle at Christ Church, Oxford, by Aldrich, the first palatial Palladian composition in Britain (PLATE 9). The fourth side of this Quad acquired the gigantic Library, based on Michelangelo's palatial structures on the Capitol, Rome, and was started in 1717: the original ideas came from Aldrich, but the architect was George Clarke (1661–1736), who became the leading architectural guru at Oxford. Christ Church Library has a Giant Corinthian Order of seven bays, with a lower Order of Doric clearly derived from the Capitoline Palace. Clarke had been consulted about the design of the Clarendon Building, which was erected to designs by Hawksmoor in 1712–15. Clarke also had an important role, with Hawksmoor, in the design of Queen's College, Oxford (1710–21), and Clarke provided the master-mason William Townesend with designs for the New Buildings at Magdalen College of 1733. Clarke was closely involved in the design of Worcester College.

So Oxford, at the beginning of the Georgian period, not only embraced the Baroque language of Vanbrugh and Hawksmoor, but was in the vanguard of Palladianism before

Lord Burlington took up the cudgels on behalf of the Revival. Furthermore, Oxford saw not only the Gothic Survival of the seventeenth century, but the beginnings of Gothic Revival as at All Souls' College, erected in 1716–35 to designs by Hawksmoor: the towers are loosely based on those of Beverley Minster in Yorkshire, but the church of St Anne, Limehouse, has an echo in the crowning concoctions. Hawksmoor was also responsible for the breathtaking Radcliffe Square, Oxford: the Bodleian Library, Brasenose, and St Mary's church were there already, but Hawksmoor provided the Codrington Library and the enchanting screen-wall and gate linking the Codrington to the Medieval chapel to the south, and he proposed a large domed free-standing structure in the centre. Gibbs developed this central idea when he created the Radcliffe Camera (in which Palladian and Baroque motifs are cleverly mixed) to stand in the middle of the square, in 1737 (PLATE 45). It is one of the finest architectural ensembles in England.

Gibbs's Cambridge Senate House of 1721–30 also mingles Baroque and Palladian themes, and he built the Fellows' Building at King's College in 1723–29. The latter with its rusticated base, central pediment, thermal window over the curiously over-sized central aedicule containing the entrance, and keystones over the windows, is cleverly related to the soaring verticality of the Medieval chapel. However, before Gibbs arrived on the scene, Cambridge's equivalent to Aldrich and Clarke, Sir James Burrough (1691–1764), of Gonville and Caius, had produced a design for the Senate House not unlike that built by Gibbs. Burrough was responsible for the Palladian Fellows' Building at Peterhouse (1738–42) and for the refronting of the principal court there (1754–56), as well as other works in Cambridge.

The Gothic Revival came later to Cambridge, but included the charming screen at King's College, with Perpendicular tracery and gatehouse (in which reminiscences of the turrets of the chapel, of Wren's Tom Tower at Oxford, and of Hawksmoor's All Souls' gate at Oxford occur), by William Wilkins, of 1824–28. Wilkins, who could often be insufferably dull, was anything but stodgy here: he also designed the New Buildings opposite the chapel. He was responsible for New Court at Trinity (1821–23, in Tudor Gothic), and New Court at Corpus Christi (1823–27, in Gothic). Thomas Rickman designed the pretty New Court at St John's College of 1827-31 with Henry Hutchinson (1800–31), who was responsible for the Gothic Bridge at St John's.

But of course it was Wilkins's Downing College at Cambridge of 1804–21 which heralded a full-blooded Greek Revival, largely through the influence of Thomas Hope. In 1806–09 Wilkins built the East India (now Haileybury) College, Hertfordshire, in the Greek Revival style, with noble Ionic porticoes breaking up the forty-two bays (the gigantic, even monstrous *Rundbogenstil* dome is not by Wilkins, but by Arthur Blomfield, who ought to have known better). (Sir) William Tite (1798–1873) designed Mill Hill School, Middlesex, of 1825–27, in a Greek Revival style, much influenced by Wilkins's work at Haileybury, but Oxford appears to have avoided early nineteenth-century antiquarianism with the exception of the Clarendon Press building of 1826–30 by Daniel Robertson (with the north wing completed by Edward Blore [1787–1879]), an essay in Roman Classicism, complete with triumphal arch as the entrance to Walton Street.

Theodore Jacobsen's main quadrangle of Trinity College, Dublin, of 1752–59, with its west front derived from Campbell's third design for Wanstead, is one of the noblest Palladian collegiate compositions in the British Isles. Trinity also has Colonel Thomas Burgh's (n 1670) grand and solemn Library of 1712–32, and Sir William Chambers's facing blocks of the Examination School and Chapel of 1775–1800. The Provost's House is derived from Burlington's house for General Wade in London (in turn descended from Palladio), but it has a remarkable and original saloon which extends the full length of the first floor. The architect is not known, although John Smyth was paid for plans in 1759, and Henry Keene may have been involved, as may John Sanderson, but the evidence is so far lacking. Whoever was responsible for the Provost's House, however, was no mean architect, and a cut above the ordinary Palladian. In London, incidentally, Theodore Jacobsen was influenced by Kent in his designs for the Foundlings' Hospital, Coram's Fields, of 1742–52, executed by James Horne (ob 1756).

Edinburgh University acquired a handsome Neo-Classical quadrangle designed by Robert Adam in 1789, and completed (with certain modifications) by William Henry Playfair in 1817–26. The street frontage has a great portico. Then there was the Greek Revival composition of University College, London, by William Wilkins, from 1827, a serene work that has a certain grandeur.

Many fine Georgian charity schools were associated with almshouses. One of the most beautiful is the Southwell School, Downpatrick, Co Down, a charming composition in brick with two pavilions linked by means of quadrants, and with a simple belfry over the centre block (PLATE 176). Regrettably, it has been obscured by the raising of the road at the east end of the Cathedral Church of the Holy Trinity. It was built in 1733, possibly to designs by Sir Edward Lovett Pearce, and was one of many so-called 'Bluecoat' schools, named after the uniforms worn by the pupils. There were other schools provided by individuals, or, more commonly by Companies, such as the worshipful Company of Drapers of the City of London: these schools were often of the 'Lancasterian' type, that is, based on the monitorial form of instruction established by Joseph Lancaster (1778–1838).

There was a fine example at Moneymore, Co Londonderry of 1820, by Jesse Gibson (*c* 1748–1828), for The Drapers' Company, and another at Ballykelly, of 1829–30, by Richard Suter, for The Fishmongers' Company.[9] These simple Neo-Classical buildings consisted of a central block (usually the Master's house) flanked by school-rooms for boys and girls, with a yard and privies. Compositions were symmetrical. Often, such charity schools were built with courts, open or closed, and are usually very plain in terms of architecture, the only embellishment being the tablet recording the gift, or some nod towards grandeur in the entrance. The line between schools, almshouses, and infirmaries is often blurred.

Much grander were the purpose-built schools, like Haileybury or Mill Hill. Other examples are Dollar Academy by W. H. Playfair of 1818–20 (Greek Revival) and the magnificent Royal High School, Edinburgh, of 1825–29 by Thomas Hamilton (PLATE 95). The latter is comparable with the finest Neo-Classical work on the Continent, and is composed on a platform of stone, with various pavilions. Severe Greek Doric was also employed by William Burn in his John Watson's School, Edinburgh, of 1825–28. Tudor Gothic was used for

some schools, such as Elizabeth College, Guernsey, of 1826 by John Wilson (*ob* 1866), and the extensions to Harrow by C. R. Cockerell of 1818.

As indicated above, the line between almshouses, infirmaries, and schools is often unclear, and it is common to find two or all functions in the one building. By 1820, however, schools were often purpose-built, and only contained the class-rooms and accommodation for the Schoolmaster, as in the Lancastrian Schools at Moneymore and Ballykelly. The Belfast Charitable Society's Clifton House (PLATE 174) combined almshouse and infirmary, where from 1776 for a period poor children were taken in to be educated and supported, but from 1868 they were segregated from the aged residents, and by 1882 no more children were taken in.[10] From the very beginning the Southwell Charity in Downpatrick (PLATE 176) was a school and almshouses, but there were many buildings that were partly almshouses, and remained so. The almshouses at Boyton in Suffolk of 1736, with a wing to the west of 1828 and another to the east of 1860 (both continuing the plain brick architectural language) are as plain as possible, and were always almshouses, pure and simple.

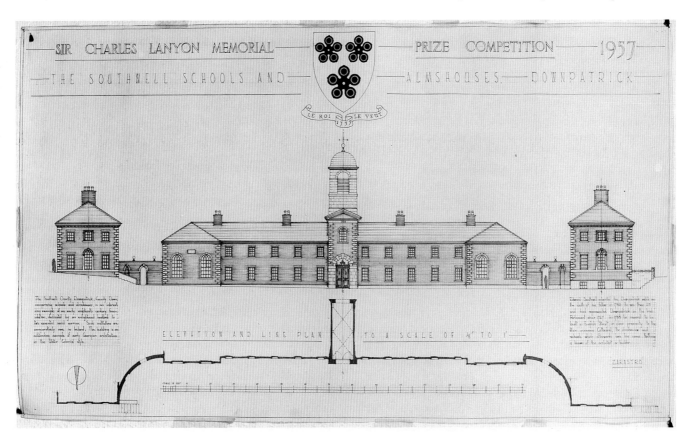

PLATE 176 *Southwell Schools and Almshouses, Downpatrick, Co Down, of 1733. From a measured drawing by the Author* (JSC).

Buildings for Professional Organisations

The colleges of Oxford and Cambridge, with their quads and courts, stairs and sets of rooms, and communal dining- and common-rooms were the models for the Inns of Court. These latter housed not only the legal profession in apartments in long ranges of terraces around or in courts, but members of other professions as well. Mention has already been made of Sir Robert Taylor's Offices at Lincoln's Inn Fields of 1774–80 which were designed as such, but this was rare. Verulam Buildings, Gray's Inn, of 1805–11, was a conventional terrace of rooms served by communal stone stairs with iron balustrades, and it contained the offices of many non-legal people, including the occasional architect.

PLATE 177 *The Royal Institution, Edinburgh, of 1822–26, by W.H. Playfair. An essay in Graeco-Egyptian Neo-Classicism* (RCAHMS ED/7842).

The King's Inns in Dublin by James Gandon of 1795 was designed as offices for the legal profession, with chambers, a library, and a dining-hall. The same architect's Four Courts in Dublin (begun in 1777 by Thomas Cooley) not only has a fine Neo-Classical plan in which the Four Courts are arranged round the Rotunda, but had purpose-built offices associated with the Courts. Gandon's Custom House in Dublin is, of course, another singularly important Georgian Classical building, purpose-made for its function. Gandon, as has been noted, was influenced by Sir William Chambers's Somerset House in London of 1776–1801, another purpose-built structure designed to house centralised offices for the Government (Audit Office, Salt and Land Tax Office, Stamp Office, offices of the Duchies of Cornwall and Lancaster, and Navy offices) as well as the Royal Academy and the Society of

Antiquaries. The Royal Academy Picture Gallery was top-lit, with Thermal windows with semi-elliptical arches instead of the usual semicircle, and was one of the first such galleries. It is now back in use as a gallery as part of the Courtauld Art Gallery. Somerset House is the grandest essay in Anglo-French Neo-Classicism in England, and was much more assured, masculine, and tough than the work of Chambers's rival, Adam, whose attenuated delicacies were starting to pall. While Chambers successfully merged grandly Roman flavours, French Neo-Classicism, and Palladian compositional techniques, the fact that Somerset House is one of the first offices for bureaucrats and Government tax-collectors and administrators in Britain makes it important as a precedent (PLATES 112–113). But the great palatial building also housed those two important institutions of the Georgian period, the Academy and the Antiquaries, both of which did much to promote Taste and Scholarship.

George Dance Junior built the Royal College of Surgeons in Lincoln's Inn Fields in collaboration with James Lewis in 1806–13: it had a tough unfluted Greek Doric portico, the first in London, but later fluted when Charles Barry rebuilt the College in 1835–37. Robert Smirke followed with the Royal College of Physicians building in Trafalgar Square in 1822–25, in Greek Ionic (the southern portico was added in 1925). Lewis Vulliamy (1791–1871) designed the Law Society's Hall, Chancery Lane, of 1828–32 in the Greek

Revival style, while the Royal Society of Edinburgh, Society of Antiquaries of Scotland, the Institution for the Encouragement of Fine Arts, and the Board of Trustees for the Manufactories and Fisheries were housed in the extraordinary Graeco-Egyptian Royal Institution in Edinburgh by W. H. Playfair of 1822–35 (PLATE 177). Playfair also designed the Surgeons' Hall, Nicolson Street, Edinburgh, of 1829, a fine Ionic pile with prostyle hexastyle portico.

Conclusion

There is no doubt that there was an immense amount of pleasing architecture created during the Georgian period, some of it astonishingly powerful and full of poetry, and most of it, at the least, agreeable. From enormous ranges of buildings such as the Royal Artillery Barracks at Woolwich to the lock-keeper's cottage on a canal, the Georgians seemed to get their proportions right. One has to admire the utter simplicity and rightness, the use of materials, and the junctions, found in canal lock-gates, warehouses, docks, bridges, gate-lodges, and forts. Refined austerity, clarity, and logic, in Sir Albert Richardson's words, sum it all up.

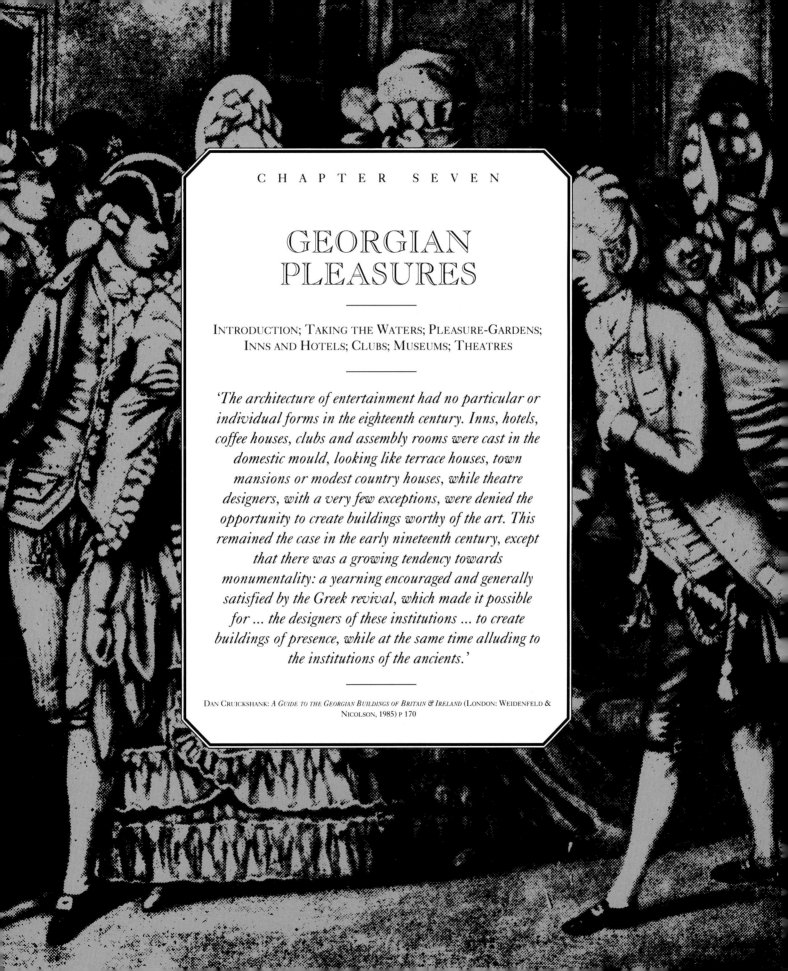

CHAPTER SEVEN

GEORGIAN PLEASURES

INTRODUCTION; TAKING THE WATERS; PLEASURE-GARDENS;
INNS AND HOTELS; CLUBS; MUSEUMS; THEATRES

*'The architecture of entertainment had no particular or
individual forms in the eighteenth century. Inns, hotels,
coffee houses, clubs and assembly rooms were cast in the
domestic mould, looking like terrace houses, town
mansions or modest country houses, while theatre
designers, with a very few exceptions, were denied the
opportunity to create buildings worthy of the art. This
remained the case in the early nineteenth century, except
that there was a growing tendency towards
monumentality: a yearning encouraged and generally
satisfied by the Greek revival, which made it possible
for ... the designers of these institutions ... to create
buildings of presence, while at the same time alluding to
the institutions of the ancients.'*

DAN CRUICKSHANK: *A GUIDE TO THE GEORGIAN BUILDINGS OF BRITAIN & IRELAND* (LONDON: WEIDENFELD &
NICOLSON, 1985) P 170

Introduction

Walter Ison, in *The Georgian Buildings of Bath*,[1] has described how Bath 'underwent a complete metamorphosis' in the Georgian period. 'It was no ordinary city of haphazard form …, but a pleasure resort, a fashionable metropolis designed as a setting for the brilliant social parade'. This place, with its medicinal springs and beautiful site, was chosen by the 'arbiters of fashion to be their summer retreat, and following in their wake came all of those possessed of rank or fortune, ostensibly seeking health from the waters, and enjoyment of simple rustic pleasures'.[2] However, it was not all country dances on the bowling-green, gentle perambulations around the town, or sipping of the waters, but almost continuous gambling at cards.

Many adventurers came to Bath, but one soon became virtual King and Chief Arbiter of Taste at Bath: his name was Richard 'Beau' Nash (1674–1761), who rose to eminence by dressing to the very edge of his finances, distinguishing himself by his manners, and by leading a life of polite dissipation without any visible means of support. Bath had been given the Royal *Imprimatur* in 1703 when Queen Anne visited, and Nash arrived in 1705 to cash in on the gaming-tables. To his consternation he found Poor Form was everywhere apparent, and provincialism was rife, with no code of etiquette, and none of dress. Ladies met under canvas for a Dish of Tea, and cards, and men arrived at the dance in top-boots. Lodgings were squalid and dirty, sedan-chairmen were insolent, and the tone of the place was clearly very low.

With charm and the gift of the gab Nash soon engaged a band of musicians and began to raise subscriptions for the building of Assembly Rooms. He drew up a Code of Behaviour which was posted in the Pump-Room, repaired all the roads, banned the wearing of swords (thereby reducing at a stroke the almost daily woundings and fatalities caused by duelling), laid down standards of dress, reduced the habit of promiscuous smoking (especially in mixed company), tamed the sedan-chairmen, and reduced the extortions of the lodging-house keepers. He laid down times for all balls and assemblies, and his regulations were enforced. He even compelled a Royal Princess and the Duchess of Queensberry to conform to his rules of behaviour and dress.[3] By the time Nash's rule had ended, Bath could vie with any city in Europe for the politeness of its amusements and the elegance of its buildings, accommodation, and public rooms.

Mention has already been made of the squares, circus, crescents, and terraces erected by the Woods, and how Palladianism had given Bath a homogeneity, enhanced by the use of the local limestone. As well as these there were assembly-rooms, card-rooms, tea-rooms, pump-rooms, shops, and so on. The Public Assembly, which formed a regular feature of fashionable life in the Georgian period, was a meeting of polite society of both sexes for purposes of conversation, gallantry, news, gossip, and play, while Private Assemblies were receptions or 'at-homes'. Assembly-Rooms were specially built for Public Assemblies, later used for balls, concerts, and meetings.

Assembly-Rooms were often thereafter provided in other towns. York acquired its fine Palladian Assembly-Rooms in 1731 to designs by Burlington derived from Palladio's so-called 'Egyptian' Hall (PLATE 16): this had a colonnade all around with a passage between it and the wall, and a clerestory over the colonnade, and was the model for Dance's Mansion House in London. The Rotunda, Dublin, of 1754 by John Ensor, had a card-room by which it was attached to Cassels's Hospital, and was subsequently improved by Gandon. Assembly-Rooms of circular form were unusual, one of the few being the Montpellier Pump Room at Cheltenham by George Allen Underwood (*c* 1793–1829) of 1817 to which J.B. Papworth (1775–1847) added the Rotunda in 1825. Provincial Assembly-Rooms were now unusual in Georgian times, and many towns had them, including Belfast, which had a fine room in the Old Exchange, designed by Sir Robert Taylor, of 1776. One of the most remarkable of all Assembly-Rooms was the beautiful Wellington Rooms, Mount Pleasant, Liverpool, a stupendously pure Greek Revival building by Edmund Aikin (1780–1820) of 1815–16, now the Irish Centre, and somewhat decayed. Many Assembly-Rooms were situated in buildings used for other purposes: Newtownards had Assembly-Rooms in its market-house, and Huntingdon had one in its town hall. Samuel Beazley designed the Royal Assembly-Rooms in Leamington Spa.

Taking the Waters

Bath set the scene, and it was not long before the existence or discovery of a spring might encourage other developments. Cheltenham was a spa town with elegant Assembly-Rooms, and Buxton in Derbyshire was developed from 1779 (although the springs had been known since Roman times). Carr of York designed the celebrated Crescent close to the St Ann's Well for the Fifth Duke of Devonshire, who wanted to create a new Bath in Derbyshire. But while these developments, to which must be added Leamington and other spas, were charming, and often inspired excellent architecture, springs could also help to create smaller pleasure-gardens and 'spaws', many of which were ephemeral, and had buildings that were unpretentious or 'rustick' in character.

It will be a surprise to many to know that there were many spas in what is now London. The town of Spa in Belgium gave its name to any place that became popular because of its mineral springs, and the name is derived from a word meaning 'fountain'. Several springs and wells in and around London were discovered that contained salts of magnesium, sodium, and iron, and landowners were quick to exploit these by building well-houses, pump-rooms, halls, and restaurants, and by laying out gardens. Chalybeate waters were much sought after, for 'cleansing the blood', 'opening obstructions, allaying vapours', and curing distempers. At a time when alcohol was consumed on a tremendous scale, such waters were recognised as palliatives for liver, spleen, pancreas, and stomach disorders, while jaundice, scurvy, and even 'Cholerick Passion' could be eased, or so we are assured by the broadsheets that advertised those long-defunct spas of London.

Pancras Well, for example, was sited south of Old St Pancras church, and lies somewhere underneath the Midland Railway Terminus. The Wells buildings were extensive, and included two pump-rooms, a Long-Room, a House of Entertainment, a Ladies' Walk and Hall, and extensive gardens, landscaped and planted. The Wells, with waters both purgative and chalybeate (meaning impregnated with iron), were said to be successful in 'Curing the most Obstinate Scurvy, Kings-Evil, Leprosy, and all other breakings out and defilements of the Skin'. Success was also claimed for the curing of 'Running Sores, Cancers, Eating Ulcers', and 'The Piles'. In addition, the waters could cure any 'Corruption of the Blood', all 'Inflammatory Distempers', disorders of the stomach and bowels, and even 'Sinking of the Spirits and Vapours'. Colds, Worms, Stones, and Gravels, and even 'Decays of Nature' in either sex could not prevail against these powerful Waters. Wines and ales were also sold on the premises, and a herd of cows was kept in the extensive grounds so that fresh milk, cream, and syllabubs were available.

Adjacent to the St Pancras Wells was St Chad's Well, at Battle Bridge, near what is now King's Cross Station. St Chad was the Patron Saint of medicinal springs, and the Well was noted as a purging spring: it had pleasant gardens attached to it, and, unlike many other London 'spaws', was always respectable, in deference, perchance, to its sacred origins. The waters were rich in sodium and potassium, and were heated before being drunk: they were celebrated for the alleviation of liver disorders, dropsy, and scrofula, and were 'mildly tonic, and powerfully diuretic'. The pump-room was clapboarded and rustic in appearance.

Bagnigge Wells was situated in King's Cross Road, and in the 1760s became fashionable. Pumps were erected in a

PLATE 178 *Bagnigge Wells, London, from the* Sunday Ramble *of 1774, engraved by Page* (JSC).

pavilion under a 'dome superb', gardens were hastily planted, and arbours and gazebos were created. An engraving by Page (PLATE 178), published in the *Sunday Ramble* in 1774, shows the gardens, where

> *'Salubrious Waters, Tea, and Wine,*
> *'Here you may have, and also dine;*
> *But, as ye through the Garden rove,*
> *Beware, fond Youths, the Darts of Love.'*

This gives an indication of the tone of the place, which clearly became a rendezvous early in its heyday. The gardens seem to have been pretty: the trees were arranged in espalier fashion and clipped; there was a Chinee-Bridge; a Cupid held the neck of a swan out of the beak of which rose a fountain of Spa-water; and Dishes of Tea were taken among the trellises and leafy arbours. A notion of the swank and high fashion of Bagnigge Wells may be gleaned from a picture of *The Bread and Butter Manufactory; or the Humours of Bagnigge Wells*, published by J. R. Smith in 1772 (PLATE 179). This is an interesting view, for it shows the interior of a typical London Spa Long Room of the period. A fashionable gathering is

PLATE 179 The Bread and Butter Manufactory: or the Humours of Bagnigge Wells, *published by J.R.Smith in 1772. The scene is the Long Room of the Spa* (JSC).

promenading, while other persons are taking Dishes of Tea; the room is lighted by brazen candelabra with waxen tapers, and music was provided on an organ. The moods of the company are clearly shown, and much ogling and quizzing is evident. In the middle of the picture a richly clad lady on the arm of one gallant is receiving a salute from another, to the mortification of her escort. The swagger, the elegance, and the gossiping company are vividly displayed. Such detailed pictures of the ephemeral life of a London spa are rare. Garrick's *Bon Ton* of 1775 has an allusion to Bagnigge Wells in the Prologue:

> *'Bon Ton's the space' twixt Saturday and Monday,*
> *And riding in a one-horse chair on Sunday:*
> *'Tis drinking Tea on summer afternoons*
> *At Bagnigge Wells with china and gilt spoons.'*

The poet Churchill noted in 1779 that at Bagnigge Wells

'Unfledged Templars first as fops parade,
And new-made Ensigns sport their first Cockade.'

By Regency times, however, the Wells became less fashionable, but remained popular with local people, the men indulging in the drinking of ale and the playing of bowls, while their families consumed vast quantities of muffins and tea, and listened to the threepenny concerts in the surroundings once frequented by the Exquisite Mob. In 1844 the gardens were closed, for, as Pinks observed in his study of Clerkenwell, it had long been the case that persons of

'The City to Bagnigge Wells repair,
To swallow dust, and call it air.'

Yet the name was perpetuated in The New Bagnigge Wells, otherwise the Bayswater Tea Gardens, opened as London expanded northwards and the purity of waters could no longer be guaranteed. To judge from the numerous illustrations of The New Bagnigge Wells, however, the place does not appear to have been noted for its tone, and remained in essence a Tea Garden until around 1850.

The fame of Tunbridge Wells, in Kent, led entrepreneurs to ape the establishment there, and the Islington Spa, for example, was called the 'new Tunbridge Wells'. St Pancras Wells was also called Pancridge Wells, to give it added respectability. Such attempts, however, were not always successful, for most of the London Spas were frequented by a mixed company of

'Wits, Captains, Politicians, Trulls,
Sots, Devotees, Pimps, Poets, Gulls,'

as the author of *The Humours of Tunbridge Wells* declared in 1734. The spas therefore had reputations not only as watering-places, but as convenient spots for all dalliance where one could

'Scud away to Tunbridge Wells,
To mix with vulgar Beaux and Belles.'

Islington Spa was near what is now Rosebery Avenue, and entertainments there included a dance-hall, a card-room, and a gaming-room, as well as extensive gardens and good restaurants which ensured that the Spa became popular with society anxious 'promiscuously to chatter'. Beau Nash and Royalty attended the Islington Spa, and it became the 'Tunbridge Wells of London' by 1733.[4] There, 'Lords, Milkmaids, Duchesses, and Clowns, in all their various Dishabille', gathered together to take the Waters. An Exquisite Mob, led by a Beau, adorned the gardens and Long Room, and masquerades

of suitable style to attract high fashion were held from time to time, when Intrigue and Passion were indulged. No doubt many gowns, like My Lady Bunbutter's, in Compton Mackenzie's *The Passionate Elopement*, were torn 'on a monkey's tail', during some Chinee Masquerade. In the latter part of the eighteenth century Islington Spa declined, but was used as an amusement-and-afternoon-tea-garden until the early 1800s.

Most 'Spaw' gardens appear to have been of the instant variety, and fairly large trees were in great demand to grace the walks. Trellis-work supported climbing plants, and regiments of gardeners were employed to ensure that the gardens were kept as spruce as possible. Espalier growths were encouraged, and many trees and shrubs were in large pots, so that they could be moved in inclement weather. Yet even some of the arbours had an ephemeral quality, and were essentially the backcloth against which parades, fopperies, and intrigues could take place. Today, there is hardly a trace, save for street names, and the Spas have vanished with the Beaux and Belles whose Exquisite Passions were once inflamed by the music, wine, and foods of the vanished Spas of London.

Sadler's Wells has some claim to have been a holy well with medicinal qualities in the Middle Ages. However, it got its present name from an impresario who founded a concert-room there. Sadler rediscovered the well, which was found to contain chalybeate water, and judicious advertising soon encouraged the public to take the Waters at Sadler's Wells. The liquid was made more palatable by the addition of *Capillaire*, a flavoured syrup, and retailed at the vast price of sixpence per glass. A season's treatment would cost a guinea. The Waters were regarded as a cure for all 'hectic and hypochondriacal Heat, for beginning Consumptions, for Scurvy, Diabetes, for bringing away Gravel, Stones in the Kidney, &c'. The Wells incurred the jealous wrath of the owners of nearby Spas, and a campaign of denunciation soon reduced the popularity of Sadler's Wells as a Watering-Place. The 'Musick-House' continued to thrive, however, as a resort of 'strolling damsels, half-pay officers, peripatetic tars, butchers, and others that are musically inclined', so doubtless other Spas did well out of the increase in Pox that would be traced to such promiscuous company. However, the Sadler's Wells Theatre far outshone the Spa in fame, but the gardens and buildings were very pretty, and remained popular well into the last century.

Not far from Sadler's Wells was the London Spaw, which enjoyed a dubious reputation as a Spa until around 1810. It was situated on the Duck, or Ducking-Pond Fields, in Clerkenwell, which later became known as Spa Fields. The 'Spaw' was apparently founded by a publican who discovered a spring in his garden, and saw that it might increase trade. Beer sold was brewed on the premises, using the spring water, and medicinal properties were claimed for it. The London Spaw was frequented by the Lower Orders, and a contemporary jingle claimed:

> *'Some go but just to drink the water*
> *Some for the ale which they like better.'*

The 'Spaw' had arbours, trees arranged in espalier fashion, and trellis-works, but the tone of the place never seems to have been noted for its politeness. It is remembered today in the name of a public house near Finsbury Town Hall.

Unquestionably, one of the most important of the Spas of London was Hampstead. A medicinal spring was known from early times, and in 1698 this spring and some acres of land, later known as the Wells Charity Estate, were given to the Hampstead poor by Susannah Noel, Countess of Gainsborough, and her son, Baptist, the Third Earl. In the early years of the eighteenth century the waters were on sale in flasks, and both the ephemeral flasks and chalybeate wells are celebrated in Hampstead's present-day street-names.

Buildings associated with the spring were erected in what is now Well Walk, and gardens were laid out and planted. The largest room of the complex was known as the Assembly-Room, and could accommodate five hundred people at concerts. Inevitably, there were also a Long-Room, and a Pump-Room where the water was dispensed to those taking the cure. The medical profession had a high regard for the waters, which were thought of as being superior to almost any of the chalybeate springs of England. Thus, the beauties of the surroundings, and the quality of the concerts in the Assembly-Rooms, ensured that Hampstead Spa had a gratifyingly higher tone than that of many of the London Spas. At Hampstead, courtesans with airs and scanty dress vied with amateur ladies, overdressed but with no airs, for the favours of the Exquisites. Even working-girls, dressed to the nines in creations of their own labours, danced minuets, while their 'Cloaths hung as loose about them as their Reputations'. The Season at Hampstead lasted from May to October, and, while many people lodged near by, most habitués could easily drive out from Town for the day. There were gaming-tables, dancing-rooms, and plenty of 'consorts of both vocal and instrumental musick'. Inevitably, the Spa developed a raffish reputation as a rendezvous and place of pleasure. Nemesis came in 1725 when some of the buildings changed their use and became a Dissenters' Chapel.

Attempts were made subsequently to revive Hampstead Spa, and a new set of buildings was erected in Well Walk. The 'Inexhaustable Fountain of Health', as Hampstead Wells was called, was extolled by physicians, and Hampstead remained popular among middle-class Londoners who enjoyed the fresh air and the waters.

Comparable with the brief reign of Hampstead Spa was that of Acton Wells, popular in the early-Georgian period. The waters at Acton were said to be cathartic, and contained Glauber's Salts claimed to be even more efficacious than the powerful sulphate springs of Cheltenham Spa. Acton Wells attracted its clientèle in much the same way as did Hampstead Spa, but the amusements do not appear to have been on the same scale, and Acton was a much more sober, respectable, and serious place. Acton had an Assembly-Room that was pleasantly proportioned, but had none of the grand style of Hampstead, and was free from any dubious reputation as a haunt of courtesans.

There were many other spas, including one at Kilburn, at the junction of what is now Kilburn High Road and Belsize Road: this was an alkaline spring which fed a reservoir in the garden of the Bell Tavern. The waters were heavily charged with carbon dioxide, and so probably resembled the waters of the springs of Saint-Yorre or Célestine at Vichy. The Bell Tavern had fine gardens and salubrious buildings where 'musick', dancing, and other diversions could be enjoyed, and they were still in use as Tea-Gardens until well into Queen Victoria's reign. The New Wells, near the London Spaw in Clerkenwell, also had gardens, but it also had a theatre, a grotto, and even a menagerie. Sydenham Wells was situated in the country, and the Spa was 'Rustick', with no amusements except a gypsy fortune-teller and unlimited supplies of brandy. The waters, however, could open all obstructions of the liver, spleen, 'Mesaraick Veins, Pancreas, the Biliary, Uterine, and Urinary Passages', and could cure 'Haemorrhoides', 'Fits, Hypochondriacks, Barrenness, Worms, and all manner of Cutaneous Distempers'; proud boasts indeed. Streatham acquired a pretty well-house with a bust of Aesculapius in a niche over the door, and there were other spas at Finch's Grotto Gardens near St George's Fields, Dulwich, and Biggin Hill. Even Hoxton had a well of 'Aromatick Waters', supposedly 'Balsamic', which had remarkable powers as a purgative, responsible for much 'bustle and ferment'. The mind boggles.

Pleasure-Gardens

Far to the west, near the Parish church of St Marylebone, was a Spa of late foundation at Marylebone Gardens, which themselves originated in the joining of a place of public resort known as The Rose to a large bowling-green. These gardens were improved in 1738, and theatres, tea-arbours, musick-rooms, and other attractions were added. Buildings were elegant, with the upper floors

PLATE 184 *The Tontine Inn at Stourport-on-Severn, from* A South-West
Prospect or Perspective View of Stourport, *of 1776. Note the locks,
basin, and handsome bridge* (Worcester County Council Records).

brewing trade and with the hop-growing areas of Herefordshire and Worcestershire. The little town itself has some excellent Georgian buildings.

One of the largest and most ambitious of Georgian Hotels was built as a political gesture by the local Tory candidate to curry favour among the residents of Stamford, Lincolnshire, who favoured the Whigs, led by the Cecils. This was the handsome Greek Revival Stamford Hotel, beside St Mary's church, which features a Giant Order derived from the Choragic Monument of Lysicrates in Athens. The architect was John Linnell Bond (1764–1837), who carried out other works for the Noel family, Earls of Gainsborough. The Stamford Hotel dates from c 1810–29. Inside were Graeco-Egyptian chimney-pieces of marble, and a statue of Justice by J. C. F. Rossi of 1810 in artificial stone (Rossi also carried out work for the handsome hotel in Leicester, as previously noted above). Regrettably, the Stamford Hotel has been gutted in recent years.

The Georgian town offered diversions of many kinds, including concerts, operas, oratorios, plays, and pleasure-gardens. There were plenty of bookshops, and shops selling goods of all kinds were common. There were 'cook-shops' with meat on spits, and all classes could go and eat there, asking for whatever cut took the fancy: this was placed on a plate with salt and mustard, and served with a roll of bread and a bottle of beer. Slightly more up-market were the chop-houses, beefsteak-houses, and coffee-houses. Chop-houses were large, comfortable rooms, fitted out with large tables and benches, top-hat racks, and usually partitions between each table with its benches. Such an arrangement survives at Simpson's, Cornhill, in the City of London. Meat, bread, and beer were served. There were cheaper establishments called dining-cellars, where broth, bread, cheese, and occasionally meat could be had.

The fact that London had a very large number of cook-shops, chop-houses, and dining-rooms suggests that a significant proportion of the populace did not dine at home, and this was probably because most people lived in rooms (or even one room) where conditions were less than congenial, and to entertain friends would have been impossible. Coffee-houses served coffee, provided a fire, and were agreeable places where gossip, business, and news could be exchanged or transacted. Meals could also be ordered and delivered to lodgings. In addition, there were taverns offering congenial and comfortable surroundings, various rooms, and food and drink. Taverns usually had a public parlour, a tap-room, kitchen, private parlour, and a 'coffee-room' which meant a restaurant divided into stalls for each table. There was no bar in the modern sense, and drinks were brought to customers by waiters, barmaids, or pot-boys. The 'bar' was a room where the public could not enter, but where orders could be given or issued: it was a kind of reception-desk with a glazed partition around it.[7]

Some taverns hired rooms out for meetings, or for members of Clubs to meet before they acquired premises of their own. So the Georgian city, especially London or Bath, could offer a variety of accommodation, diversions and eating-places.

Clubs

Purpose-built clubhouses were erected for Georgian gentry who felt that the like-minded should meet in salubrious premises rather than in coffee-houses and taverns. Standards of comfort were rising rapidly, and in 1775 John Crunden (c 1745–1835) designed the Savoir Vivre Club, later called Boodle's, in St James's Street, London. Crunden also designed the Assembly Rooms of the Castle Hotel, Brighton, around the same time. Boodle's has a handsome symmetrical façade: on the ground floor is a bow-window, and above is a Serliana within an arched opening, with a bats-wing treatment. The elegant elevation looks Adamesque, and indeed it has resemblances to Robert Adam's Royal Society of Arts building in John Adam Street, Adelphi, if 1772–74, although the latter has an Ionic Order applied to the brick façade (PLATE 185).

Brooks's Club, also in St James's Street, was designed by Henry Holland, and, as befitted a Club for Whigs, was suitably Palladian, although with Grecian touches. The date was 1776. Then came James Wyatt's White's Club for the Tories, in the same street, of 1787–88. In Waterloo Place two important Clubs, the United Services by John Nash (1826) and the Athenæum by Decimus Burton (1827) (PLATE 94) set standards for spacious grandeur. The Athenæum, with its Greek frieze (a copy from the Parthenon) and Statue of Athene, has a splendid staircase and library. Two years later Charles Barry designed the Travellers' Club in Pall Mall, an astylar building with *cornicione* based on an Italian *palazzo*. The 'Italianate' Renaissance style thus appeared in the last year of the Georgian period.

Thomas Harrison's splendid Lycæum Club, Liverpool, of 1800–02, is in the Greek Revival style, with a fine Ionic recessed portico, and contains a magnificent domed room inside which contained the gentleman's subscription library. Such subscription libraries were features of the Georgian period although the Liverpool library was the first, established in 1758. Belfast's Linen Hall Library was founded in 1788, and was typical of eighteenth-century interest in learning, for the Georgian period saw the phenomenal rise of the educated professional and middle classes, hungry for knowledge. Throughout the land, literary and philosophical societies were founded, with their own libraries and

ARTS AND COMMERCE PROMOTED.

PLATE 185 *Elevation of the House of the Society for the Encouragement of*
Arts, Manufactures, and Commerce, situated in John Adam Street, Adelphi,
London, by Adam, from his Works in Architecture, *Vol I, No IV,*
Plate IV (SM).

reading-rooms, and the 'Lit-and-Phil' was a feature of most of the larger towns, like Newcastle-upon-Tyne, which acquired a handsome building by John Green (1787-1852) in 1822-25. These buildings were usually Grecian in style, for the Greek Revival, untainted by Absolutism, Papistry, Toryism, or Whiggery, was ideally suited to the serious high-mindedness of the middle classes. Barry's superbly handsome Institution of Fine Arts in Manchester of 1824-25 (now the City Art Gallery) has fine interiors and a noble porticoed exterior, again pronouncedly Greek, and contrasting with the same architect's Athenæum next door, of 1837, which is a *palazzo*.

Museums

Parallel to the rise of the 'Lit-and-Phil' reading-rooms and libraries was the notion of raising the tone of society by providing temples to the arts. From 1812 Soane created a remarkable house and museum at 13 Lincoln's Inn Fields, with extraordinary and complex interiors, where the interpenetration of the spaces is ingenious in the extreme. Here were antiquities, plaster-casts, models, drawings, paintings, and cinerary urns in profusion. The great sarcophagus of Seti I was the centre-piece of the museum, but the collection of Piranesi drawings, the Hogarth paintings and the splendid architectural library are of great importance. Soane's picture-gallery at Dulwich of 1811–14, top-lit, and with a mausoleum attached, is an example of his extraordinary stripped Classicism.

Special top-lit galleries were built to exhibit works of art, notably Chambers's Royal Academy Picture-Gallery at Somerset House (1776), Adam's galleries at Newby Hall, Yorkshire, for Classical sculpture (1767), and the Rotunda at Ince Blundell Hall, South Lancashire, (1802) by John Hope, the architect of Halifax's Piece Hall. At Attingham, near Shrewsbury (PLATE 97), Nash added a top-lit picture-gallery to George Steuart's great house in 1807 which incorporates a cast-iron roof-structure. York acquired a fine Greek Revival museum of 1827–30 by William Wilkins and Richard Hey Sharp (*c* 1793–1853): Sharp also designed the Rotunda Museum at Scarborough of 1828–30. The greatest of all Georgian museums, however, was the British Museum, that fine Greek Revival building in Bloomsbury, begun in 1823 to designs by Robert Smirke (PLATES 91–93).

Theatres

There are not many Georgian theatres left, because most have fallen victim to fire, to changing fashion, or to development. Robert Adam designed the theatre and Market-Hall at Bury St Edmunds, while William Wilkins's charming Theatre Royal (also in Bury) of 1819 has a fine Grecian exterior and delightful auditorium. Benjamin Dean Wyatt (1775–1855) was the designer of the splendid Theatre Royal, Drury Lane, of 1811–12, although the auditorium was reconstructed by Samuel Beazley (1786-1851) in 1822, who also added the colonnade in Little Russell Street, with its cast-iron Ionic columns. Beazley designed many theatres, but most have been demolished, and was the author of the County Library and Reading Room (1820–21) and the Royal Assembly Rooms (1820), both in Leamington Spa.

However, most theatres were surprisingly modest and self-effacing, for it was not until the late nineteenth century that showy theatres were built in numbers. Robert Smirke's Covent Garden Theatre of 1808 had a Greek Doric portico, and was a building of some grandeur: it was burned down in 1855 and replaced by the present structure. Henry Holland's Drury Lane Theatre had many other facilities such as shops and a tavern, but it only lasted from 1791 to 1809. Nash's Haymarket Theatre of 1820–21 has a noble Corinthian prostyle portico, the first example of a theatre designed as part of an axial scheme (the portico was lined up with St James's Square). There is a small theatre at Richmond in Yorkshire of 1788, complete with Tuscan columns between the boxes, and with plain benches in the pit. In addition, of course, there were places where theatrical performances could be given in the pleasure-grounds and 'spaws' mentioned above. Unlike Continental countries, Georgian theatres did not enjoy public funding, nor did Kings and Princes run their own theatres. All British theatres had proprietors, and were businesses, so architectural grandeur was generally eschewed, while maximum seating capacity was eagerly sought.

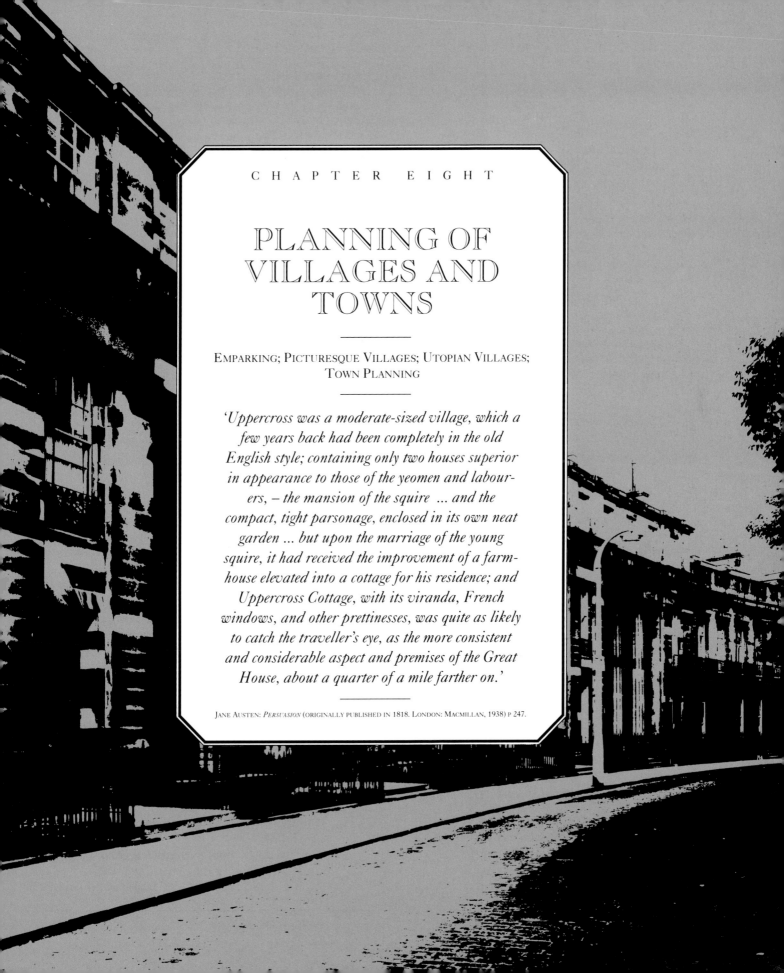

CHAPTER EIGHT

PLANNING OF VILLAGES AND TOWNS

EMPARKING; PICTURESQUE VILLAGES; UTOPIAN VILLAGES;
TOWN PLANNING

'*Uppercross was a moderate-sized village, which a
few years back had been completely in the old
English style; containing only two houses superior
in appearance to those of the yeomen and labourers, – the mansion of the squire ... and the
compact, tight parsonage, enclosed in its own neat
garden ... but upon the marriage of the young
squire, it had received the improvement of a farm-
house elevated into a cottage for his residence; and
Uppercross Cottage, with its viranda, French
windows, and other prettinesses, was quite as likely
to catch the traveller's eye, as the more consistent
and considerable aspect and premises of the Great
House, about a quarter of a mile farther on.*'

JANE AUSTEN: *PERSUASION* (ORIGINALLY PUBLISHED IN 1818. LONDON: MACMILLAN, 1938) P 247.

Emparking

This curious word implies enclosing or shutting up in a park, or to enclose or fence in land for a park. With the rise of the Whig Oligarchy and the desire to build fine new Palladian mansions in parks came the need to demolish the untidy Medieval village and to rehouse the population in a new model settlement. Often the new, planned village was designed as an entrance to the park, or as a foretaste of the grandeur to come. We can see the results of this radical change in many places today: the isolated church in the park or sited next to the great house, and the formal rows of cottages outside the gates of the park, or laid out along neighbouring roads. Very often the area to be occupied by the park was dotted with workers' dwellings, so these had to be removed before the pleasing vistas of the contrived landskip could be created, or the artificial lake flooded the smallholdings. The new houses were erected well out of sight of the windows of the great house: there was no nonsense of allowing 'rustick' villagers to meander pleasingly over the grounds.

Several architects laid out planned villages for their clients, and so the provision of new housing was not merely utilitarian but had aesthetic considerations. One of the first planned villages as a result of emparking was at Chippenham, Cambridgeshire, and dates from 1702–14. The houses are semi-detached, of one-and-a-half storeys (that is with dormers in the roofs), and there is a handsome symmetrical brick schoolhouse. The village was developed by Lord Oxford. Sir Robert Walpole in 1729 built groups of cottages both semi-detached and in terraces) at the gates of Houghton Hall in Norfolk, and there the church, now isolated in the park, is a testimony to the removal of the earlier village. Both Chippenham and New Houghton houses have very large gardens so that the villagers had some compensation for land lost after Enclosure.

Now in both these instances better housing for the tenants resulted, and at Holkham, also in Norfolk, the housing conditions were also excellent. At Well in Lincolnshire the church became a garden eye-catcher, a Classical temple (PLATE 204), and the cottages were built outside the park. Nuneham Courtenay in Oxfordshire was built in the 1760s along the Oxford-Henley road, and consists of pairs of identical semi-detached cottages in a vernacular style, all in brick. Oliver Goldsmith's *The Deserted Village* (1770) was a protest against the reorganisation of villages caused by emparking, and was prompted by Nuneham Courtenay. Lord Harcourt, the builder of the village, also erected a Classical temple as the village church, a mile away from the cottages, which was mightily inconvenient for the people. Nuneham Courtenay, with its inn (*The Harcourt Arms*, of course), was greatly admired by contemporaries, for there dirt and poverty were superseded by cleanliness and ordered prosperity. However, Nuneham was too regular for Uvedale Price and devotees of the Picturesque, for it had no surprise elements, and nothing of associationism. To Price, Nuneham was formal and insipid.

Edward Lascelles, First Earl of Harewood (1739–1820), hired Carr of York to design the village, consisting of terraces of houses, with bigger residences for the physician and land-agent, and a factory for making ribbons. The village is very urban in character, and dates from 1760: it won the approval of contemporaries for its 'neatness bordering upon elegance', a splendid inn was provided, and a school was built in 1768.

In the 1760s, too, the Adam Brothers designed Lowther Village, Westmorland, which was to have consisted of two large squares linked by an even larger circus, but it was only partially built. Milton Abbas in Dorset was laid out for the first Lord Milton in 1744–80 to designs by Sir William Chambers, with landscaping by Lancelot Brown. The cottages are uniform, whitewashed, and thatched, set on either side of the curved street which falls to the valley floor, and there are wide grass verges on each side. The cottages look as though they are big symmetrical double-fronted houses, but they are actually semi-detached, with a common front door. The walls were of cob. The ensemble was completed with a new church and reconstructed almshouses.

George Dance the Younger designed the model village of East Stratton, Hampshire, for Sir Francis Baring, Bart, in 1806: the houses are pairs of thatched cottages, and there was a well between each brick pair. Again, gardens were large, and entry to each house was at the side. The layout was formal and symmetrical.

Picturesque Villages

The Picturesque demands for more informal layouts, and the attractions of groups of cottages around the village green began to change the linear, formal patterns. At Marford, Flintshire, between 1805 and 1816, the local landowner, Boscawen, rebuilt the village, each structure being of different design, and windows are of every shape and size. There are the prettiest Gothick pairs of cottages, and roofs were deliberately constructed to make them look as though they are sagging and old. Very different is the Neo-Classical village of Belsay, Northumberland, by Monck, Gell, and Dobson, the creators of Belsay, the great Greek Revival house. The houses are built over arcaded ground floors, and the effect is very Italian: they date from 1807–17. There is a pretty Tudor-Gothic model village at Ripley, near

Knaresborough, complete with crenellated 'Hôtel de Ville', as its creator, Ingilby, named it.

Peter Frederick Robinson (1776–1858) published his *Rural Architecture; or a Series of Designs for Ornamental Cottages* in 1823, *Designs for Ornamental Villas* in 1825–57, and *Designs for Village Architecture, being a Series of Designs illustrating the Observations contained in the Essay on the Picturesque by Sir Uvedale Price* in 1830. These miscellanies of designs were in various styles, and decorative barge-boards, elaborate chimneys, thatch, and intricate detail were much in evidence. Vernacular styles and timber-framed domestic architecture were ransacked to provide the designs for pattern-books, and soon the Picturesque village was to come into being.

The great protopype of the Picturesque village, however, was Blaise Hamlet, near Henbury, Bristol, Somerset, for J. S. Harford, of 1810–11 by John Nash and Humphry Repton. Here, nostalgia for a rural never-never land, the clichés of 'rustick' cottage architecture, and the Picturesque all merged in a heady brew of thatch, leaded lights, elaborate chimneys, asymmetry, and olde worlde charm. The designs of the cottages were based loosely on vernacular forms, and the cottage designs were lithographed in 1826. So, with Robinson's books, Blaise Hamlet, and Repton's flair for bucolic detail, the Romantic Picturesque cottage movement was launched. Of course the *cottage orné* had already been in vogue for some time, but to design a whole model village of Picturesque cottages was something new. The layout was very 'random', with the cottages spaced in irregular fashion around a green, and called 'Sweet Briar', 'Jessamine', and other redolent names. Repton recognised the importance of lean-to elements and sheds in creating his effects of Picturesqueness.

Park Villages (East and West), Regent's Park, followed, as suburban fringes to the more formal layouts around the Park itself. Nash had designed many individual asymmetrical villas in the country: at Park Villages he placed asymmetrical villas in a setting that was both urban and rural, and the remarkable compositions of individually designed villas (in the Italianate and Tudor Revival styles) placed quite closely together were models of Picturesque theory realised. Work began in 1824, and was completed under Pennethorne. Nash also laid out a model village at Atcham opposite the gates of Attingham Park, Shropshire, traces of which survive, but only traces.

Model villages with model farms, churches, dispensaries, schools, and houses, were also built by the London Livery Companies[1] in the 1820s in Co Londonderry. The best examples are Ballykelly (Fishmongers), Moneymore (Drapers), and Eglinton (Grocers).

Utopian Villages

The enchanting planned Georgian village of Gracehill, Co Antrim, was a Moravian settlement, planned around a square green. The Moravians were Bohemian Protestants who had left Central Europe after the religious upheavals of the seventeenth century, and from 1744 to the 1780s seven Moravian villages were built in the British Isles. Fulneck, near Pudsey, Yorkshire, was the first such settlement, and consisted of a long terrace of the principal buildings overlooking the valley, with a parallel row containing the church and housing. Benjamin Latrobe was born there. Moravians carried out several trades, including the production of textiles, and profits were ploughed back into the community. Later villages were laid out around a square, each had a church where there was some attempt at Classical enrichment, and there were houses, schools, shops and workshops. Fairfield, near Manchester, was the last to be laid out, in 1785, and was a square within a square. The buildings, like all Moravian settlements, were severely simple and refined. Compared with the miserable conditions in many conventional industrial settlements, amenities in the Moravian settlements were excellent, and the sense of community was very strong.

New Lanark, south of Glasgow, was an industrial village founded *c* 1784 by (Sir) Richard Arkwright (1732–92) and David Dale (1739–1806). From the late 1790s Robert Owen (1771–1858) applied his revolutionary ideas to the running of the village, providing the Institute for the Formation of Character (1812), the new Institution (1816), and housing. Owen's village provided good standards of accommodation, work in the mills by the Clyde, and possibilities of instilling good habits in the children of the ignorant parents. In 1800 Owen had applied his rules and regulations, temperance, discipline, and lessons in economy and cleanliness to nearly two thousand working-class Scots, turning this unpromising material into a civilised and prosperous community. Owen provided an infants' school, so that mothers could work, and in the evenings encouraged education, musical activity, and dancing. The buildings are tall, mostly of four storeys, and very plain, with sash-windows in the stone walls. Only a Classical belfry, a plain pediment, and one bow-front made any concessions to enrichment. Owenite settlements were also founded in America, notably at New Harmony, where he worked with the architect Thomas Stedman Whitwell (*ob* 1840), a pupil of Soane, from 1825.

The Reverend Robert Rennie proposed formal planned villages for the Scottish Highlands to the Highland Society from 1803, and Sir John Sinclair, in his *Analysis of the Statistical Account of Scotland* of 1825, proposed regular planned villages to raise the tone of Scottish rural society as a whole. There were many planned villages and plenty of new ideas in Georgian Britain. Among the planned villages designed to bring prosperity and civilisation to wild parts, the most successful architecturally were Inveraray, Ullapool, and Pultneytown (later called Wick).

Town Planning

The first formal, Italian-inspired, urban planned development of architectural quality in England was Inigo Jones's Covent Garden in the seventeenth century, with its houses on arcades and its use of a Giant Order of pilasters. This was carried out for the Fourth Earl of Bedford: it was for William, Fifth Earl and First Duke of Bedford, that Bloomsbury Square was laid out in the 1660s. St James's Square (for the Earl of St Albans) with which Richard Frith (died 1695) was concerned, was part of an urban development of various types of houses, with a market and a church (St James's, Piccadilly, by Wren).

In spite of such schemes, nearly all the domestic architecture of Georgian times was carried out in a speculative manner by individuals. Where there were unified façades, as in the grander parts of Bath, each house was individually built, with varied layouts and different backs, although the frontispiece had to conform to the unified pattern. Most of these speculators were builders with limited capital, so they were only able to build a few houses at any one time.

On the Grosvenor Estate in London there were attempts to provide unified palatial terraces, and Campbell designed one such for Grosvenor Square which was not realised. John Simmons (*ob* 1737 or 1738) was the 'undertaker' for the houses eventually erected in Grosvenor Square between 1725 and 1735: these were astylar, but had a pediment over the central house and attic storeys over the end-houses, so there was a nod towards formal symmetry. Generally, however, most developments consisted of individual buildings following approximately similar forms, so homogeneity was achieved by building materials, by windows of similar size and proportion, by standard details, by equal frontages, and by the constraints of building regulations. Attempts to call in architects to try to improve the elevations were not really successful.

The first uniform square in Georgian London was Bedford Square of 1776–86, and this was achieved because of the determination of the Bedford Estate, the freeholders. The design of the elevations may have been by Thomas Leverton (1743–1824), but William Scott and Robert Grew were also

involved. Houses are of brick, and there is much tuck-pointing: each range is an attempt at a palatial composition, with a six-bay rendered centre-piece (the central four bays with a Giant Order of pilasters and a pediment over) and the end houses also projecting forward with taller parapets. Each house has elaborate Coade Stone keys, voussoirs, and rusticated blocks around the doors. The four-bay centre-pieces mean, of course, that there is a pilaster in the centre instead of a void, which is rather uncomfortable. A similar solecism occurs on the centre-piece of John Eveleigh's Camden Crescent in Bath of 1788 (PLATE 36).

The machinery of development on the Bedford Estate was typical of Georgian times. A builder would acquire a building-lease from the freeholder, and the lease would vary in length. Sixty-one years was the usual term of the Bedford Estate in the early-Georgian period, but longer leases (usually ninety-nine years) became common in the 1780s. The builder would then run up the shell of the house, the elevation conforming to a predetermined pattern, then floor and roof the structure, and apply a rough coat of plaster to internal walls. This would be done as quickly as possible, then the builder could sell to an occupier, who would then fit out the house to his own taste with chimney-pieces, plasterwork, and so on. This system was fraught with dangers, for fickle fashion could intervene. If the house were not in the right area (or even street), or a slump occurred, the builder could be left with an unfinished house, no capital, and a debt to the freeholder.

Later in the century it became common in better-class work for the builder to finish the houses internally, as the Adam Brothers did at their enormous development at the Adelphi, a scheme which nearly ruined them, for they were obliged to get rid of the houses by running a lottery, with the properties as prizes. The huge financial risks made dodgy workmanship and poor materials common, and the gracious fronts of brick were often merely applied to inferior construction, the headers being snapped, and not true bonding headers at all.

Although the façades were not palatial, they were uniform, and the details were repetitive at Merrion Square, Dublin, of 1762 and after, probably designed by John Ensor, a pupil of Cassels, and his brother, George Ensor, was also involved.[2] This huge and monumental square, with its plain brick fronts and fine doorcases with fanlights, is one of the great achievements of Georgian speculative development, this time on the land of Lord Fitzwilliam. The scale of Merrion Square, and the grandeur of Georgian Dublin, were in no small measure due to the activities of the Wide Street Commissioners, established by Act of Parliament in 1758,[3] the year in which Viscount Charlemont (created Earl 1763) began building the wonderful Casino at Marino, near Dublin, to designs by Chambers (PLATE 111). The Dublin Vestries were empowered to levy a lighting tax to illuminate streets in 1760,[4] and by the 1770s there was great determination to make the streets of Dublin as noble and as uniform as possible: in the 1780s the Commissioners showed their teeth by getting windows in a recently completed house changed because they did not conform to those of their neighbours, and in 1799 both Westmorland and d'Olier Streets had uniform fronts and shop-fronts.

In Belfast, too, developments moved ahead when the Earl of Donegall in 1767 granted new leases for nearly all holdings in Belfast, obliging tenants to redevelop. The handsome Donegall Square, laid out around the White Linen Hall, and other gracious Georgian Streets in the vicinity made Belfast, by 1800, a very pleasing town. But it was in Edinburgh and Bath that the greatest domestic architecture was created.

James Craig (1744–95), a nephew of the poet James Thomson (of *The Seasons* fame), won the competition for the laying out of the New Town of Edinburgh in 1766. The plan consisted of a series of rectilinear streets, with a square at each end. Two of the streets (Queen and Princes) were to have buildings on one side only, so there were to be uninterrupted views across to the dramatic Old Town from Princes Street and over the Firth of Forth from Queen Street. Craig designed the uniform St James Square of 1773 (demolished) and the Physicians' Hall in George Street in the Palladian manner of 1775 (demolished 1843). The grandest houses were in St Andrew Square to the east and Charlotte Square to the west. St James Square contained the first attempt at uniform terrace design in Edinburgh, but Robert Adam's Charlotte Square was entirely designed (in 1791) to be unified and palatial, mixing late-Palladian and Neo-Classical elements (PLATE 109). There are noble pedimented centre-pieces with engaged columns and wide end-pavilions. As with Dublin, Edinburgh New Town has elevations to the principal streets that are coherently joined, and, in spite of the different contractors, are very alike.

Where does the First New Town plan come from? John Adam was one of the judges in the competition, and he and his father had planned Inveraray in 1747: Inveraray has an axial square, central street, and back streets, and a single-sided outer street overlooking Loch Fyne, and it is echoed in Craig's scheme. Other precedents are Covent Garden and Richelieu in France of 1633. The positioning of the church of St Paul at Covent Garden is also recalled in Adam's church of St George, which terminates the vista from George Street, while Sir William Chambers's house for Sir Laurence Dundas of 1771, based on Marble Hill at Twickenham, but grander, terminates the vista at the east end.[5]

The Northern New Town was planned by Robert Reid and William Sibbald (*ob* 1809) in 1801–02, and is the largest scheme in the development of Georgian Edinburgh. It was built with remarkable unity, and remains virtually complete apart from Heriot Row and Jamaica Street. Like the First New Town it has a powerful east-west axis with smaller parallel streets and other streets cutting across at right angles. On the centre axis of Great King Street is Drummond Place (with its palatial façades), and tucked away at the west end is the brilliant Royal Circus by W. H. Playfair of 1820–23, again with a palatial centre-piece.

The Moray Estate followed, consisting of Moray Place, Ainslie Place, and Randolph Crescent, in 1822–36. William Burn produced a layout, but the detailed architecture and plans were made by James Gillespie Graham (1776–1855). The polygonal Moray Place, with its Giant Tuscan Order of engaged columns, is handled in a masterly fashion, with Darnaway, Forrest, and Great Stuart Streets and Doune Terrace running off it. Perhaps even more magnificent is Playfair's Calton, designed in 1819, with two converging terraces of enormous splendour, Royal and Regent Terraces. Royal Terrace of 1824 has forty houses, with an arcaded and rusticated ground floor, and the long plain façade broken up by three Giant Corinthian colonnades carrying attics, with balustrades between. At Stockbridge can be found the charming St Bernard's Crescent of 1824 by James Milne (flourished 1809–34) with its pavilions with attics and *in antis* Greek Doric columns and miniature Doric colonnade at ground-floor level: it is one of the most daring uses of Greek Doric in domestic architecture (PLATE 186).

In the Georgian period the size of a house was related to the width of the street in front of it, which ensured a certain regularity of front. Other enactments insisted that party-walls and external walls should be made of brick or stone, and all this helped to regulate appearance to a certain extent. The general fashion for sash-windows of various standard sizes also ensured that window-openings were vertical and related to multiples of the average-sized piece of glass, for large sheets were too expensive for domestic use. All this, with the prevailing fashion for Classical, and especially Palladian, architecture, ensured a homogeneity we have not enjoyed since the Picturesque movement triumphed. Furthermore, the various Acts of Parliament designed to prevent the spread of fire (the first great enactment was the year after the Great Fire of London in 1666) affected the appearance of buildings. In 1707 timber-eaves-cornices were prohibited in London because in unified façades fire would spread easily along them, and it became usual to raise the front of the house above the eaves, so roofs began to disappear behind parapets. In 1709 sash-boxes (which up until then were set flush with the façade) began to be set back from the fronts as a precaution against fire.

Another enactment was window-tax, imposed on houses with a certain number of windows (in 1784 if a house had only six windows it was liable). Blocked-up windows were

PLATE 186 *St Bernard's Crescent, Stockbridge, Edinburgh, by James Milne, of 1824: one of the most remarkable of Greek Revival terraces of houses* (RCAHMS ED/2461).

sometimes a result of this tax, but often blank windows were introduced for decorative effect or so as not to interrupt the repetition of a window range: in such cases a false frame or a *trompe l'oeil* window might be painted on the panel. Fashions established by London Building Acts were copied in the provinces. The great Act of 1774 consolidated earlier Acts and enabled standards of construction and design to be enforced and, most importantly, insisted that sash-boxes should be built in behind the outer brick skin so that it was no longer exposed. This Act determined the design of late-Georgian domestic architecture.

Bath[6] is an instance where the lovely, warm, local limestone gave a further ingredient to contribute to harmony of design. The hilly nature of Bath ensured that there was less of the grid pattern and more of the curve. John Wood the Elder's Queen Square of 1729–36 has a unified palatial façade on one side with three-bay end-pavilions and a five-bay pedimented centre-piece, all with a Giant Corinthian Order of engaged columns set on a rusticated ground floor: the six-bay fronts between the wings and the centre-piece have pilasters. Now although this is later than Peckwater Quadrangle in Oxford, the Queen Square range is the earliest realised purely domestic range of houses devised as a palatial front, although Campbell's Grosvenor Square scheme would have been the earliest if it had been built. Wood also designed houses in Wood Street, John Street, and Old King Street in the same period, and the North and South Parades, with Pierrepoint and Duke Streets of 1740–43. He designed Gay Street (*c* 1735–55) which joined the Square to the Circus, begun in 1754 and completed by his son. As stated above, the Circus has superimposed Orders (unfluted Roman Doric, Ionic, and Corinthian) consisting of paired columns separating each bay.

Ison states that 'the elder Wood surely reached the summit of his powers with his design for the King's Circus, where he translated the general grandeur and detailed multiplicity of the exterior of a Roman amphitheatre into terms of domestic architecture, and produced a work of extraordinary magnificence and subtlety of effect … The grouping of the houses into three equal segments is a brilliant contrivance of planning, designed to give the effect of a continuous range of building confronting the spectator and closing the vista from each of the entering streets … The elevations "in theatrical style" are of the most elaborate description, a *tour-de-force* of external decoration solely contrived to impress the beholders at close quarters. The three stories are enriched with superimposed orders of Roman Doric, Ionic and Corinthian plain-shafted three-quarter columns, carrying their appropriate entablatures … Each bay of the main wall face above the third-story windows is decorated with a frieze carrying a female mask, linked by garlands with the Corinthian capitals … The pedestal parapet is broken forward over each

pair of columns to form bases for the crowning ornaments of stone acorns'.[7] These masks and acorns are probably references to the female deity (Sulis) who presided over the waters at Bath, and whom the Romans identified with Minerva, and to the legends of Bladud (PLATE 34). Wood's slightly dotty historical Romanticism can best be savoured in his *The Origin of Building, or the Plagiarism of the Heathens Detected* of 1741, a heady brew of Freemasonic legend and speculations about Classicism, and *An Essay Toward a Description of Bath* of 1742, in which the Druids, Ancient Britons, and his antiquarian researches combine in a mind-boggling confection.

The Circus is joined by means of the plainish Brock Street (where there is a charming Batty Langleyesque Gothick doorcase on the south side and many windows derived from the Venetian type but without architraves or entablatures, giving a diversified rhythm to the street frontages) to the stunning Royal Crescent of 1767–74 by John Wood the Younger, a hemi-ellipse facing a greensward slope to the south (PLATE 35). Originally, the Crescent, with its Giant Order of engaged Ionic columns, faced open fields, a completely new conception in town planning applied to a terrace of houses, although the pattern may derive from Prior Park, and therefore, by proxy, from Palladio. Here, too, the shape of the crescent is employed for the first time in England. This majestic and noble design is one of the finest ranges of terrace-houses anywhere in Europe.

Mr Ison, in his definitive and indispensable *Georgian Buildings of Bath*, writes that instead of a totality of development, one should look instead for a 'series of *coups d'oeil* of accidental and remarkable beauty'. Yes, indeed, and these *coups* were undoubtedly designed to achieve variety and surprise, surely an essential element of the Picturesque? Other planned developments in Bath include Lansdown Crescent by John Palmer (*c* 1738–1817) of 1789–93, and Camden Crescent, 1788, mentioned earlier (PLATE 36). But east of the river is the spectacular wide Great Pulteney Street by Thomas Baldwin (1750–1820) of 1788, and Laura Place (a lozenge-shaped junction between Johnson, Henrietta, and Great Pulteney Streets) of 1789–1805. This great development at Bathwick starts with the beautiful Pulteney Bridge of Robert Adam of 1770 and ends with Sydney Gardens and the former hotel of 1796, looking like a country mansion with a Corinthian portico. The gardens were to be laid out as a 'Vauxhall', with a fake castle, Chinese cast-iron bridges, thatched 'umbrellos' and the like. The Bathwick developments have a unity and a civic grandeur not uninfluenced by the developments of the Adam Brothers. Baldwin favoured a Giant Order of Corinthian pilasters, and the ranges in Great Pulteney Street and in Laura Place exhibit these features.

Mention has been made above of Coade Stone and cast-iron components. Coade Stone was a remarkably hard and durable

artificial stone which could be used to make architectural ornament. It was used in some profusion at Bedford Square,[8] and
figures and ornaments made of it were prepared by artists of
distinction. It was often used for repetitive elements such as
capitals, for it was far cheaper to prepare moulds for Coade
Stone than to carve each one individually in stone. So artificial
stone like Coade Stone, or another similar preparation by James
George Bubb (1782–1853), who went into partnership with
Rossi in the preparation of terracotta designs, was widely used
during the Georgian period. The Paestum capitals at
Hammerwood Lodge by Latrobe were made by Coade, but the
commonest Coade capitals were Ionic: examples include
Wyatt's Heaton Hall, Lancashire, and Ashdown House, Sussex,
by Latrobe. Similar rusticated door details to those in Bedford
Square occur in 61–63 New Cavendish Street, London, by John
Johnson, while the details of the same architect's Hotel in
Leicester are all of Coade Stone. There are many good examples of Coade funerary monuments (J. Booth in St John's
church, Stamford, Lincolnshire) and garden ornaments
(Antinoüs in Buscot Park, Berkshire). The fine Neo-Classical
friezes at Ickworth in Suffolk, too, are of Coade Stone.

John Nash was in partnership with Repton from 1796 to
1802, and the Picturesque asymmetrical composition was
developed by them, derived from Payne Knight's Downton
Castle (PLATES 61–62). Nash's enchanting Italianate
Cronkhill, Shropshire, of c 1802, is also asymmetrical, and
incorporates an arched loggia, a circular tower, and wide over-
hanging Italian roofs, the whole derived from images of buildings in paintings by Claude (PLATE 2). His Regent's Park,
designed from 1811 and realised in the 1820s, has grand
ranges of palatial terraces, all stuccoed, around it, and the
scheme also included a large number of Picturesque villas.
What Nash did by applying the theories of composition to the
West End of London was to import the Picturesque from its
rural habitat. At Regent's Park the landscaped country-house
park was married to palatial terrace-houses and picturesque
villas, so combining the best of town and country.

London acquired its spectacular town-planning scheme by
which Waterloo Place was linked to Regent's Park via
Portland Place quite late in the Georgian period. John Nash
created Piccadilly Circus as the hub around which he swung
the axis of Lower Regent Street westwards into Piccadilly and
northwards to the County Fire Office, at which point the
Regent Street Quadrant proceeded west, then north, with the
building blocks reading as a series of episodes towards Oxford
Circus, then stopping at the church of All Souls, Langham
Place, where again the street swung west, then north into
Portland Place. At the north end of the latter, the street
opened into a large space with the curves of Park Crescent on
either side, and then the expanses of Regent's Park lay ahead,
with the great palatial terraces laid out around its perimeter.

Piccadilly Circus had four quadrants with an Ionic Order on
the ground floor, above which was a system of vertical and
horizontal moulded strips. The Quadrant, of 1818–20, led
from Abraham's Fire Office (based on part of Old Somerset
House, then supposed to be by Inigo Jones), and was lined
with Roman Doric cast-iron columns carrying an entablature
and balustrade, which was for show and which acted as a
colonnaded covered promenade for shoppers. The buildings
behind had plain façades. Beyond, north of the Quadrant,
were houses with shop-fronts inserted, and Nash produced
designs for long symmetrical frontages between the junctions
with the side-streets, and of course the lengths varied.

Regent Street was not straight, and it was not possible to
see All Souls' church (1822–25) until a position well northwards was reached. Nash admired Oxford's High Street,
which is laid out on a curve before it straightens towards
Carfax, and consists of a series of architectural events which
are revealed as one walks from Magdalen Bridge. The grander
buildings, and the great tree which has become a famous
landmark, are interspersed with humble buildings. So it was
with Nash's Regent Street: the long symmetrical fronts
(PLATE 187) were placed among less pretentious material. For
the uniform blocks Nash did his best to control shop fronts by
bringing a Giant Order of pilasters down to the pavement
(PLATE 188) at 171–195 Regent's Street, and by other
devices, but commercialism, flashiness, and advertising were
soon put before architecture, and the unfortunate pilasters
were soon truncated. It should be remembered that at this
time plate-glass became cheaper to make, and so shop-fronts
got larger and glazing-bars were removed, with disastrous
results for proportions. Favourite Nashian motifs such as
shell-and-fan windows, curved corners with cupolas over, and
showy stucco fronts abounded. Nash did not design all the
blocks, for 156–170, for example, was a block designed by
Soane in his developed reductionist manner. 224–240 was
probably by Nash, and incorporated everything that was
'Regency', including recessed columns, Greek windows,
incised patterns in the Greek-key type, and acroteria-blocks *à
la Soane*. In short, Regent's Street was a series of episodic
happenings, and in spite of its 'Regency' showiness, must be
regarded as Picturesque.

To the north lay the curved peristyle wrapped round the
drum of All Souls', Langham Place, which thus became a
pivot round which the street swung. Then the route moved
into the breathtakingly wide and grand Portland Place of
1776–c 1780 by the Adam Brothers: the fine façades with their
elegant frontispieces must have looked splendid, but, like so
much of London, they have been shamefully vandalised by
piecemeal redevelopment and crude alterations. At the northern end Nash added Park Crescent of 1812–22, and around
the Park he designed the terrace façades, the siting of the

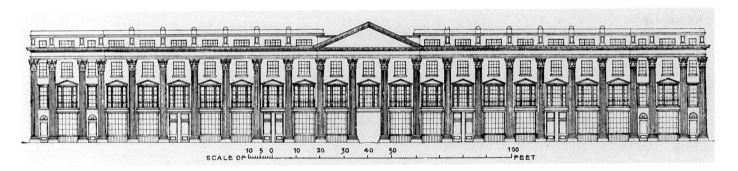

villas, and the planting. Cornwall and Clarence Terraces were designed by Decimus Burton. Nash's spectacular Cumberland Gate and Terrace were carried out under the direction of James Thomson, but Nash seems to have been solely responsible for Ulster Terrace, York Terrace, York Gate, Sussex Place, Hanover, Kent, Chester, Cambridge, and St Andrew's Terraces, and Park Square. The Park Villages have already been mentioned. When Carlton House was demolished, Nash also designed the superb Carlton House Terraces of 1827–33, on The Mall.

Many of these schemes employ cast-iron columns (eg the Doric columns at Carlton House Terrace), while Cumberland Terrace (described by Mr Cruickshank as 'the last word in grandiose palace-fronted terrace design'[9]) has the tympanum sculpture and other enrichments of artificial stone by J. G. Bubb, who also carried out the figures of British Worthies for Chester Terrace. Even more exotic was Sussex Place, with its canted bays rising to octagonal turrets with curiously oriental-looking cupolas, and recessed frontage with a Giant Order of Classical columns standing proud of the façade between the bays.

PLATE 187 *One of the façades on the east side of Regent Street, London, by John Nash, showing the design of the shop-fronts in relation to the Greek-influenced upper storeys. From Richardson (BTB/SH).*

PLATE 188 *Nos 171–195 Regent Street, London, by John Nash, showing a group with a Giant Order of pilasters with shop-fronts between. From Richardson (BTB/SH).*

Peter Nicholson (1765–1844) designed a palatial façade for Carlton Place, Laurieston, Glasgow, in 1802–18 (PLATE 189), and more modest palatial fronts were built in Blythswood Square in *c* 1823 to designs by John Brash. Nicholson also made a town plan for Ardrossan in Ayrshire for the Twelfth Earl of Eglinton, the harbour of which was constructed under the direction of Telford. The plan consisted of a long crescent of detached villas set out on either side of a central church, and the houses facing Ardrossan Bay were to be formal palatial terraces, with crescents breaking up the long frontage (PLATE 190).

Nicholson illustrated various categories of London houses established under the London Building Act of 1774: the First-

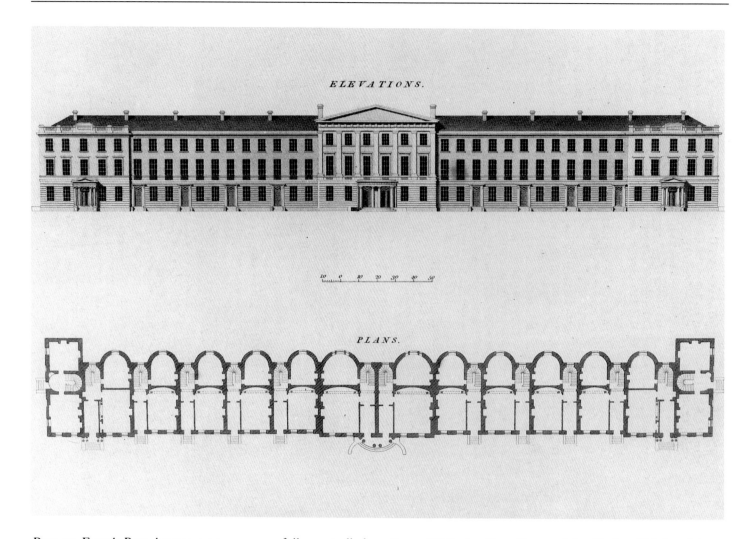

ELEVATIONS.

PLANS.

Rate to Fourth-Rate houses were very carefully controlled (PLATES 191–194). Every builder or owner had to inform the District Surveyor of the intention to build or alter any structure within the seven 'rates'. The 'rate' was determined by the number of 'squares' measured on the ground floor: a 'square' was 100 square feet. Any house of more than nine squares on the ground floor was deemed 'first-rate', and the measurements included the internal and external walls. Houses exceeding five squares and not more than nine were 'second-rate'; those exceeding three-and-a-half squares but not more than five were 'third-rate', and houses not exceeding three-and-a-half squares were 'fourth-rate'. The fifth, sixth, and seventh rates were not subject to the same restrictions: fifth- and sixth-rate properties were on isolated sites, and the seventh embraced special structures such as windmills.

A first-rate house had to have external and party walls two bricks thick, but the party wall of the cellar had to be two-and-a-half bricks thick, and the external wall from the first floor upwards one-and-a-half bricks thick. Party walls in the

PLATE 189 *Carlton Place, Glasgow, designed by Peter Nicholson. It is a unified palatial façade. Note the bows to the rear, and the curved ends to the front rooms. From Nicholson's* Architectural and Engineering Dictionary, *Vol II (JSC).*

roof-space were one-and-a-half bricks thick. For second-rate houses the party wall could be one-and-a-half bricks thick from the second floor up, and the external wall could be one brick thick from the first floor up. Third-rate houses had party walls one-and-a-half bricks thick except in the cellar, where they were two bricks thick. The external walls were one brick thick except in the cellar, where they were one-and-a-half bricks thick. For fourth-rate houses all walls were one brick thick except in the cellars, where they were one-and-a-half. Furthermore, party walls had to be carried up at least eighteen inches above the roofs. Materials used in construction were subject to control, and, as has been described, exposed timber, such as sash-frames and eaves-cornices, had been outlawed.

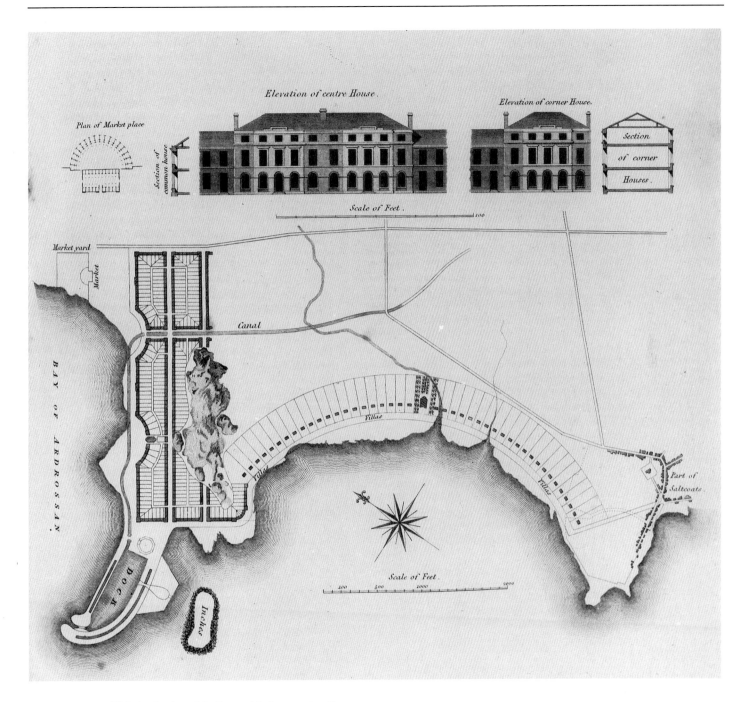

PLATE 190 *Peter Nicholson's plan of the Town of Ardrossan, Ayrshire, with villas and terraces. From his* Architectural and Engineering Dictionary *(JSC).*

PLATE 191 *First-Rate House, designed by Michael Angelo Nicholson (c 1796–1842), from Peter Nicholson's* New Practical Builder *of 1823* (JSC).

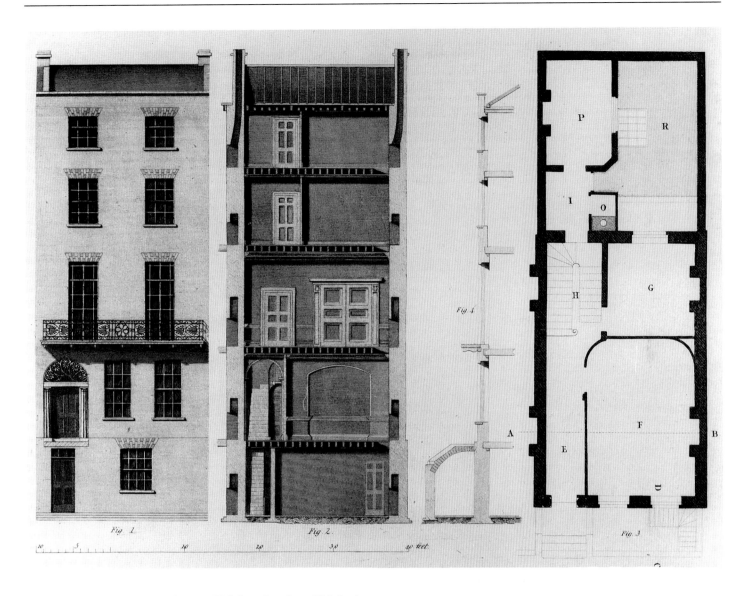

PLATE 192 *Second-Rate House by M.A. Nicholson, from Peter Nicholson's*
New Practical Builder (JSC).

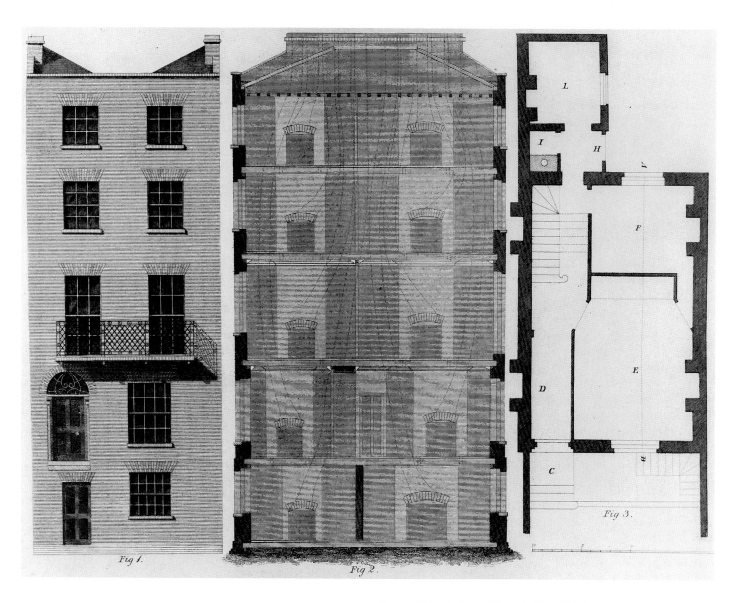

PLATE 193 *Third-Rate House by M.A. Nicholson, from Peter Nicholson's New Practical Builder* (JSC).

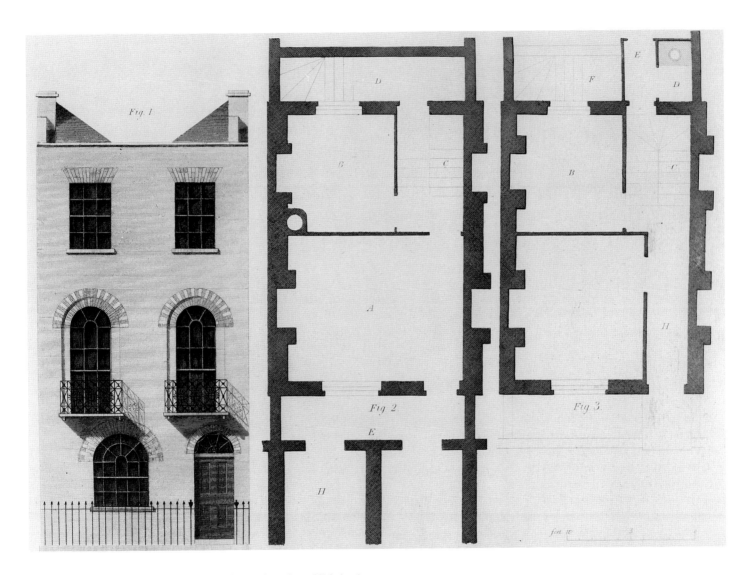

PLATE 194 *Fourth-Rate House by M.A. Nicholson, from Peter Nicholson's*
New Practical Builder (JSC).

A further variation on the terrace or crescent was the arrangement of houses in a terrace with set-backs (usually the parts behind the doors), so that they appear as semi-detached dwellings. Michael Searles (1750–1813) designed a crescent at Gloucester Circus, Greenwich, of 1790–91, with two-window-wide pedimented elements linked by set-backs containing the doors, and with four-window-wide blocks with parapets and arcaded ground floors flanking each pair of pedimented blocks. Terraces designed to look like pedimented pairs of houses with the doors set back between them were built on the Lloyd-Baker Estate in Clerkenwell from 1819, to designs by John Booth (c 1760–1843). Searles also designed the Paragon at Blackheath in 1793–1807, a wonderful composition of semi-detached blocks linked by six-bay colonnades (PLATE 195). John Buonarotti Papworth designed Lansdowne Place and Crescent at Cheltenham of 1825–29 in which pairs of houses are joined by the entrances which are lower and set back. Papworth was responsible for several developments in the Gloucestershire Spa.

A further remarkable point to be made about Georgian

PLATE 195 *The Paragon, Blackheath, by Michael Searles, of 1793–1807* (JSC).

planned developments is the enormous range of variations on themes to be found. Round-arched and square-headed windows, Venetian windows, Wyatt windows, fanlights, doors with side-lights, pilasters and engaged columns, colonnades and arcades, flat terraces, curved terraces, and terraces broken up to look like semi-detached houses – all were mixed in a marvellous brew. Bows and canted bays, Gothick and Palladian detail, and Greek elements all added variety to the planned streets of the Georgian town.

It is perhaps indicative of the low esteem in which Architecture and Town Planning are held in Britain that of the stupendously grand conception devised by Nash for Piccadilly Circus-Regent Street-Langham Place, not much remains except the shapes of the streets, the church of All Souls, and, of course, the façades north of Portland Place. Of Nash's Regent Street nothing remains save its line: it was totally rebuilt during the 1920s.

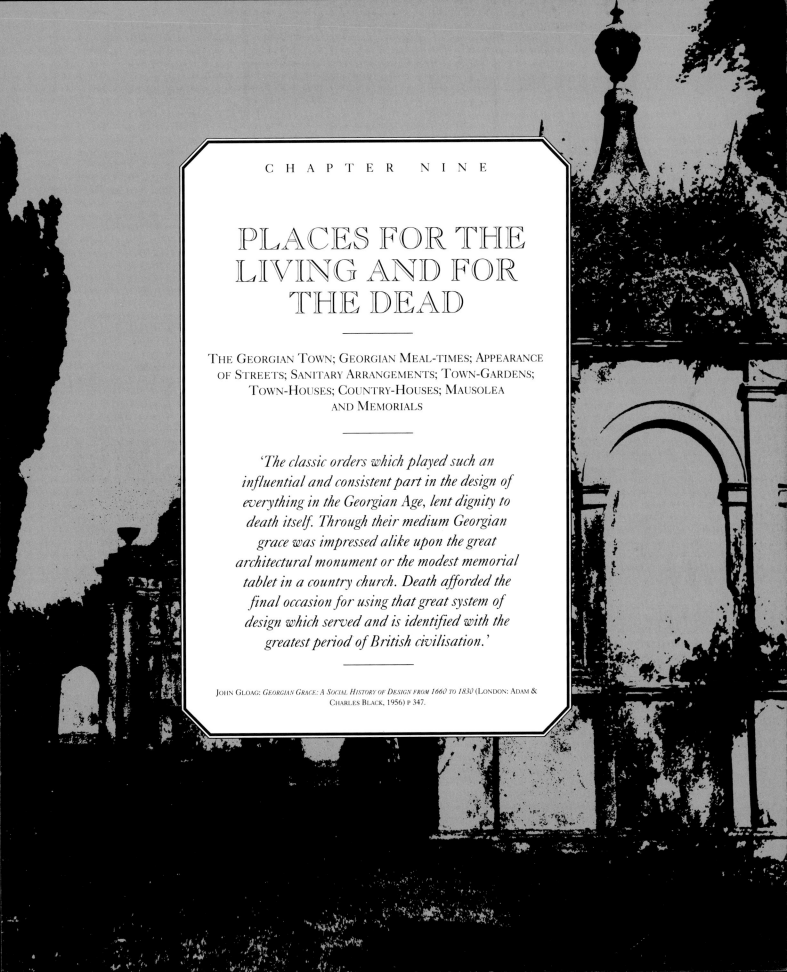

CHAPTER NINE

PLACES FOR THE LIVING AND FOR THE DEAD

THE GEORGIAN TOWN; GEORGIAN MEAL-TIMES; APPEARANCE
OF STREETS; SANITARY ARRANGEMENTS; TOWN-GARDENS;
TOWN-HOUSES; COUNTRY-HOUSES; MAUSOLEA
AND MEMORIALS

*'The classic orders which played such an
influential and consistent part in the design of
everything in the Georgian Age, lent dignity to
death itself. Through their medium Georgian
grace was impressed alike upon the great
architectural monument or the modest memorial
tablet in a country church. Death afforded the
final occasion for using that great system of
design which served and is identified with the
greatest period of British civilisation.'*

JOHN GLOAG: *GEORGIAN GRACE: A SOCIAL HISTORY OF DESIGN FROM 1660 TO 1830* (LONDON: ADAM &
CHARLES BLACK, 1956) P 347.

The Georgian Town

Many commentators, long before the Victorian period, were less than enthusiastic about the monotonous appearance of Georgian towns, especially the streets of 'parallel and uniformly extended brick walls..., with equally extended ranges of windows and doors, all precisely alike, and without any appearance of being distinct houses'.[1] The ranges of terrace-houses could easily be mistaken for hospitals, arsenals, or public granaries, according to contemporary observers. Many visitors to London felt that the usual Georgian street of terrace-houses was dark and gloomy, yet others viewed it as majestic, and as a clever way of using land in an economical way. In fact the London terrace-house was an extraordinarily compact arrangement considering the small plot of ground on which it stood.

We often think of the grimy town as a dark Victorian invention, but it is quite clear that the Georgian town was grimy too, the reason being the Briton's fondness for coal-fires in his home, something visitors from Central Europe, used to stoves, found very strange. Black smoke and sulphurous air appalled foreign visitors,[2] but nevertheless caused amusement because the cause, the domestic fire, was so inefficient, most of the heat going up the chimney. Continentals felt that the British did not realise what a warm room was, for porcelain stoves (normal in the Netherlands and throughout Germany) were unknown.

If, to the visitor, London looked like a gigantic murky warehouse of brick, inhabited by people who, if they ever looked at the sky, saw it filled with smoke,[3] paving and lighting excited favourable comment. Many streetlights in Georgian Britain were protected by globes of glass held on decorative iron supports, and consisted of wicks in oil. After 1740 streetlighting in London was regulated by Acts of Parliament, and the principle was one of levying annual rates on residents so that light could be provided when required. Lighting was often associated with 'watching', that is the provision of a night-watchman who would keep an eye on property and ensure orderliness. Rates were calculated on the *value* of a house, and the figure was arrived at on the basis of the rent a property could command. It should be remembered that most people rented property for a fixed term, a practice that was usual until the 1940s and early 1950s, when Parliamentary enactments virtually killed off the private rented sector, forcing the populace to buy property (usually by borrowing) or live in Council housing (the long-term result has been to inflate the cost of property and cause far too great a proportion of income to be expended on housing). Some occupants were, of course, freeholders, but the rate was still levied on the rent the property was reckoned to be worth. Often householders provided their own lamps to mark the entrances to their properties, so many areas were illuminated by a combination of private and Parish lights. Naturally the system failed to provide adequate lighting where there were few houses, as on the outskirts of a town, so the streets in such areas were murky and dangerous.

Shops were often illuminated with candles, but in the latter part of the eighteenth century oil-lamps became usual, and main thoroughfares were thus well lit. Gaslight was introduced in the 1790s, and in 1807 the first gas-lamps were erected in Pall Mall. By 1827 gaslight was being provided to thousands of public and private lamps. Often a lamp was included as a fixed element in the centre of a Georgian fanlight.

With regard to paving, from the 1760s responsibility began to pass from individuals to public bodies with powers to levy rates. Before this every occupant or owner of a house was required to pave the street in front of the house to the middle of the street, and many of the great estates made such requirements part of any leasing arrangement. That part of the street nearest the house was usually raised slightly and paved with stone flags, but the carriageway was often paved with round pebbles or cobbles, creating a very poor surface for the hard-wheeled horse-drawn carriages. From the time of the Westminster Paving Act (1762) raised pavements and smoother stone carriageways (often of Purbeck stone) were provided, and the central drainage channel was superseded by gutters below and parallel to the kerbs, a system that is now almost universally used. Towards the end of the Georgian period squared stones (setts) were used for the carriageways, and Tarmacadam began also to make its appearance.

In addition to the above matters households were obliged to sweep and clean the pavements and roads in front of the properties, and the dirt was removed by scavengers paid by the Parish. These scavengers could sell the ashes from fires to brick manufacturers, and doubtless there were other pickings to be had. Streets were cleaned by water-carts, and dust was removed in a cart by dustmen. At street corners were sweepers who, for a small consideration, cleared a path for pedestrians across the frequently muddy or dung-covered carriageway.

However, there was another great problem which impositions on tenants and landlords could not solve. British cities, especially London, had a sizeable proportion of population that was unemployed, casually employed, or itinerant, of no fixed abode, and those people ('the Mob') were difficult to control, or even to potty-train. Descriptions of 'extremely unpleasant' streets in the summer in the vicinity of drinking-dens indicate that vomit, urine, and fæces were common sights on the streets in Georgian times. It should be remembered that the Watch was by no means like an efficient public police-force, and the respectable citizen was no doubt both frightened and appalled by the drunken, dirty, anti-social Mob, and even by the poor, who, renting single rooms, would empty their chamber-pots into the gutters, thereby causing a frightful stench. The Watch was supposed to apprehend anyone casting 'night-soil' into the street, but catching anyone in the overcrowded houses in multiple occupancy was almost impossible.

The Georgian town was therefore noisy, often dirty, frequently smelly, and the traffic was a hazard. Foreign visitors were often knocked down by surly rogues carrying sedan-chairs, had their legs bruised by street-porters, or were injured by the thousands of carts, carriages, and horses that passed through the streets. To the clatter of hooves and wheels on the rough carriageways were added the cries of the vendors of everything from oysters to garlic, the jangle of hand-bells, the noise of musical instruments of itinerant performers, the shouts of drunken men and women, the uproar when a thief made off with a watch or a handkerchief, and the calls of the purveyors of food at the street-corner stalls.

Added to the noise, the smells, the dung-covered streets, and the hazards, were problems from above. Views of early eighteenth-century London and other towns show the main streets lined with large signs hanging from elaborate metal brackets fixed to the fronts of buildings to advertise shops, wares, and taverns. It was not unusual for these to fall down, especially in windy conditions, killing or injuring pedestrians below, and perhaps bringing down parts of the façades as well. The fact that the population was packed densely into the urban fabric meant that upper-level 'penthouses' and rooms let out individually were common, so the passer-by could be brained by a falling flower-pot, injured by a deliberately aimed missile, sprinkled with a watering-can intended for the plants on a balcony or window-sill, or plastered with the contents of a chamber-pot. The hanging signs were thought to prevent the free circulation of air, and they certainly obscured views of the street, so they began to disappear from the 1760s, for the Georgians began to worry about 'miasmas', or stagnant air which could be debilitating or downright dangerous. The Westminster Paving Act of 1762 also prohibited hanging signs. If signs encroached upon pavements, and hung over pedestrians like Swords of Damocles, another favourite encroachment was the bow-window which gave shopkeepers more space inside, but forced the pedestrian nearer the posts or bollards which lined the kerbs. And if there were dangers and unpleasantnesses above, too much attention given to protecting the head could result in further catastrophes: coal-holes in pavements, steps down to areas or cellars, and unprotected abysses could maim or kill if the luckless pedestrian blundered into them.

Finding one's way around could be difficult as well, for at the beginning of the Georgian period streets were not labelled, so the stranger would have to enquire his way. By the 1760s it was also apparent that names of streets, roads, and alleys should be placed in conspicuous positions on corners. At this time, many individuals had their names inscribed on brass plates, and houses acquired numbers, either on the doors, or on the fanlights, walls, or railings. By the 1780s London streets were all named by means of painted signs on each corner, and all doors were numbered. Cast-iron or enamelled signs came in later.

Georgian Meal-Times

In the course of the eighteenth century habits changed. In the early-Georgian period it was customary to dine at one in the afternoon, but in the course of the century the hour was gradually put back so that activities in the Exchange would not be interrupted. London bankers and merchants would start the day by drinking tea at home, with toast, butter and marmalade, the toast being made on a fork before the fire. Breakfast could be a leisurely affair, and could be at 9, 10, or 11am. Working-class journeymen usually began work at 6, breakfasting around 8 at a public house or a street-stall, usually off bread, butter, and tea, but workmen could also drink beer, eat bread-and-cheese, and consume gruel with toast, butter, and nutmeg.[4]

City bankers and merchants would use coffee-houses, often staying for an hour to gossip and transact business, and were involved in the Exchange or in offices until dinner, which moved back to 2, then to 4pm. Workmen usually dined between noon and 1pm, and stopped work at 6pm. Tradesmen took breakfast between 6 and 9am, consuming toast, tea, coffee, or cocoa, and dined between 1 and 4pm. Tea was taken later, and a light supper consumed at 9pm. Cards and the Play provided diversion in the evening. The better-off tradesman, like the banker and merchant, had servants, breakfasted late (as late as 11am), dined between 4 and 6pm, and drank wine with other gentlemen until they rejoined the ladies for tea around 9pm. This was followed by supper and more drinking.

The aristocracy rose late, read reviews and newspapers, breakfasted around 11am, dined between 5 and 7pm, drank tea or coffee before the wines and fruit were removed, then drank until supper at 10pm, which could last until 2am with or without more drink. The drinking of toasts seems to have been a part of the entertainment when the gentlemen were alone, and the conversation was free, often indecent. Foreigners were amazed by the fact that chamber-pots were provided on the sideboard so that gentlemen could relieve themselves without any interruption of the conversation. French visitors supposed this was why English ladies withdrew from the company before the toasts. When the gentlemen rejoined the ladies for tea in the drawing-room (foreigners noted how weak was the coffee), readings could form part of the entertainment, or musical activity, such as songs accompanied by a keyboard instrument.

Appearance of Streets

In the course of the eighteenth century the appearance of streets changed further, not only because of the paving, lighting, and signs, but because of enactments designed to protect buildings from fire. Sash-windows had been introduced in the late seventeenth century, with wide glazing-bars and exposed sash-boxes. In 1707 and 1709 cornices constructed of timber were prohibited and sash-boxes had to be set back in reveals. In 1774 standards of construction were determined, and sash-boxes had to be set back *and concealed* behind the jambs in rebates. All this was to prevent the spread of fire. Colour, too, played its part. In the 1730s external timber was painted with white lead, but by the 1780s colours were darkening. Glazing-bars had become extremely fine, and, to reduce their prominence further, darker colours were used. Dark-brown, grained, and dark-green sashes became usual, and almost universal by 1810. Nash specified that the sash-windows of the terraces in Regent's Park should be grained every four years, and should resemble oak. Doors were usually painted, often green or blue-green, but were grained later.

When stucco became fashionable, instead of the bland Georgian stock-bricks, the Roman-Cement façades were often lined to resemble ashlar, and were 'frescoed' or colour-washed with iron sulphate in water, with the 'joints' coloured in umber to suggest stonework. Sometimes stucco finishes were given three coats of oil paint, the last lightly sanded to suggest a stone surface. Timber or stucco shop-fronts were painted to suggest rich stone such as porphyry: the Georgian period saw a remarkable development of skills in suggesting, by means of paint, marble, stone, rich woods, and other materials. Ironwork was usually black, but sometimes (especially in the early nineteenth century) was a rich black-green colour. Very occasionally some gilding was applied, especially to hanging shop-signs, for iron railings were generally painted in one colour, usually dark, although early-Georgian railings were often of a steely blue or indigo shade. In the 1770s a

royal blue was occasionally used for ironwork until it was superseded by the greeny-bronze shades of the Regency period. Trellises, too, were usually green, and green was favoured for front doors from about 1800.

Sanitary Arrangements

With regard to sanitary arrangements, the Georgian house was primitively equipped by modern standards. Most houses had a cesspool, sometimes with an outflow leading to a sewer if one were available, but more usually not provided with an outlet. The better type of cesspool was constructed of brick, with a domed top, but more often the cesspool was a hole in the ground and the liquid simply oozed into the ground. Cesspools had to be emptied, and this was done by the 'nightmen' who had carts, and removed the 'night-soil' by the bucket. This operation was carried out between midnight and 5am by law, so the Georgian street, with its regular cries from the Watch, or the 'Charley' as the Watchman was called, and the noise of the nightman and his cart, was by no means quiet.[5]

Privies were usually sited over or near cesspools in the corner of the rear garden, or at the back of a yard, because they were evil-smelling places. In town-houses privies were sometimes sited in the vaulted structures under the pavements which contained the coal-cellar and other offices, or in the front part of the basement 'area', but these would have been used by the servants. Water-closets were simply pans which could be flushed from a tank or a pipe, and they were not uncommon in the better type of house: probably most of the aristocratic and upper middle-class houses were equipped with water-closets by the 1780s, and these were often sited in a small room sited off the rear staircase. Nonetheless, from early-Georgian times most town-houses would have had the family privy sited in the garden, and this would have been of the non-flushing variety.

Town-Gardens

Town-gardens were most commonly rectangular, and were laid out formally with hedges of elm or other trees, a gravel path round the garden (sometimes edged with box), and a central bed planted with flowering shrubs such as almond, lilac, or laburnum. Sometimes there was an arbour in the centre, or a trellis structure, and usually the 'conveniency' or 'Temple of Cloacina' sited in a corner, sometimes coyly draped with honeysuckle or some other sweet-smelling climbing plant to make the privy less offensive and obvious. Occasionally pergolas were provided, but more often the arrangement of paths and beds was formal, symmetrical, and simple. Town-gardens were walled, and the hedges were formed of trees (elm and poplar were common) arranged in espalier fashion.

However, the extremely sooty atmosphere of London even in Georgian times made the creation of gardens a problem, so often the plants were potted, being brought indoors if things got too foul outside. To judge from the many paintings of Georgian family life and Georgian interiors that have survived, house-plants were greatly liked, and were a feature of the Georgian drawing-room. Occasionally gardens were planted with evergreens for topiary, but more often the arrangement included espaliered trees, often fruit. Cherry, fig, and mulberry were favoured, and vines were not unusual on south-facing walls, or where there were trellises or pergolas. Peach and nectarine were greatly prized. Roses were popular, as were stocks, honeysuckles, laburnum, and lilac. Sometimes the end of a town-garden was embellished with an architectural feature such as a pediment over an arch, with niches on either side, Coade Stone medallions, and the like.

Then there were the gardens in the centres of Georgian Squares. At the beginning of the Georgian period town squares such as St James's Square were simply gravelled, but in the 1720s it acquired a water-basin. Some smaller squares, such as Soho Square, had four areas of grass and trimmed trees set in gravel. In the 1760s and 1770s the centres of several squares were railed off and very densely planted.

Town-Houses

It is clear from the impressions of foreign visitors that the exteriors of Georgian town-houses were dingy and dull, but that the interiors were clean and fresh, probably because the Georgians *washed* their rooms once a week.[6] The basement contained the kitchen, stores, various offices, and servants' rooms, and was illuminated from the 'area' or sunken yard at the front and rear. Coal was stored in the vaults, usually under the pavement. The ground floor contained the entrance-hall, usually reached from a few steps rising from the pavement, often carried on a vault over the 'area'. The stair rose from this hall, and off the hall was the front parlour, and one of the two ground-floor rooms was

often used for dining, although the dining-room could also be located in the rear room of the *piano-nobile* level, on the first floor. Dining-rooms seem to have moved between ground- and first-floor rooms at various times during the Georgian period.

The drawing-room was almost always on the first floor at the front of the house, and the formal breakfast-parlour was on the ground floor. Sometimes the drawing-room would be towards the rear, and a bedroom was located over the entrance-hall, but more usually the bedrooms were on the second floor, with sometimes an attic-storey above (that is over the main cornice, and with ceilings that were flat). Garrets were ill-lit rooms with matchboard partitions situated in the roof-space, and used as sleeping-quarters for servants. In addition, there would be 'closets' to the rear of the house, often on several floors, used as dressing-rooms or small bedrooms. In larger houses a separate staircase for servants would be provided so that chamber-pots and soiled linen could be moved downstairs without offending the sensibilities of visitors or the rest of the family. Occupants of town-houses would normally consist of a married couple, several children, a butler, footman, a cook, housemaids, a housekeeper, and a governess, so there would be as many as eighteen inhabitants of a ten to fifteen-roomed house, but the usual number of occupants, including servants, seems to have been around twelve.

Of course, there were even more people in houses that were occupied by tenants not connected with each other. The hall and stairs would be used by everyone, and would probably not be very clean. The most usual arrangement would be for tenants to take a set of rooms, or a floor, but individual rooms could also be let independently. The basement kitchen and the privies would be used by everyone, an arrangement that must have been both revolting and a cause of endless friction. Kitchens were equipped with lead cisterns supplied with water by a water-company, and the water could be pumped up to higher levels. Water was also provided from public conduits or fountains, collected in water-butts from rain-water pipes, drawn from private wells in gardens or areas (these became polluted from cesspools in the latter part of the eighteenth century), or drawn from the carts of the water-carriers. In towns, of course, piped supplies were possible, but the supply-pipes were not watertight, so loss of pressure, and pollution, were constant problems. In 1817 the suppliers of water in London were required by law to lay iron pipes.

Sinks were of stone, or of timber lined with thick lead. Cooking was done on a fire, or on a primitive kitchen-range consisting of a grate with an iron hinged bracket from which pots could be suspended. Stoves appeared late in the eighteenth century, so most Georgian cooking was done on an open fire, food being boiled or roasted on some kind of spit. Proper 'ranges' with iron ovens and hot-water boilers only appeared in the 1780s, and even then they were inefficient things.

Baths, if used at all, were movable tubs, placed in closets or bedrooms, and laboriously filled with water brought up from the kitchen. Washing of dirty linens was done in a wash-house, paved, like the kitchen, in stone, and fitted out with sinks, boilers, and deal shelves and draining-boards.

While heating was provided by means of coal fires, lighting was by means of a pith of rushes dipped into hot melted animal-fat, and held in clips on a stand: a long rush light would burn for about an hour, but cannot have been pleasant. Tallow candles, made from processed animal-fat congealed around a wick, also stank, and needed constant trimming. Candles made from beeswax were very expensive, but were not unpleasant to smell, and needed less attention. Candles mounted in sconces on walls with mirrors behind increased the brightness, but the average Georgian room at night-time was very dark and underlit. By the 1790s oil-lamps with wicks, a reservoir, and a glass shade which acted as a chimney were coming into use, giving a far better light than candles, and burning oil made from rape. Paraffin was not introduced until the 1860s. Although streets were lit by gas increasingly from 1807, this fuel does not seem to have been usual in houses until well into the Victorian period, and even then it was usually only provided in the hall and main rooms.

Much interior decoration was by means of paint based on white lead and linseed oil, and often involved 'graining' to imitate olive, walnut, marble, and other materials. Shadows were often suggested by means of paint. Plain buff colours were common, however, and 'stone colour' was popular, as were biscuit and cream. Sometimes 'stone colour' had a greyish hue created by adding a little lamp-black to the last coat, or had small amounts of rose, orange, or vermilion added to make it warmer. Grey, made with white lead, Prussian blue, black, and lake, was often used, as were olive greens made from Prussian blue and yellow ochre, while lighter greens were made of white lead, Prussian blue, and the more refined yellows. Neutral tints of white lead and burnt umber were also very common.[7] Wallpapers, plain or patterned, were also used, but only above the light-painted dado-rail. Many Georgian rooms, however, were panelled, and there was a ceiling-cornice. Fire-surrounds were of marble, stone, slate, or wood. Wall-hangings came back into vogue around the middle of the eighteenth century, while stencilled patterns and frescoes enjoyed a popularity at the end of the century. When panelling above the dado fell from grace in the 1740s, wallpapers and fabric hangings came back, but wallpaper from 1770 was almost universal. Plaster decorations and mouldings were found in grand houses, but not in the humbler terrace-house.

Country-Houses

Of course, there were great country-houses, churches, public buildings, commercial buildings, clubs, places of assembly, institutional and government buildings, palaces, garden-buildings, and many other types, many of which have been discussed above. This chapter is an attempt to give a flavour of what the Georgian period offered in terms of the built fabric, and so is really composed of broad brush-strokes.

It seems clear that there was a remarkable amount of building activity involving country-houses between 1715 and 1740,[8] and that the building boom was partly caused by the desire to construct houses in the new style of the moment, Palladianism. In most cases the new houses were erected on the sites of older properties on inherited lands, and were undertaken either to promote or to denote success in public life. Of course landed gentry had an interest in politics, and if the land produced profit, then political ambition could be satisfied. A great country-house was not only a symbol of aspiration: it was indicative of prestige, that the landowner had 'made it', and that in the house he could not only dispense lavish hospitality but show that he was prosperous.

In addition to the larger houses there were estates purchased as investments on which more modest houses might be built, perhaps as a base for a further generation to assume political responsibilities, but more often to provide the ideal for a leisured retirement on the Virgilian model: such houses were of the 'villa' type, associated with Pliny. Such a house was where friendship could be cultivated and leisure could be enjoyed.

The Palladian style, previously discussed, began as a variety of the cult of Inigo Jones: it was only after the intervention of Burlington that Palladio's influence grew. In the course of the Georgian period the Classical villa (the innovation of the century) slowly began to supersede the grander status-house on the palatial scale, and eventually became transmogrified into something else. Great houses such as Castle Howard, Wanstead (PLATES 8, 12, 13), or Wentworth Woodhouse (PLATE 18), were essentially palaces. Campbell's designs for Wanstead were the models for Prior Park, Bath, Wentworth Woodhouse, Yorkshire and Nostell Priory, Yorkshire. In fact, as Sir John Summerson has observed,[9] any house of the 1730s, 1740s, or 1750s 'with a hall-and-saloon plan' in the centre, 'a regular three-storey multi-windowed front of Palladian ratio and a portico contains at least a streak of Wanstead'. Carr's plan for Harewood House, Yorkshire, was a reduction of the third Wanstead design, and, as Summerson has noted, something new started to happen, for schemes like Harewood and Ware's Wrotham Park, Hertfordshire (formerly in Middlesex),

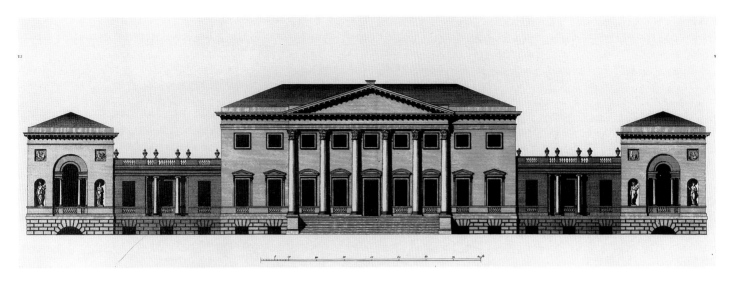

PLATE 196 *Design for the north-west elevation of Harewood House, Yorkshire, by John Carr. From* VB, *Vol V, Plates 25-26* (BAL/RIBA).

show both a reduction of a great house and an expansion of the villa type 'by means of wings and pavilions.' (PLATE 196).

At Houghton, Norfolk (PLATES 20–21), Campbell took themes from Belton, Lincolnshire, Shobdon, Herefordshire (itself derived from Talman's sketch for a country house in Wren's collection of drawings),[10] and mixed them with the south front of Wilton, Wiltshire, Jones's great Classical house of 1636. The towers, as designed by Campbell (PLATE 20), at Houghton derive directly from Wilton and from Campbell's third design for Wanstead (PLATE 13). The hall at Houghton, however, is modelled on that of the Queen's House at Greenwich. At Houghton the grouping of rooms on either side of the great central hall and saloon, with square rooms in towers at the corners of the block, and the wings connected to the main house, became the precedent for Holkham Hall, but this time there were four wings connected to the main house by low linking elements (PLATE 25). Yet Holkham, with its clear Palladian themes, also has affinities with Burlington's Tottenham Park, Wiltshire, and with Chiswick Villa (PLATE 15), but the towers derive from Wanstead, and the portico, too, comes from the Wanstead model.

The great innovation at Holkham is that, instead of the Jonesian hall, a Roman basilica on a podium appears in the guise of a hall (PLATE 27). The four-winged house probably derives from Palladio's Mocenigo project, but the links are straight rather than Palladian quadrants, and so are probably based on the Tottenham Park scheme. Again, the Holkham wings, with their triple-pedimented fronts, are like villas themselves. At Kedleston, clearly derived from Holkham, the four wings were to be connected to the main house by means

of quadrants, and Brettingham (from Holkham) designed these pavilions. Paine then designed the main block on lines unlike either Houghton or Holkham (PLATE 99), and the corner towers were dispensed with. Kedleston, with its two internal walls dividing the main block into three parts is derived from a villa plan, but the great basilican hall comes from Holkham, and the front with portico and *perron* is derived from Wanstead. Paine also introduced a novelty: this was the Pantheon-like drawing-room on the hall axis which projected from the south front, and was derived from Roman *Thermae* and from circular Roman temples (PLATES 100–101).

Paine's Kedleston was a model for Wyatt's Heaton Hall, Lancashire, with its projecting bow and low colonnaded wings joined to canted pavilions (PLATE 116), but by the 1770s the monumentality of Kedleston had been superseded by a much more modest scale. While the pavilions at Kedleston were separate buildings connected to the main house by passages in quadrants, at Heaton the pavilions and wings consisted of rooms fully integrated with the house. At both Kedleston and Heaton, however, were central blocks with curved domed bays flanked by Venetian windows set in blind arches, and with subsidiary Orders in the linking wings. Venetian windows recur in the pavilions. At Heaton the main Order sits on a plinth rather than on a high rusticated podium. Furthermore, the detailing at Heaton is lighter and more elegant: Greek Orders had appeared. It was Robert Adam who was responsible for bringing the main Order down to the ground, or down to a low plinth, rather than putting it on a rusticated ground floor at *piano-nobile* level: the model was Adam's screen at the Admiralty, Whitehall, of 1760, where the colonnade stands almost at ground level (PLATE 197). To Adam also must be credited the models for the attenuated Greek Ionic Order, the paterae, and the swags found at Heaton.

PLATE 197 *Robert Adam's screen of 1760 at the Admiralty, Whitehall, London, with Tuscan columns and Roman Doric entablature, concealing Thomas Ripley's Admiralty building of 1723–26. From* Works in Architecture, *Vol I, No IV, Plate I* (SM).

With the elimination of the rusticated base, the kitchens and service-rooms had to be placed on the same level as that of the principal rooms, or possibly in a wing. At Heaton the kitchens were in one of the canted pavilions, while the other contained the library. Even so, Adam and Borra remodelled Stowe, Buckinghamshire, in the 1770s, in the older Palladian manner.

Yet although the grander palatial house was going out of fashion, the notion of the villa as an ideal had been sown by Campbell much earlier. A *casa di villa* meant to Palladio a house on an estate, so *villa* meant a country estate rather than the house. By the time Gibbs published his *Book of Architecture* in 1728 he was using the term *villa* to mean a nobleman's secondary house, usually in the suburbs or in the country around the town. Horace Walpole used *villa* to describe a very small house. *Villa* also meant 'village' as opposed to town. However, by the 1770s a *villa* seems to have been accepted as meaning a country-house with farm and outbuildings, or a residence in the country or neighbourhood of a town, usually with some architectural pretensions. The

word was intended to suggest a house not quite grand or big enough to be a mansion or main seat, but one of distinction and one which commanded many views: in short, it was applied to a gentleman's country-house, roughly square, compact, pleasing, and modest in scale. A villa was the occasional retreat used by persons who had town-houses, and was therefore accessible from a town, or it was the country-house of a wealthy person, also not far from a town. It was, as well, a small provincial house, hunting seat, or country place for a person of relatively modest means, but was elegant, compact, and convenient.

Obvious early Palladian villas are Campbell's Mereworth Castle, near Tunbridge Wells, in Kent (and therefore used for a short season each year when the Spa was visited), derived from Palladio's Villa Capra, Vicenza (PLATES 22–24);

Campbell's Stourhead, Wiltshire, derived from Palladio's designs for the villa of Leonardo Emo at Fanzolo (PLATES 10–11); Sir William Robinson's Newby-on-Swale, now Baldersby, near Ripon, derived from a Campbell design (PLATE 19); Roger Morris's Marble Hill, Twickenham, and Lord Burlington's celebrated villa at Chiswick, also derived from Villa Capra (PLATE 15).

Flitcroft's Bower House, Havering, Essex, is a charming and very simple villa, five windows wide, with a pediment over the central three. Grander is Frampton Court in Gloucestershire, a somewhat clumsily detailed house by John Strahan (*ob c* 1740), which resembles Redland Court in Bristol, and which has wings with strange towers over them. Interestingly, Strahan worked with William Halfpenny, who, with his son John, probably designed the Orangery at Frampton Court (PLATE 50). The combination of Palladian and Gothick raises possible connections with Castle Ward, Co Down (PLATES 37–38), which, although *c* 1760, is both a villa and a structure incorporating detail which looks very like that of the Orangery. The connections between Bath and Bristol Architects and the landed gentry of Ulster, and especially of Co Down, has previously been mentioned.

Other villas included Linley Hall, Bishop's Castle, Shropshire, of the 1740s, designed by Henry Joynes (*c* 1684–1754), which has a rusticated base, overemphasised keystones (Joynes had worked with Vanbrugh), and a Palladian and a Thermal window. Sir Robert Taylor's Danson Hill, Kent, of 1756, was designed with wings so that it was like a mini-version of Holkham, but Taylor introduced the canted bay in the side elevations, a theme he again used at Asgill House, Richmond, a building which also incorporates the half-pedimented wing, later a common motif of the villa type (PLATE 198). The canted bay, of course, remained popular virtually until 1939, but its origins derive from parts of octagons, and seem to date from the time of Burlington. They were common in the Georgian period, and were called octangular bows.

Isaac Ware's Wrotham Park of 1754 incorporated elements derived from Burlington's villa at Chiswick with wings terminating in canted pavilions, and it clearly influenced other designs, such as Heaton Hall. The villa, with or without wings and pavilions, was obviously coming into its own from the 1740s. Sir William Chambers's Duddingston, near Edinburgh, of 1763–68, is not unlike Campbell's Stourhead, but has no rusticated basement, and the prostyle tetrastyle Corinthian portico sits on a platform only four steps high (PLATE 199). All Chambers's houses are examples of the villa type. His Peper Harow House, Surrey, of 1765–68, was the model for Lancelot Brown's Claremont, Esher, Surrey, which in turn derives from Stourhead. The basis, as has been mentioned above, was the Villa Emo, and was an approximately square arrangement

divided into three in both directions: in the central compartment were the top-lit staircases, with the rooms arranged all around, communicating with each other and, sometimes, with the staircase compartment. Of this type too is Berrington Hall, Herefordshire, by Henry Holland, of the 1770s. Soane, Holland's pupil, used this basic arrangement at Tendring Hall, Essex, of the 1780s, but reintroduced the segmental bay on the garden front, looking back to Paine at Kedleston and Wyatt at Heaton Hall. A similar plan, with a bow-fronted entrance and drawing-room, was used by Soane at Tyringham, Buckinghamshire, of the 1790s, but there the stairs were moved to one side.

Thus by 1775 the villa type, with or without wings and pavilions, was fashionable, and the middle classes who had made their piles were busy erecting villas. High rusticated ground-floor basements were going out of fashion, and the *piano-nobile* dropped to ground level, or just above it. Service-wings were therefore necessary, grouped around a courtyard, attached to the house, or kept well secreted behind shrubberies. At the same time, architectural details tended to become attenuated and delicate, often with Grecian elements, much influenced by Adam And Wyatt. The tall attenuated columns and pilasters used by Steuart at Attingham are a case in point.

Finally, with Castle Coole, Co Fermanagh (PLATE 117, Wyatt combined the bow-fronted saloon and a more severe type of Neo-Classicism. With Grange Park, Hampshire, however, Wilkins accentuated the Greek temple, and the theme of the villa was almost obscured (PLATE 88). Architects such as Peter Nicholson, however, did not abandon the villa, and provided many fine designs in which a new simplicity, grace, gravity, and delicacy became paramount.

Mausolea and Memorials

The design of tombs and memorials can reveal much about a period, its tastes, its beliefs, and its craftmanship. Georgian memorials were derived from Classical models, and even the lettering was often of the Roman type, although cursive lettering was frequently used. Georgian design for death was rooted in the Orders and in the architectural language of Greece and Rome. The cartouche, or parchment-like surface of marble on which an inscription would be placed, was very common in the Baroque period, and examples were still being made in the early eighteenth century. Like doorcases and the surrounds of niches, Georgian memorials in churches often had broken pediments with urns between them, and featured all the elements of architrave,

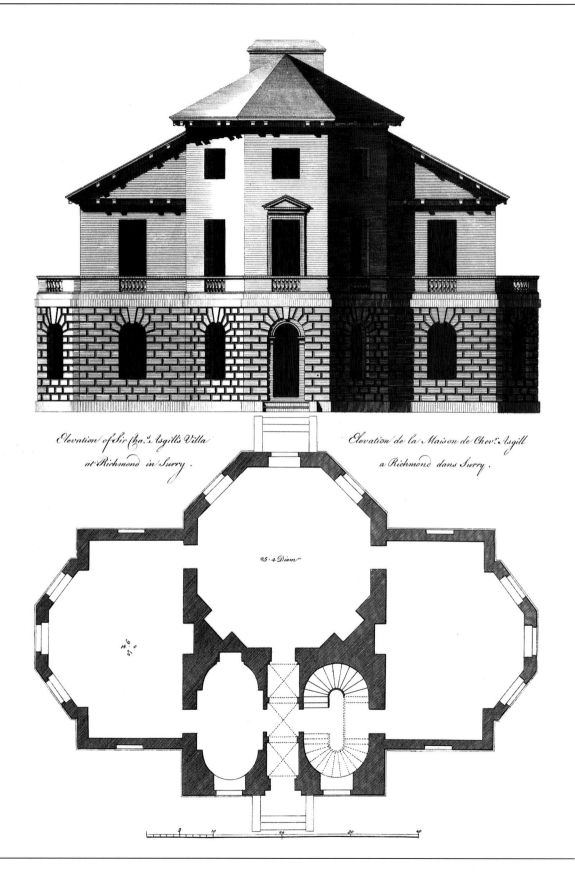

Elevation of Sir Chas Asgill's Villa
at Richmond in Surry.

Elevation de la Maison de Chev.^r Asgill
a Richmond dans Surry.

PLATE 198 *Sir Robert Taylor's Asgill House, Richmond, Surrey, from* VB, *Vol IV, Plate 74* (SM).

entablature, and pediment (PLATE 200). In addition, of course, were the draped urns, weeping mourners, *putti* with inverted torches, cherubs, effigies in full periwig and contemporary dress, medallions, and so on, usually carved in marbles. By the time of Neo-Classicism, however, pure Roman and then Greek elements came in, and predominantly white marble memorials in churches became normal.

When death occurred in the Georgian Age all bodies were buried, or entombed in vaults, shafts, or built mausolea. The rich could be entombed in magnificent coffins in their family vaults, usually under a mortuary-chapel or former chantry-chapel attached to a church, or in a mausoleum in parkland, or under the church in the park. Such modes of burial involved the use of lead coffins, usually protected in outer wooden cases covered with velvet and embellished with handles, plates, and nail-heads, silver or gilt. Others were entombed in brick-lined shafts under churches, each coffin resting on iron bars built into the sides of the shafts, and the shafts were sealed with inscribed ledger-stones of slate or black marble. If burial occurred, it was in the churchyard attached to a church, or, in the case of overcrowded city churchyards, often in 'over-spill' grounds physically removed from the church. An example of a Parish graveyard not attached to the church because the original graveyard had become completely full (and therefore unwholesome) is that of St Giles-in-the-Fields, London, situated beside Old St Pancras church behind the Midland Railway terminus at St Pancras: in it were buried Johann Christian Bach (1735–85) and the architect Sir John Soane (1753–1837) – who built a remarkable mausoleum (PLATE 128) for himself and his wife there. Mausolea (roofed tombs built above ground on which or under which coffins were placed) were unusual in Parish churchyards, although examples can be found (PLATE 201).

Funerals usually took place at night in the first half of the eighteenth century, the church service beginning late in the evening, and the mourners following the corpse from the house to the church. Armigerous families had their achievements painted on square panels set with the corners of the panel at the top, bottom, and sides, and these 'hatchments' were hung up in the church after the burial: many hatchments survive and can be seen in Parish churches to this day.

While it was doubtless useful to have a mausoleum as an

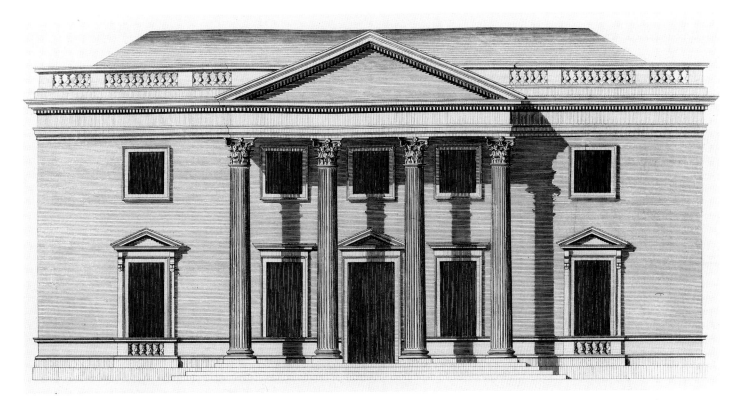

PLATE 199 *Elevation of the Earl of Abercorn's house at Duddingston, near Edinburgh, by Sir William Chambers, of 1763–68. Note that the prostyle tetrastyle Corinthian portico sits on four steps rather than on a basement storey. From* VB, *Vol IV, Plate 14* (SM).

PLATE 200 *Baroque monument to John Moore, Bishop of Ely, in the south choir-aisle of Ely Cathedral, Cambridgeshire. It has two standing cherubs (winged), and the Order is Composite, with a scrolled pediment in the centre of which is a flaming urn. Note the lettering on marble 'drapery', and the achievements within a Baroque cartouche frame (JSC).*

PLATE 201 *Some eighteenth-century mausolea in the church-yard of Knockbreda Parish church, Co Down. Note the urns and tall pyramids* (JSC).

PLATE 202 '*Grand National Cemetery Intended for the prevention of the Danger and Inconvenience of burying the Dead within the Metropolis Proposed to be erected by a Capital of 400,000l in 16,000 shares at 25l each, designed by Francis Goodwin, Architect.*' *A late-Georgian proposal for what would have been the grandest necropolis ever built* (GLCL).

eye-catcher to ornament the park or terminate the vista, the entombment of families in mausolea reflected a new sensibility. If the individual mausoleum could not be had, then entombment in a chapel or within a church was the next best thing, for families often had interests in one-time chantry-chapels which were by Georgian times only mortuary-chapels. Burial in a church or vault was preferred to interment in the churchyard because there was a universal fear of body-snatchers who disinterred freshly buried bodies for sale to the anatomists. Many churchyards were therefore protected by high walls with spiked railings on top, and were watched by paid night-watchmen who, however, could be bribed or threatened by the 'Resurrection-Men'. Burial in a churchyard almost invariably meant disturbing previous graves, and in overcrowded churchyards there were often revolting scenes and unpleasant smells.[11]

Commemoration involved the erection of a headstone in a churchyard, usually of local stone or slate, and frequently decorated with Baroque and Rococo ornament, hour-glasses, winged cherubs' heads, skulls and bones, picks and mattocks, and weeping widows with draped urns. Lettering was often exquisite and elaborate, especially when cut into slate: excellent slate headstones survive in the churchyard of St Mary de Castro, Leicester, where one stone depicts a skeleton climbing out of its tomb at the Last Trump. Altar-tombs were common, covering the whole grave, and inscribed at the sides, while table-tombs and flat slabs laid over brick or stone shafts were also found.

Ledger-stones in churches had inscriptions and often other decorations such as achievements inscribed on them. The well-off were commemorated by elaborate memorials mounted on the walls of churches, and Georgian memorials unquestionably reflect architectural styles and tastes throughout the period. Architectural aedicules, drapery with urns and mourners, obelisks and triangular compositions, sarcophagi, medallions, carved reliefs, and a vast array of carved tablets in frames of various shapes and sizes, often featuring differently coloured marbles, demonstrate the great variety of one of the finest legacies of the Georgian Age. The last phase was dominated by Neo-Classicism, and the flavour became severe and Greek in the hands of John Flaxman, Sir Richard Westmacott, Sir Francis Legatt Chantrey, and others.[12] Parish churches in the British Isles contain a marvellous collection of funerary monuments of all periods, but the richest and finest memorials are those of the Georgians, erected between 1714 and 1830.

From the literature of the period, however, it is clear that the conditions in urban burial-grounds were appalling, and various ideas began to be floated to improve matters. Liverpool acquired two cemeteries, unattached to churches, in the 1820s, and at the very end of the Georgian Age, in 1830, Francis Goodwin (1784–1835) proposed a new and enormous metropolitan cemetery which, if realised, would have been the most magnificent necropolis in the world (Plate 202): as it was, however, it was not built, as landscaped cemeteries, of which the first was the General Cemetery of All Souls, Kensal Green, were preferred.

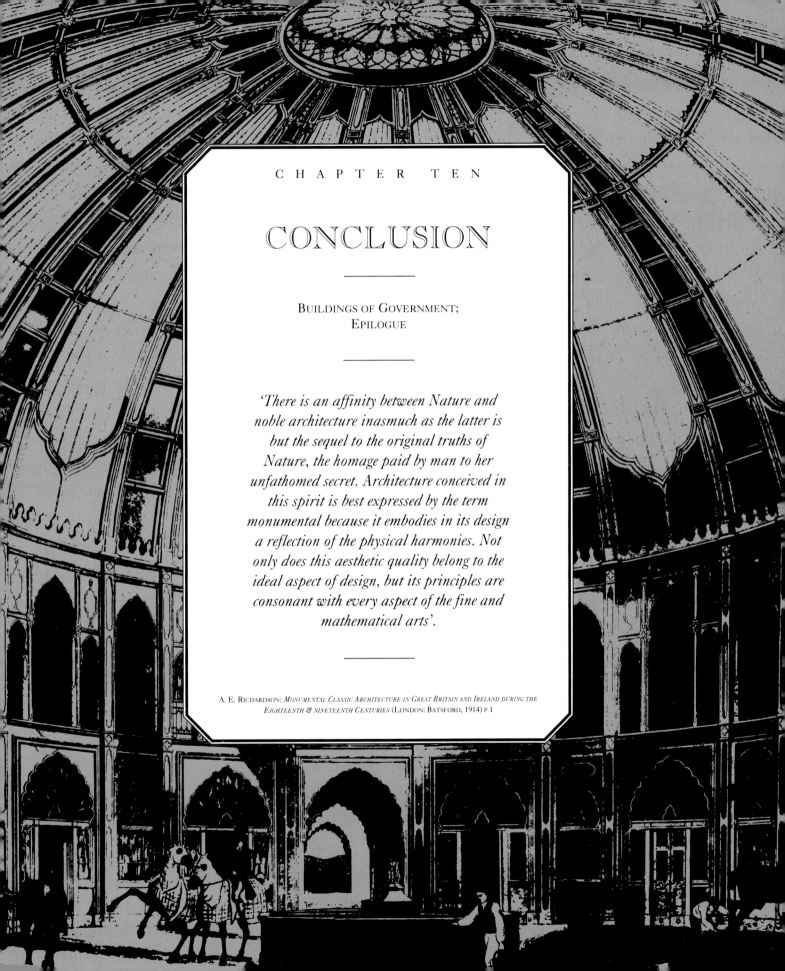

CHAPTER TEN

CONCLUSION

BUILDINGS OF GOVERNMENT;
EPILOGUE

'There is an affinity between Nature and noble architecture inasmuch as the latter is but the sequel to the original truths of Nature, the homage paid by man to her unfathomed secret. Architecture conceived in this spirit is best expressed by the term monumental because it embodies in its design a reflection of the physical harmonies. Not only does this aesthetic quality belong to the ideal aspect of design, but its principles are consonant with every aspect of the fine and mathematical arts'.

A. E. RICHARDSON: *MONUMENTAL CLASSIC ARCHITECTURE IN GREAT BRITAIN AND IRELAND DURING THE EIGHTEENTH & NINETEENTH CENTURIES* (LONDON: BATSFORD, 1914) P 1

Buildings of Government

Many works of architecture and building types have been mentioned above. Here, purpose-built structures for Government of the Georgian period will be reviewed. Until after 1725 the organisation of Government took place in old buildings, altered piecemeal as needs changed. The splendid hospitals of Greenwich (naval), Chelsea (military), and Kilmainham in Dublin (military) were all established in the reigns of Charles II and William and Mary, and, of course, were modelled on the huge Hôtel des Invalides in Paris, founded by Louis XIV. The new Hanoverian monarchs inhabited the ancient buildings at Whitehall, Kensington, and St James's, and Government offices were spread through the old Palace of Westminster and sundry buildings in Whitehall.

Inigo Jones had proposed a grand palace at Whitehall, but only the celebrated Banqueting House was built. Then Thomas Ripley (c 1683–1758), under the patronage of Sir Robert Walpole, succeeded Grinling Gibbons as Master-Carpenter in 1721, and, after the death of Vanbrugh in 1726, became Comptroller of the Works. Ripley designed the Admiralty (1723–26), the first Georgian building of Government, but it was a feeble and stylistically antiquated work of architecture, and ill-proportioned to boot (PLATE 197). Indeed, it was so awful that the portico and court were eventually hidden by the colonnade of Adam built in 1760 (PLATE 197). Ripley was appointed executive architect at Houghton Hall, which experience had a remarkable effect on improving his style. At Wolterton Hall (1727–41), in Norfolk, for example, Ripley unusually incorporated architectural features normally found on the exteriors of buildings in the great staircase. When Vanbrugh, in 1721, saw Ripley's name in the public prints, he laughed so much at the 'Esquire' that he 'had like to Beshit' himself. So bad was Ripley's architecture, and so shameless and meteoric his rise under Walpole, that not only Vanbrugh despised him: Alexander Pope recognised Ripley as a model of 'Dulness', destroying everything that Burlington and Jones had achieved.

> '*See under Ripley rise a new White-hall,*
> *While Jones' and Boyle's united labours fall;*
> *While Wren with sorrow to the grave descends;*
> *Gay dies unpensioned with a hundred friends...*' [1]

wrote Pope in *The Dunciad*, Book III, of 1743. In his *Moral Essays* of 1731 Pope's fourth Epistle was addressed to Richard Boyle, Earl of Burlington. In it, Pope noted that

> '*Heav'n visits with a taste the wealthy fool,*
> *And needs no rod but Ripley with a rule*'. [2]

Pope, in a footnote to *Moral Essays*, states that Ripley 'was a carpenter, employed by a first minister, who raised him to an architect, without any genius in the art; and after some wretched proofs of his insufficiency in public buildings, made him Comptroller of the Board of Works'. [3] In the same *Essay* Pope warned Burlington, who had shown

> '*Rome was glorious, not profuse,*
> *And pompous buildings once were things of use*',

that pattern-books and rules could, in turn create problems:

> '*Yet shall, my lord, your just, your noble rules*
> *Fill half the land with imitating-fools;*
> *Who random drawings from your sheets shall take,*
> *And of one beauty many blunders make;*
> *Load some vain church with old theatric state,*
> *Turn arcs of triumph to a garden-gate;*
> *Reverse your ornaments, and hang them all*
> *On some patched dog-hole eked with ends of wall;*
> *Then clap four slices of pilaster on't,*
> *That, laced with bits of rustic, makes a front.*
> *Shall call the winds through long arcades to roar,*
> *Proud to catch cold at a Venetian door;*
> *Conscious they act a true Palladian part,*
> *And, if they starve, they starve by rules of art.*' [4]

Though the Admiralty was a disaster, however, the new Parliament House in Dublin by Sir Edward Lovett Pearce, begun 1729, was a triumph (PLATE 32). It is a noble and dignified building with a portico flanked by colonnaded wings which break forward to enclose a court, and terminate in pedimented arched elements. Kent's Treasury Building, Whitehall, of 1733–36 followed, with a fully rusticated seven-window-wide façade, the front three bays of which break forward with a tetrastyle engaged temple-front above the first floor: the composition appears rather tall and squashed, and looks more like a town mansion than a Government Building. Kent followed this not altogether successful work with his celebrated Horse Guards of c 1745–60: it consists of a wide central block with a centre-piece and pavilions that project forward, a rusticated base, and an attic storey; two wings each five windows wide set back; and two three-window-wide pedimented end pavilions. There are no fewer than five Serlianas within arches, and there is a tall clock-tower over the centre (PLATE 17). The building is very fussy, and the Palladian insistence on relating external elevations to internal spaces was ignored, for many of the windows are fake, and even some of the Venetian windows illuminate minor rooms. The composition, linking various almost disparate parts, was referred to as 'concatenated', or formed of a chain, joining the pieces in an interdependent sequence of elements. Sir William Chambers spotted one of the problems:

'whenever there is a considerable difference of dimension, in objects of the same figure, both will equally suffer by it; the largest will appear insupportably heavy; the smallest ridiculously trifling: and wherever the difference of dimension is inconsiderable, it will always strike the beholder as the effect of inaccuracy in the workmen, or of inattention in the contriver; as may be verified by inspection of the arches in the basement story of the Horse Guards towards St James's Park.' [5]

Chambers went on to say that Burlington 'left no means unused to raise the reputation' of Kent: his Lordship lodged Kent 'in his house when living, and in his family vault at Chiswick when dead'. Joseph Gwilt noted sourly that 'whatever is good' in Kent's architectural designs may be traced to Burlington's 'skill and direction'. The Horse Guards was completed under the direction of John Vardy (*ob* 1765) after the death of both Kent and Burlington. Chambers noted that the Horse Guards was a building not much liked, and criticised what he saw as Kent's use of unnecessary complexity.

Chambers's own Somerset House was gravely severe, much influenced by French Neo-Classicism, and, as previously noted, was a purpose-made office building for various Government departments. While the elevations are very successful, with their plain ranges of rusticated wall and Giant Order centre-pieces, it must be admitted that the drum and dome on the river frontage and the low towers on the other ranges are far too small, and really do not work (PLATES 112–113).

Also monumental was the Royal Mint at Tower Hill of 1807–12 by James Johnson (*ob* 1807) and Robert Smirke, a Palladianesque building with severe Grecian gate-lodges. Certainly monumental was Nash's Buckingham Palace of 1825–27, which had a *Cour d'Honneur* with building around three sides facing the Mall. Edward Blore (1787–1879) filled in the fourth side of the court with a very clumsy and dismal east wing of 1847–50, subsequently refronted by Sir Aston Webb (1849–1930) in 1913. Nash's building was noble yet showy, with Greek and other allusions, and was perfectly in tune with the styles of the Regency and of the reign of George IV.

Sir Robert Taylor's monumental houses (Gorhambury, Hertfordshire, of 1777–90, Heveningham, Suffolk, of 1777–80 [PLATE 30]) were certainly grand, but his Bank of England, with its superb Pantheon-like Stock Room, and the other Transfer offices, was a *tour-de-force* of grand official architecture. At Stone Buildings, Lincoln's Inn (1774–80) and the Six Clerks' and Enrolment Offices, Chancery Lane (1775–77), Taylor produced purpose-designed chambers and office-

buildings (PLATE 203), but at his Guildhall in Salisbury of 1788 he gave England one of its first truly grand Local Government buildings. This extraordinary free-standing single-storey building employs Taylor's favourite vermiculated rusticated quoins and voussoirs, has Serlianas set in the powerful blocky elements of the design, and in the Council Chamber a bow contained within a canted bay. The entrance was approached through a screen of unfluted Roman Doric columns set between the projecting wings. Central rooms were top-lit, like parts of the Bank of England. In this great Guildhall Taylor created a building of originality and presence quite unlike the average Town Hall or Guildhall of the period. Stamford Town Hall, Lincolnshire, for example, of 1776–79, probably Henry Tatam, has rusticated window-openings, channels, and very thin detailing, suggesting more an overblown domestic building than a civic structure, and in this respect it was usual of the Georgian Age. Newark's Town Hall, Nottinghamshire, of *c* 1774–76, is a Palladian mansion plonked down in a Market-Square, as is James Wyatt's Town Hall in the Market-Square in Ripon, Yorkshire; in the latter instance, however, a civic flavour is given by the frieze inscribed:

EXCEPT YE LORD KEEP YE CITTIE, YE WAKEMAN
WAKETH IN VAIN.

Palladianism was the dominant style for Town Halls. Occasionally, quotations from churches can be found, as in Roger Morris's Council House at Chichester of the 1730s, where a variation on Palladio's façade of San Giorgio Maggiore in Venice occurs over a plain brick arcaded ground floor. The arcade occurs also at the Bastard Brothers's Town Hall at Blandford in Dorset and at the Guildhall in High Wycombe, Buckinghamshire: the first is set in a terrace, and the latter, by Henry Keene, of 1757, is free-standing with an open ground floor with Tuscan arcading. Dance's celebrated front to Guildhall in London (PLATE 67), mentioned earlier, is monumental, in the 'Hindoo' style of Gothick. The earlier Worcester Guildhall of 1721–23 by Thomas White (*c* 1674–1748) is heavily Baroque, with a Giant Composite Order carrying an ornate segmental pediment, a façade with segmental-headed windows, and two projecting wings: yet this Guildhall is not really monumental, but looks vaguely institutional. Liverpool Town Hall, formerly the Exchange, of 1749–54, was monumental, like a vast Whig country mansion, unlike Robert Adam's Shire and Town Hall, Hertford, of 1767–69, a loose and somewhat feeble composition, which looks like the old mixture of Town Hall and Market-House/Exchange. Leith Town Hall of 1827–28 by Richard (1792–1857) and Robert (*c* 1794–1865) Dickson has Graeco-Palladian elements, and is severely stark, as befits a building for Local Government of the period. There are many fine

WEST ELEVATION

examples of Town and Shire Halls, many of which display Palladian elements (one of the best is Sanderson Miller's Warwick Shire Hall of 1754–58, a single-storey building with a pedimented centre-piece).

At the turn of the century, however, a very much larger and more complicated set of monumental buildings was heralded by Chester Castle by Thomas Harrison, housing courts, gaol, barracks, treasury, offices, and Shire Hall. These buildings comprise a fine Greek Revival complex. Robert Smirke's Assize Courts at Carlisle, of 1810–11, is monumental in a different way, consisting of two round court rooms in two round towers, with Gothic two-light windows and crenellations.

Of course Soane, Wyatt, and others carried out works for the Palace of Westminster, but these were tacked onto or fitted within older fabric. Soane, however, designed the New State Paper Office in St James's Park of 1830, and, of course, the Bank of England: he also prepared unexecuted designs for a new House of Lords. It was not until Chambers's Somerset House that London acquired her first great Georgian riverside building (PLATES 112–113), for the new Palace of Westminster was not to rise until Victoria was on the Throne. Then, in 1817 David Laing's Custom House was finished: it was a long, bold Neo-Classical building with an astylar central portico pierced by tall semicircular-headed windows. Unfortunately the piles failed, and Robert Smirke rebuilt the central portion to his own design. Smirke's General Post Office of 1824–29 was another long façade impeccably Greek in manner.

It has to be said, however, that the riverside buildings in Dublin (the Custom House and Four Courts) (PLATES 114 and 115) were far grander than anything by Thames-side, not least because of their unfussy detail and very fine cupolas. Edinburgh, too, acquired its elegant Register House to designs by Robert Adam in 1774–89, the first important Government Building in Great Britain since Kent's Horse Guards: it is basically Palladian, with a *piano nobile* over rusti-

PLATE 203 *Stone Buildings, Lincoln's Inn, and the Six Clerks' and Enrolment Offices, Chancery Lane, London, of 1775–77, by Sir Robert Taylor, from Richardson (BTB/SH).*

cated arches, but the character is more Neo-Classical (PLATES 106–108). Robert Reid's scheme for Edinburgh's Parliament Square of 1803–38 quotes Adam's unexecuted designs for the University quadrangle in the quadrants, and is an elegant and gracious mixture of Palladian, Neo-Classical, and Adamesque motifs. Even earlier, in 1754, John Adam had produced designs for City Chambers, Edinburgh, modified by John Fergus: the building was originally called the Royal Exchange, was a three-sided courtyard with rusticated arcaded ground floor and a centre-piece with Corinthian pilasters and pediment, and contained public offices. It became City Chambers in 1811.

It would be tedious to list every Georgian building associated with Government. Pevsner's *Buildings of England, Scotland, and Ireland* series mentions these, while, within the Georgian period, the Gazetteer in Dan Cruickshank's *A Guide to the Georgian Buildings of Britain & Ireland* covers the field, is comprehensive in scope, and is elegantly written.

Epilogue

The general acceptance of Classicism during the Georgian period was neither fortuitous nor due to mere fashion. Britain, like the rest of Europe, was still enjoying the results of the Italian Renaissance, and Classical detail and design were accepted as modern, civilised, and universal. Even when the Greek Revival triumphed, the essential qualities of Classical Palladianism were retained, while even Georgian Gothick is, for the most part, Classical with pointed arches and certain details applied to something which could just as easily have been dressed in Classical Roman or Greek garb.

There were many architects of modest talent in the Georgian period, but there were also giants. The Adams, Alexander, Archer, Beazley, Bedford, Bond, Bonomi, the Booths, the Brettinghams, Brown, Browning, Brunel, Burlington, Burn, Burton, Campbell, Carr, Cassels, Chambers, the Cockerells, Cooley, Craig, Cubitt, the Dances, Dobson, Donaldson, the Elliots, Elmes, Essex, Flitcroft, Foster, Foulston, Fowler, Galilei, Gandon, Gandy, Gibbs, Gibson, Goodwin, Graham, Gwilt, Hakewill, the Halfpennys, the Hamiltons, Hanson, the Hardwicks, Harrison, Hawksmoor, the Hiornes, Holland, Hopper, the Inwoods, James, Johnson, Johnston, Keene, Kent, Laing, the Langleys, Latrobe, Leoni, Leverton, Miller, Milne, Monck, Moneypenny, the Morrises, the Morrisons, Mulholland, Müntz, Mylne, Nash, the Nicholsons, Paine, the Pains, Papworth, Pearce, Pembroke, Plaw, the Playfairs, Porden, Priestley, Reid, Rennie, Repton, Revett, Richardson, Rickman, the Robinsons, Sandys, Savage, Shanahan, Simpson, Smirke, the Smiths, Soane, Stark, Steuart, Stuart, Suter, Tatham, Taylor, Telford, Thomson, Tite, Vanbrugh, Walpole, Ware, Wilkins, the Woods, Wren, and the Wyatts were just a few names of those who contributed to the architecture of the Georgian period (although one or two, like Wren, were very old, and died soon after the beginning of the Hanoverian reigns). There were hundreds of provincial architects and designers who also worked within the language, vocabulary, and syntax of Classicism, and here the importance of printed designs cannot be over-stressed. True, there were clumsinesses and solecisms, but generally, in spite of Pope's

concerns, the rules and the patterns ensured a degree of harmony in design that was not seen before 1714 and which began to vanish after 1830.

'Georgian architecture', Sir Albert Richardson wrote, 'was democratic; it admitted to its purpose hosts of lesser men. Its benefits, as a style, were world-wide; it favoured many qualities. Where else can be found stylistic truths to replace the Colonial architecture of British America? Where else could be found works of similar status to those which adorn Ireland? In what other part of the world can we discover the simple statement and the unerring senses of proportion which seems to belong to this English style alone?'.[6]

Quite so: it 'admitted to its purpose hosts of lesser men', and that was the strength of Georgian architecture. Design is extraordinarily difficult, and most people cannot do it: it is debatable as to whether most people who read Architecture

PLATE 204 *Church of St Margaret, Well, Lincolnshire, of 1733, designed as a point de vue for the Park. An example of the Palladian Inigo Jones Revival. The Tuscan portico is based on the front of the church of St Paul, Covent Garden, by Jones, which is in turn based on Palladio and Vitruvius* (JSC)

are really proficient in design, and matters are made worse these days because there are few rules, and there is no universally agreed vocabulary, syntax, or architectural language. Classicism had all these, and the excellent pattern-books, rules of proportions, and the like enabled duff designers to produce something passable. There was nothing shameful in it. These days, when 'self-expression' and 'originality' (usually euphemisms for carelessness or worse) are everywhere claimed (and the results are lamentable design, ham-fisted junctions, and abysmal understanding of materials), a system of rules, of proportion, and a series of carefully designed parts might not be so bad. Certainly the system in the Georgian period produced marvellous buildings, townscapes, and architecture. Edinburgh New Town, Bath, Clifton, Dublin, Cheltenham, Brighton, Bloomsbury, Marylebone, Armagh, and many other places would not have been possible without pattern-books, rules, architectural language, and a universal acceptance of the rightness of Classicism. Mrs Coade could not have produced her stoneware architectural components and decorative motifs without that universal language, and it is not without significance that her factory ceased production in *c* 1850 when the certainties of Classicism had been destroyed by the pseudo-moralising of Goths and Christians. Gone was that Augustan equipoise.

And the Georgians not only gave us fine streets, towns, squares, buildings, but beautiful gardens and landscapes as well.

> *'To build, to plant, whatever you intend,*
> *To rear the column, or the arch to bend,*
> *To swell the terrace, or to sink the grot;*
> *In all, let nature never be forgot.*
> *But treat the goddess like a modest fair,*
> *Nor over-dress, nor leave her wholly bare;*
> *Let not each beauty ev'rywhere be spied,*

> *Where half the skill is decently to hide.*
> *He gains all points, who pleasingly confounds,*
> *Surprises, varies, and conceals the bounds.'* [7]

Pope also hit the nail on the head when he advised:

> *'Consult the* genius of the place[8] *in all;*
> *That tells the waters or to rise, or fall;*
> *Or helps the ambitious hill the heav'ns to scale,*
> *Or scoops in circling theatres the vale;*
> *Calls in the country, catches op'ning glades,*
> *Joins willing woods, and varies shades from shades*
> *Now breaks, or now directs, th'intending lines;*
> *Paints as you plant, and, as you work, designs.*

> *Still follow sense, of ev'ry art the soul,*
> *Parts answ'ring parts shall slide into a whole,*
> *Spontaneous beauties all around advance,*
> *Start ev'n from difficulty, strike from chance;*
> *Nature shall join you; time shall make it grow*
> *A work to wonder at - perhaps a Stowe.'* [9]

Finally, he exhorted Lord Burlington:

> *'You too proceed! make falling arts your care,*
> *Erect new wonders, and the old repair;*
> *Jones and Palladio to themselves restore,*
> *And be whate'er Vitruvius was before.'* [10]

Pope shall have the last words: they are apposite, and the Georgians understand harmonious design, as few have done, before or since, for they 'implored the genius of the place' (*Geniumque loci precatur*).[11]

NON EQUIDEM INVIDEO, MIROR MAGIS [12]

REFERENCES

---

*'The Georgian manner represents an
amalgam of motifs and theories taken
from divers sources. In one sense it was
eclectic and bookish, in another it
epitomized the practical side of an
Englishman's taste.'*

A.E. RICHARDSON: *An Introduction to Georgian Architecture*
(LONDON: ART & TECHNICS, 1949) P 20

CHAPTER I THE GEORGIAN PERIOD

1 27 George II, c 3

2 See Hutcheson, Francis *An Inquiry into the Original of our Ideas of Beauty and Virtue* (London: np, 1725); Hume, David 'Of the Standard of Taste' in *Essays Moral, Political, and Literary* (London: A. Murray, 1875); Alison, Archibald *Essays on the Nature and Principles of Taste* (London: J. & G. Robinson, and Edinburgh: Bell & Bradgate, 1790); and Stewart, Dugald *Works*, collected by Sir William Hamilton (London: Hamilton & Adams, and Edinburgh: Thomas Constable, 1854–60)

3 Burke, Edmund *A Philosophical Enquiry into the Origin of our Ideas of the Sublime and Beautiful* (London: J. Dodsley, 1782)

4 Alison *Essays* pp 2, 127–133. See also Crook, J. Mordaunt *The Dilemma of Style. Architectural Ideas from the Picturesque to the Post-Modern* (London: Murray, 1987) pp 17–21 and *passim*

5 Ettlinger, L. D. 'A German Architect's Visit to England in 1826' *The Architectural Review* 97 (May 1945)

6 See Hunt, John Dixon *William Kent: Landscape Garden Design* (London: Zwemmer, 1987)

7 See Hunt, John Dixon and Willis, Peter *The Genius of the Place: The English Landscape Garden 1620–1820* (London: Elek, 1975) pp 17–20

8 See Curl, James Stevens *The Londonderry Plantation 1609–1914* (Chichester: Phillimore, 1986)

9 In his *Biographical Dictionary of British Architects 1600–1840* (London: Murray, 1978) p 469

10 Jacob, Margaret C. *The Radical Enlightenment: Pantheists, Freemasons, and Republicans* (London: Allen & Unwin, 1981) p 121

11 *Ibid*

12 See Curl, James Stevens *The Art and Architecture of Freemasonry* (London: Batsford, 1991)

CHAPTER II PALLADIANISM

1 From Jones's Roman Sketchbook at Chatsworth, fol 76*r* See also Harris, John and Higgott, Gordon *Inigo Jones: Complete Architectural Drawings* (New York and London: Zwemmer, 1989)

2 *Second Characters, or the Language of Forms*

3 Bodleian Library, MS Rawlinson B 376, f 9

4 9 Anne, c 22 public

5 For Georgian gardens see Jacques, David *Georgian Gardens: The Reign of Nature* (London: Batsford, 1983); Hunt, John Dixon and Willis, Peter *The Genius of the Place: The English Landscape Garden 1620–1820* (London: Elek, 1975); Hussey, Christopher *English Gardens and Landscapes 1700–1750* (London: Country Life, 1967), and many others

6 See Curl, James Stevens *The Art and Architecture of Freemasonry* (London: Batsford, 1991)

7 Colvin, Howard *A Biographical Dictionary of British Architects 1600–1840* (London: Murray, 1978) p 560

8 Cruickshank, Dan *A Guide to the Georgian Buildings of Britain & Ireland* (London: Weidenfeld & Nicolson, 1985) p 12. Mr Cruickshank's work has been invaluable to the present writer, who is indebted to the former for his friendship and generosity.

9 See Ison, Walter *The Georgian Buildings of Bath* (London: Faber, 1948)

10 Attributed by McCarthy, Michael *The Origins of the Gothic Revival* (New Haven and London: Yale UP, 1987), although Howard Colvin has suggested Flitcroft was the Architect.

11 For a very full discussion of this see Crook, J. Mordaunt *The Dilemma of Style: Architectural Ideas from the Picturesque to the Post-Modern* (London: Murray, 1987)

CHAPTER III THE ROMANTIC REVOLUTION

1 See Little, Bryan *The Life and Work of James Gibbs 1682–1754* (London: Batsford, 1955)

2 Colvin, Howard *A Biographical Dictionary of British Architects 1600–1840* (London: Murray, 1978) p 504

3 Harris, Eileen 'Batty Langley, Tutor of Free-Masons', *The Burlington Magazine* CXIX 890 (May 1977) pp 327–35. See also Rowan, Alistair 'Batty Langley's Gothic' *Studies in Memory of David Talbot Rice* (Edinburgh, 1975) pp 197–215

4 Harris *op cit* in note 3

5 *Ibid* p 199

6 In *Palladio and English Palladianism* (New York: Braziller, 1974) pp 73–112

7 See Clark, Kenneth *The Gothic Revival* (London: Murray, 1962) and especially McCarthy, Michael *The Origins of the Gothic Revival* (New Haven and London: Yate UP, 1987) esp pp 4–11

8 Note 15 p 183 McCarthy *op cit*

9 See Rowan *op cit*

10 Breman, P (*ed*) *The Architecture of the Early Eighteenth Century* (London: Weinreb, 1965) Item 46 Catalogue 11

11 McCarthy *op cit* p 8

12 For a development of this theme see Crook, J. Mordaunt *The Dilemma of Style: Architectural Ideas from the Picturesque to the Post-Modern* (London: Murray, 1987)

13 *Op cit* pp 549–51

14 Williams, M. (*ed*) *Letters of William Shenstone* (Oxford: Blackwell, 1939) p 204

15 Lewis, W. S. (*ed*) *Horace Walpole's Correspondence* (New Haven: Yale UP, 1973) Vol XXXV p 359

16 Chambers, William *Plans etc. of the Gardens and Buildings at Kew in Surrey* (London: The Author, 1763), plate 29

17 Illustrated in McCarthy *op cit*

18 For details of Strawberry Hill, see McCarthy *op cit* pp 63–91

19 In a letter to Miss Berry of October 1794

20 For descriptions see Lindsay, Ian G. and Cosh, Mary *Inveraray and the Dukes of Argyll* (Edinburgh: Edinburgh UP, 1973)

21 For Scottish and Northern English houses see Macaulay, James *The Gothic Revival 1745–1845* (Glasgow & London: Blackie, 1975)

22 Honour, Hugh *Chinoiserie. The Vision of Cathay* (London: Murray, 1961) p 141

23 *Ibid* p 156

24 See Stroud, Dorothy *Henry Holland. His Life and Architecture* (London: Country Life, 1966)

25 Curl, James Stevens *The Egyptian Revival: An Introductory Study of a Recurring Theme in the History of Taste* (London: Allen & Unwin, 1982)

CHAPTER IV ARCHAEOLOGY AND THE REVIVAL OF CLASSICAL ANTIQUITY

1 *The Development of a Theme in Architectural History and Theory from the Gothic Revival to the Modern Movement* (Oxford: Clarendon Press, 1977)

2 See Woodman, Francis *The Architectural History of King's College Chapel and its Place in the Development of Late Gothic Architecture in England and France* (London: Routledge & Kegan Paul, 1986)

3 Colvin, H. M. 'Gothic Survival and Gothick Revival' *The Architectural Review* Vol CIII (1948) p 91 *et seq*

4 See Clark, Kenneth *The Gothic Revival. An Essay in the History of Taste* (London: Murray, 1962)

5 See Praz, Mario *On Neoclassicism* (Evanston: Northwestern UP, 1969) and *Neo-Classicism* (London: Arts Council, 1972)

6 See Pevsner, Nikolaus and Lang, S. 'The Doric Revival' in *Studies in Art, Architecture, and Design* Vol 1 (New York: Walker & Co, 1968)

7 Chapter 1 plate 3

8 The volume is dated 1787, and the plate is number 3 in chapter 4 of volume II.

9 See Curl, James Stevens 'Altes Museum, Berlin' and 'Charlottenhof, Potsdam' *The Architects' Journal* (19 June and 24 & 31 July 1991 respectively)

10 *Treatise* 1825 edition pp 114–116

11 See Leach, Peter *James Paine* (London: Zwemmer, 1988)

12 See Rankin, Peter *Irish Building Ventures of the Earl Bishop of Derry* (Belfast: Ulster Architectural Heritage Society, 1972)

CHAPTER V GEORGIAN CHURCHES

1 See the useful volume by Clarke, Basil F. L. *The Building of the Eighteenth-Century Church* (London: SPCK, 1963)

2 Pugin, A. Welby *Contrasts: or, A Parallel between the Noble Edifices of the Middle Ages, and Corresponding Buildings of the Present Day; shewing the Present Decay of Taste* (London: Charles Dolman, 1841) p 51

3 Quoted in Crook, J. Mordaunt *The Dilemma of Style: Architectural Ideas from the Picturesque to the Post-Modern* (London: Murray, 1987) p 42

4 *Ibid* p 43

5 See Pugin, A. W. N. *An Apology for the Revival of Christian Architecture* (London: n p, 1843) pp 1–3

6 Donaldson, T. L. 'Modern Theories of Architectural Taste' *The Builder* (30 December 1854) Vol 12 p 508

7 Eastlake, Charles L. *A History of the Gothic Revival* (London: Longmans Green, 1872) p 47

8 *Ibid* p 42

9 Dutton, Ralph *The Age of Wren* (London: Batsford, 1951) p 42

10 See the scholarly Drummond, Andrew Langdale *The Church Architecture of Protestantism: an Historical and Constructive Study* (Edinburgh: Clark, 1934) p 36

11 *Ibid* p 37

12 See Little, Bryan *The Life and Work of James Gibbs 1682–1754* (London: Batsford, 1955)

13 London: Cassell, 1910

14 *Ibid* p 211

15 See Curl, James Stevens *Classical Churches in Ulster* (Belfast: Ulster Architectural Heritage Society, 1980)

16 See Brett, C. E. B. *Roger Mulholland Architect, of Belfast, 1740–1818* (Belfast: Ulster Architectural Heritage Society, 1976)

17 See Curl *Classical Churches . . . op cit*

18 See Curl, James Stevens *The Londonderry Plantation 1609–1914* (Chichester: Phillimore, 1986)

19 Craig, Maurice *The Architecture of Ireland from the earliest times to 1880* (London: Batsford, 1982)

CHAPTER VI INDUSTRIAL, COMMERCIAL, INSTITUTIONAL, AND MARKET-BUILDINGS

1 *Shropshire* (Harmondsworth: Penguin, 1958) p 157

2 NS XI (1832) pp 81-82

3 1832

4 See Curl, James Stevens *The Egyptian Revival* (London: Allen & Unwin, 1982)

5 Schinkel's Travel Diary (1826) p 53

6 In his *A Guide to the Georgian Buildings of Britain and Ireland* (London: Weidenfeld & Nicolson, 1985)

7 In *A History of Building Types* (London: Thames & Hudson, 1976) p 213

8 See Gomme, Andor and Walker, David *Architecture of Glasgow* (London: Lund Humphries, 1968) p 81, and Larmour, Paul *Belfast: An illustrated architectural guide* (Belfast: Friar's Bush Press, 1987) p 1

9 See Curl, James Stevens *The Londonderry Plantation, 1609–1914* (Chichester: Phillimore 1986)

10 Strain, R. W. M. *Belfast and its Charitable Society* (London: Oxford University Press, 1961)

CHAPTER VII GEORGIAN PLEASURES

1 London: Faber & Faber, 1948

2 *Ibid* p 29

3 *DNB*

4 Curl, James Stevens 'Taking the Waters in London' *Country Life* (2 and 9 December 1971, and 11 and 18 November 1976). See also Foord, Alfred Stanley *Springs, Streams and Spas of London* (London: T. Fisher Unwin, 1910) and Sunderland, Septimus *Old London's Spas, Baths, and Wells* (London: John Bale, Sons & Danielsson, 1915)

5 See Curl, James Stevens 'Town Life on the Waterfront. Stourport-on-Severn, Worcestershire' *Country Life* (6 December 1979)

6 A financial scheme for raising capital to build houses, hotels, etc.

7 Loudon, John Claudius *Encyclopaedia of Cottage, Farm, and Villa Architecture and Furniture* (London: Longman, Rees, Orme, Brown, Green, & Longman, 1834) pp 675–726

CHAPTER VIII PLANNING OF VILLAGES AND TOWNS

1 See Curl, James Stevens *The Londonderry Plantation 1609–1914* (Chichester: Phillimore, 1986)
2 See *Georgian Society Records* Vol V (1913) p 113
3 31 George II, c 19
4 33 George II, c 18
5 For detailed descriptions see John Gifford, Colin McWilliam, and David Walker *Edinburgh: The Buildings of Scotland* series (Harmondsworth: Penguin, 1984), and A. J. Youngson *The Making of Classical Edinburgh 1750–1840* (Edinburgh: Edinburgh UP, 1966)
6 See Ison, Walter *The Georgian Buildings of Bath from 1700 to 1830* (London: Faber, 1948)
7 *Ibid* p 151
8 See Kelly, Alison *Mrs Coade's Stone* (Upton-upon-Severn: The Self-Publishing Association, 1990)
9 See Cruickshank, Dan *A Guide to the Georgian Buildings of Britain and Ireland* (London: Weidenfeld & Nicolson, 1985) p 30. For Nash generally see Summerson, John *The Life and Work of John Nash Architect* (London: Allen & Unwin, 1980)

CHAPTER IX PLACES FOR THE LIVING AND FOR THE DEAD

1 Southey, Robert *Letters from England by Don Manuel Alvarez Espriella* (London: Longman, 1807)
2 See Cruickshank, Dan and Burton, Neil *Life in the Georgian City* (London: Viking, 1990) *passim*
3 *Ibid* p 3
4 Quoted in Cruickshank and Burton *op cit* p 29
5 *Ibid* p 94

6 See, for example, La Rochefoucauld, François de *A Frenchman in England* (Cambridge: Cambridge UP, 1933)
7 See, for example, Nicholson, Peter *The New Practical Builder and Workman's Companion* (London: Thomas Kelly, 1823) pp 410–18 and *passim*
8 Summerson, John *The Unromantic Castle and Other Essays* (London: Thames & Hudson, 1990) p 82
9 *Ibid* p 97
10 *Ibid* p 99
11 See Litten, Julian *The English Way of Death: The Common Funeral Since 1450* (London: Hale, 1991)
12 See Kemp, Brian *English Church Monuments* (London: Batsford, 1980), and Penny, Nicholas *Church Monuments in Romantic England* (New Haven and London: Yale UP, 1977)

CHAPTER X CONCLUSION

1 *The Dunciad* Book III, lines 327–28
2 Epistle IV of *Moral Essays* lines 17–18
3 *The Poetical Works of Alexander Pope* (London: Warne, n d) p 265
4 *Moral Essays* Epistle IV (to Lord Burlington), lines 23–28
5 Chambers, Sir William *A Treatise on the Decorative Part of Civil Architecture* (London: Priestley & Weale, 1825) p 318
6 *An Introduction to Georgian Architecture* (London: Art & Technics, 1949) p 127
7 Pope, Alexander *Moral Essays* Epistle IV to Lord Burlington, lines 47–56
8 My italics
9 *Moral Essays* Epistle IV, lines 57–64
10 *Ibid*, lines 191–194
11 Virgil, *Aeneid*, vii, 136. Pope got the phrase from Virgil.
12 As for me, I grudge thee not – rather I marvel! Virgil, *Eclogue* i, 11

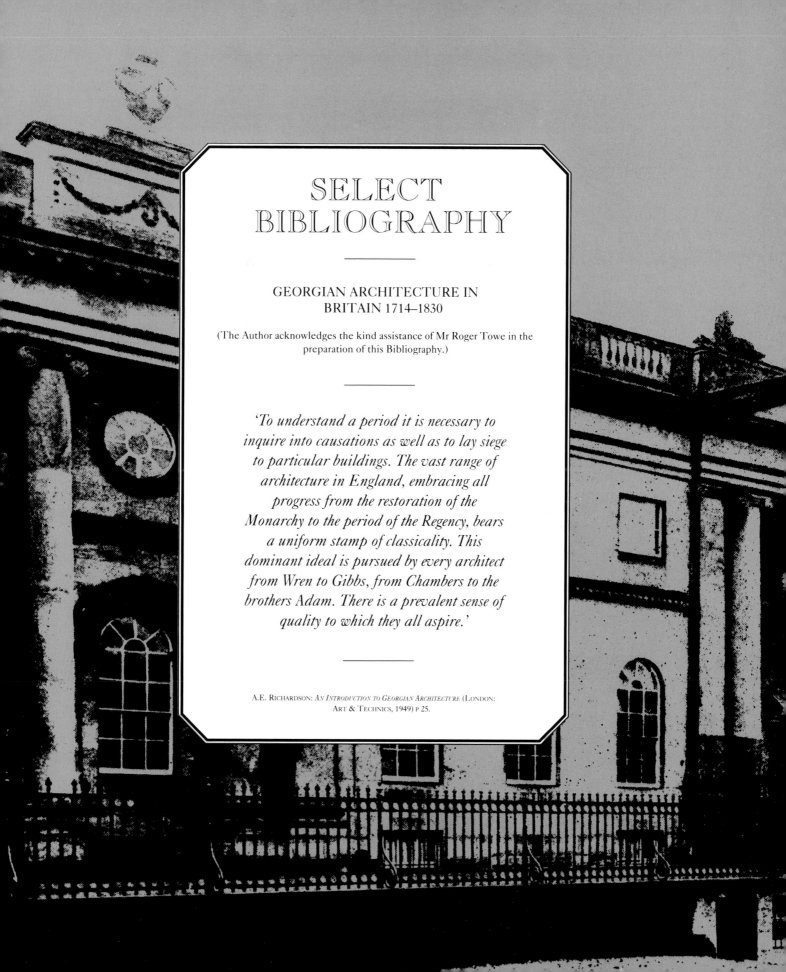

SELECT BIBLIOGRAPHY

GEORGIAN ARCHITECTURE IN BRITAIN 1714–1830

(The Author acknowledges the kind assistance of Mr Roger Towe in the preparation of this Bibliography.)

'To understand a period it is necessary to inquire into causations as well as to lay siege to particular buildings. The vast range of architecture in England, embracing all progress from the restoration of the Monarchy to the period of the Regency, bears a uniform stamp of classicality. This dominant ideal is pursued by every architect from Wren to Gibbs, from Chambers to the brothers Adam. There is a prevalent sense of quality to which they all aspire.'

A.E. RICHARDSON: *An Introduction to Georgian Architecture* (London: Art & Technics, 1949) p 25.

Amery, Colin (*ed*) *Three centuries of architectural craftmanship* (London: Architectural Press, 1977)

Beard, Geoffrey *Craftsmen and interior decoration in England, 1660–1820* (Edinburgh: Bartholomew, 1981)
— *Decorative plasterwork in Great Britain* (London: Phaidon, 1975)
— *Robert Adam's country houses* (Edinburgh: Bartholomew, 1981)
Bell, Colin and Rose *City Fathers: the early history of town planning in Britain* (Harmondsworth: Penguin 1972)
Binney, Marcus *Sir Robert Taylor: from rococo to neoclassicism* (London: Allen & Unwin, 1984)
Blomfield, Reginald and Thomas, F. Inigo *The formal garden in England* (London: Waterstone, 1985 [*orig publ* 1892])
Bolton, Arthur T. *The architecture of Robert and James Adam (1758–1794)* (London: Country Life, 1922)
— (*ed*) *The portrait of Sir John Soane, R.A. (1753–1837), set forth in letters from his friends, (1775–1837)* (London: Sir John Soane's Museum, 1927)
Bonwitt, W. *Michael Searles: a Georgian architect and surveyor* (London: Soc of Architectural Historians of GB 1987)
Breman, Paul (*ed*) *The architecture of the early eighteenth century* (London: Weinreb, 1965) Catalogue 11
Breman, Paul and Addis, Denise *Guide to Vitruvius Britannicus: annotated and analytical index to the plates* (New York: Blom, 1972)
Briggs, Martin S. *Goths and Vandals: a study of the destruction, neglect and preservation of historical buildings in England* (London: Constable, 1952)
Brownell, Morris R. *Alexander Pope and the arts of Georgian England* (Oxford: Clarendon, 1978)
Burke, Joseph *English art 1714–1800* (Oxford: Clarendon, 1976)
Burlington, Richard Boyle, 3rd Earl of *Fabbriche Antiche disegnate da Andrea Palladio Vincentino* (London: The Author, 1730)
Byrne, Andrew *London's Georgian houses* (London: Georgian Press, 1986)

Campbell, Colen *Vitruvius Britannicus, or the British Architect* (London: 1715–1725 [3 vols], republ New York: Blom, 1967)
Castell, Robert *The villas of the ancients illustrated* (London: The Author, 1728, republ New York: Garland, 1982)
Chalklin, C.W. *The provincial towns of Georgian England: a study of the building processes, 1740-1820* (London: Arnold, 1974)
Chambers, Sir William *Designs of Chinese buildings, furniture, dresses, machines, and utensils* (London: The Author, 1757, republ Farnborough: Gregg, 1969)
— *A dissertation on Oriental gardening* (London: Griffin, 1772, republ Farnborough: Gregg: 1972 with 'An heroic epistle' and 'An heroic postscript' by Wm. Mason)
— *A treatise on the decorative part of civil architecture* 3rd ed (1st ed 1759) (London: Smeeton, 1791, republ Farnborough: Gregg, 1969)
Clark, Kenneth *The Gothic Revival: an essay in the history of taste* 3rd ed (London: Murray, 1974)
Clarke, Basil F.L. *The building of the eighteenth-century church* (London: SPCK, 1963)
Colvin, H.M. *A biographical dictionary of British architects 1600–1840* (London: Murray, 1978)

Colvin, H.M. and Harris, John (*eds*) *The country seat: studies in the history of the British country house presented to Sir John Summerson . . .* (London: Allen Lane, 1970)
Colvin, H.M. (*ed*) *The history of the King's Works. Vol 5, 1660–1782* (London: HMSO, 1976)
— *The history of the King's Works. Vol 6, 1782–1851* (London: HMSO, 1973)
Cornforth, John *English interiors 1790–1848: the quest for comfort* (London: Barrie & Jenkins, 1978)
Council of Europe *The Age of Neo-Classicism* (London: Arts Council of GB, 1972)
Craig, Maurice *The architecture of Ireland from the earliest times to 1880* (London: Batsford, 1982)
— *Dublin 1660–1860: a social and architectural history* (Dublin: Figgis, 1969)
Croft-Murray, Edward *Decorative painting in England, 1537–1837. Vol 2: the eighteenth and early nineteenth centuries* (Feltham: Country Life, 1970)
Crook, J. Mordaunt *The dilemma of style: architectural ideals from the picturesque to the post-modern* (London: Murray, 1987)
— *The Greek Revival: neo-classical attitudes in British architecture 1760–1870* (London: Murray, 1972)
Crouch, Joseph *Puritanism and Art: an inquiry into a popular fallacy* (London: Cassell, 1910)
Cruickshank, Dan *A guide to the Georgian buildings of Britain and Ireland* (London: Weidenfeld & Nicolson, 1985)
Cruickshank, Dan and Burton, Neil *Life in the Georgian City* (London: Viking, 1990)
Cruickshank, Dan and Wyld, Peter *London: the art of Georgian building* (London: Architectural Press, 1975)
Curl, James Stevens *The Egyptian Revival: an introductory study of a recurring theme in the history of taste* (London: Allen & Unwin, 1982)
Refer also to *By the same author*, page 4

Dale, Anthony *James Wyatt* (Oxford: Blackwell, 1956)
Davis, Terence *The architecture of John Nash* (London: Studio, 1960)
— *The gothick taste* (Newton Abbot: David & Charles, 1974)
— *John Nash: the Prince Regent's architect* New ed (Newton Abbot: David & Charles, 1973)
Desmond, Ray *Bibliography of British gardens* (Winchester: St Paul's Bibliographies, 1984)
Downes, Kerry *The Georgian cities of Britain* (Oxford: Phaidon, 1979)
Drummond, Andrew Langdale *The church architecture of Protestantism. An historical and constructive study* (Edinburgh: T. & T. Clarke, 1934)
Dutton, Ralph *The English interior 1500–1900* (London: Batsford, 1948)
— *The age of Wren* (London: Batsford, 1951)

Edwards, Ralph and Ramsey, L.G.G. (*eds*) *The early Georgian period, 1714–1760* (London: Connoisseur, 1957)
— *The late Georgian period, 1760–1810* (London: Connoisseur, 1956)
— *The Regency period, 1810–1830* (London: Connoisseur, 1958)

Fleming, John *Robert Adam and his circle in Edinburgh and Rome* (London: Murray, 1962)

Fletcher, Sir Banister and Musgrove, John (*ed*) *A history of architecture* 19th ed (London: Butterworths, 1987)

Fowler, John and Cornforth, John *English decoration in the 18th century* 2nd ed (London: Barrie & Jenkins, 1978)

Friedman, Terry *James Gibbs* (New Haven: London: Yale UP, 1984)

Gadd, David *Georgian summer: Bath in the eighteenth century* (Bath: Adams & Dart, 1971)

Gandon, James *The life of James Gandon, Esq., MRIA, FRS, etc . . .* (Dublin: Hodges & Smith, 1846, republ London: Cornmarket, 1969)

Geffrye Museum *George Dance, the Elder 1695–1768; The Younger 1741-1825* [Catalogue] (London: Geffrye Museum, 1972)

Girouard, Mark *Life in the English country house: a social and architectural history* (New Haven: London: Yale UP, 1978)

Gloag, John *Georgian Grace. A social history of design from 1660 to 1830* (London: A. & C. Black, 1956)

Gomme, Andor and Walker, David *Architecture of Glasgow* Rev ed (London: Lund Humphries, 1987)

Gomme, Andor, Jenner, Michael and Little, Bryan *Bristol: an architectural history* (London: Lund Humphries, 1979)

Gunnis, Rupert *Dictionary of British sculptors, 1660–1851* (London: Odhams, 1963)

Harris, John *The artist and the country house: a history of country houses and garden view painting in Britain, 1540–1870* (London: Wilson, 1979)

— *The design of the English country house, 1620–1920* (London: Trefoil, 1985)

— *Georgian country houses* (Feltham: Country Life, 1968)

— *The Palladians* (London: Trefoil, 1981)

— *Sir William Chambers, Knight of the Polar Star* (London: Zwemmer, 1970)

Holmes, Michael *The country house described: an index to the country houses of Great Britain and Ireland* (Winchester: St Paul's Bibliographies, 1986)

Honour, Hugh *Chinoiserie. The vision of Cathay* (London: Murray, 1961)

— *Neo-classicism* (Harmondsworth: Penguin, 1968)

Hope, Thomas *Household furniture and interior decoration: classic style book of the Regency period* (London: Dover, 1971, orig publ 1807)

Hunt, John Dixon and Willis, Peter (*eds*) *The genius of the place: The English landscape garden, 1620–1820* (London: Elek, 1975)

Hunt, John Dixon *William Kent, landscape garden designer: an assessment and catalogue of his designs* (London: Zwemmer, 1987)

Hussey, Christopher *English country houses: early Georgian 1715–1760* Rev ed (London: Country Life, 1965)

— *English country houses: mid-Georgian 1760–1800* (London: Country Life, 1956)

— *English country houses: late Georgian 1800–1840* (London: Country Life, 1958)

— *English gardens and landscapes, 1700–1750* (London: Country Life, 1967)

— *The picturesque: studies in a point of view* (London: Cass, 1967, New imp, orig publ Putnam, 1927)

Hyams, Edward *Capability Brown and Humphry Repton* (London: Dent, 1971)

Ison, Walter *The Georgian buildings of Bath 1700–1830* (London: Faber, 1948)

— *The Georgian buildings of Bristol* (Bath: Kingsmead, 1978)

Jacques, David *Georgian gardens: the reign of nature* (London: Batsford, 1983)

Jenkins, Frank *Architect and patron: a survey of professional relations and practice in England from the sixteenth century to the present day* (London: Oxford UP, 1961)

— *John Soane* (London: Academy Editions, 1983)

Jourdain, M. *English decoration and furniture of the later XVIIIth century* (London: Batsford, 1922)

— *English interior decoration 1500–1830: a study in the development of design* (London: Batsford, 1950)

— *English interiors in smaller houses from the Restoration to the Regency 1660–1830* (London: Batsford, 1923)

Kaufmann, Emil *Architecture in the age of reason: baroque and post-baroque in England, Italy and France* (Cambridge: Harvard UP, 1955)

Kaye, Barrington *The development of the architectural profession in Britain: a sociological study* (London: Allen & Unwin, 1960)

Kersting, Anthony F. and Lindsay, Maurice *The buildings of Edinburgh* (London: Batsford, 1981)

Langley, Batty *The builder's chest book; or, A complete key to the five orders of columns in architecture* (London: Wilcox, 1727, repub Farnborough: Gregg, 1971)

— *The builder's jewel; or, The youth's instructor and workman's remembrancer* (London: Ware, 1741, republ New York: Blom, 1970 [1757 ed])

— *The city and country builder's and workman's treasury of designs; or, The art of drawing and working the ornamental parts of architecture* (London: Harding, 1745 [etc], republ Farnborough: Gregg, 1969)

— *Gothic architecture improved by rules and proportions in many grand designs* (London: Millan, 1747, republ Farnborough: Gregg, 1971)

— *New principles of gardening . . .* (London: Bettesworth, 1728, republ Farnborough: Gregg, 1971)

Leach, Peter *James Paine* (London: Zwemmer, 1988)

Leacroft, Richard *The development of the English playhouse* (London: Eyre Methuen, 1973)

Lees-Milne, James *The age of Adam* (London: Batsford, 1947)

— *Earls of creation: five great patrons of eighteenth century art* (London: Hamilton, 1962)

Leoni, Giacomo (*ed*) *The architecture of A. Palladio* (London: The Author, 1715–1720)

Liscombe, R.W. *William Wilkins, 1778–1839* (Cambridge: Cambridge UP, 1980)

Little, Bryan *The life and work of James Gibbs, 1682–1754* (London: Batsford, 1955)

Loudon, John Claudius (*ed*) *The landscape gardening and landscape architecture of the late Humphry Repton Esq.* New ed (London: Longman, 1840, republ Farnborough: Gregg, 1969)

Lowndes, William *The Royal Crescent in Bath: a fragment of English life* (Bristol: Redcliffe, 1981)

INDEX

Page numbers in *italic* refer to illustrations.